The Future of Liner Conferences in Europe

European University Studies

Europäische Hochschulschriften
Publications Universitaires Européennes

Series II
Law

Reihe II Série II
Rechtswissenschaft
Law

Vol./Bd. 3874

PETER LANG
Frankfurt am Main · Berlin · Bern · Bruxelles · New York · Oxford · Wien

Felix Dinger

The Future of Liner Conferences in Europe

A critical analysis of agreements in liner shipping under current European competition law

PETER LANG
Europäischer Verlag der Wissenschaften

Bibliographic Information published by Die Deutsche Bibliothek
Die Deutsche Bibliothek lists this publication in the Deutsche Nationalbibliografie; detailed bibliographic data is available in the internet at <http://dnb.ddb.de>.

Zugl.: Kiel, Univ., Diss., 2003

D 8
ISSN 0531-7312
ISBN 3-631-52130-8
US-ISBN 0-8204-6576-3

www.peterlang.de

Preface

This study was presented to the faculty of law of the Christian-Albrechts-University at Kiel/Germany in the autumn of 2003 in order to attain the degree of *doctor juris*. It was possible to take into account legal developments up until June 2003.

My foremost thanks go to my supervisor, Prof. Dr. Dr. Rainer Hofmann. Through his uncomplicated style he assured a speedy work process. Prof. Dr. Joachim Jickeli, who took it upon him to co-correct my study, also deserves many thanks for his participation. In addition, I thank them both for giving me the possibility to write this thesis in English. The idea to write about liner conferences took shape during my stay at the Europainstitut in Basle 2000/2001, a circumstance for which I would like to extend my gratitude to Prof. Dr. Christa Tobler.

Writing in English proved to be much more of a challenge than I thought at the outset. My good friend Sharon Miller Horn and my brother Moritz Dinger spent many hours correcting my mistakes, a work for which I am very grateful. Any remaining mistakes are entirely my fault.

Finally, I would like to thank my parents. Their financial and emotional support gave me the necessary peace of mind.

Kiel, November 2003 — Felix Dinger, MAES

Table of contents

Abbreviations

AG	Advocate General
Art.	Article
Arts.	Articles
CFI	Court of First Instance
cit.	citation
CPI	*Contemporary Policy Issues*
CMLR	*Common Market Law Review*
Co.	Company
CSC	Canadian Shippers' Council
EATA	Europe Asia Trade Agreement
EC	European Community
ECJ	European Court of Justice
ECOSOC	Economic and Social Committee
ECR	European Court Reports
EEC	European Economic Community
EG	Europäische Gemeinschaft
ESC	European Shippers' Council
ETL	*European Transport Law*
EU	European Union/Europäische Union
EWG	Europäische Wirtschaftsgemeinschaft
FEFC	Far Eastern Freight Conference
EuR	*Europa-Recht*
f	following
ff	forthfollowing
FMC	Federal Maritime Commission
FS	Festschrift
GNP	Gross National Product
GDP	Gross Domestic Product
i.e.	ipso est
lit.	litera
Ltd.	Limited
NITL	National Industrial Transportation League
NJW	*Neue Juristische Wochenschrift*
No.	Number
NVOCC	Non Vessel Operating Common Carrier
OECD	Organisation for Economic Cooperation and Development
OJ	Official Journal of the European Communities
OSRA	Ocean Shipping Reform Act (1998)
p.	page
PCJI	Permanent Court of International Justice

RabelsZ	*Zeitschrift für ausländisches und internationales Privatrecht, begründet von Ernst Rabel*
rec.	recital
Reg.	Regulation
RIO	*Review of Industrial Organisations*
RIW	*Recht der Internationalen Wirtschaft*
RMC	*Revue du marché commun et de l'Union européenne*
SEA	Single European Act
sec.	section
Ser.	Series
TAA	Trans-Atlantic Agreement
TACA	Trans-Atlantic Conference Agreement
TR	*Transportrecht*
TSA	Transpacific Stabilisation Agreement
U. K.	United Kingdom
UN	United Nations
UNCTAD	United Nations Conference on Trade and Development
U. S.	United States
v, v.	versus
Vol.	Volume
WSC	World Shipping Council
WuW	*Wirtschaft und Wettbewerb*
ZaöR	*Zeitschrift für ausländisches und öffelntliches Recht*

Introduction

The Treaty envisions a common transport policy in Art. 3 I lit. f EC. Arts. 70 to 80 (ex 74 to 84) EC lay down more detailed rules on this matter. However, these provisions primarily set out a procedure for the Council to adopt the necessary rules, they do not contain much material law themselves[1]. The reluctance of the Treaty to provide more precise rules on a common transport policy has been attributed to the fact that, at the time the Treaty was adopted, there was an unsolved debate over the question as to whether transport services were public services or whether they were an economic activity, to which commercial principles did apply[2]. It may be that this ambiguity of the Treaty contributed to the fact that a breakthrough for the development of a common transport policy only occurred in the mid-1980s[3].

Notwithstanding these difficulties in the establishment of a common transport policy is the transport sector of vital importance for the European Community. The right of free movement of persons would not be worth much if there were no adequate means to let the people move freely. The same is true for the free movement of goods. Since the European Community is also one of the three main trading blocks in the world (Asia - Europe - North America), it is equally important that the European industries have access to sufficient, cheap and reliable transport capacities on an international level, be it as exporters or as importers. In this context shipping plays an important role. Around one third of the trade between the Member States is carried by ship. It is not only internal trade, where shipping is important: trade with third countries accounts for 18 per cent of the European Community's GNP and over 90 per cent of that trade are conducted by ship[4]. These numbers display the importance of a well-working maritime transport industry for the functioning of the Common Market and the European economy as a whole. Consequently, it is necessary that the principle of free competition is ensured in this sector.

Purpose of this study is the analysis of European competition law in the field of maritime transport and the search for an answer to the question of whether the current laws on liner shipping should remain unchanged or whether it is advisable to modify the existing legal regime. The fundamental principles of EC competition law are enshrined in Arts. 81 and 82 (ex 85 and 86) EC, which operate under the basic assumption that competitive markets are the best way to ensure efficiency, increased innovation, lower prices and therefore optimal re-

---

[1] Van Miert, ETL (1999), p. 3 ff, p. 4.
[2] Van Miert, ETL (1999), p. 3 ff, p. 4.
[3] Clough/Randolph, (1991), p. 41.
[4] Sir Leon Brittain, ETL (1993), p. 337 ff, p. 337.

source allocation[5]. For a long time the liner shipping industry has developed without taking heed of this basic principle of European competition law. Rather, the international shipping industry has a history of self-regulation[6] that reaches back to the late 19th century. Its self-regulatory regime not necessarily complies with the fundamental rules of EC competition law. Liner shipping operators traditionally enter into agreements with each other that potentially restrict competition. Among these agreements are liner conferences, consortia and discussion agreements. A prominent feature most often connected with liner conferences is that the carriers agree on a common price rate for the shipping services they offer.

The background for the unique structure of the shipping industry is a proclaimed need on the part of the carriers to ensure the stability of the maritime transport sector. Potential for instability is said to arise *inter alia* from the following factors[7]:
- high fixed costs to operate a scheduled shipping service,
- easiness for competitors to enter a certain trade, as ships can be moved without difficulty from one trade lane to another,
- substantial seasonal changes in the transport volume and
- differences in transport volume on outbound and inbound legs of a journey.

The European legislator has passed Regulation 4056/86[8] and Regulation 823/2000[9] with the purpose of defining European competition law in the maritime transport sector. The chief difference between the two Regulations is, that under the first, carriers are permitted to co-operate on prices, whereas under the second, they may not do so. It is therefore not surprising that especially Regulation 4056/86 has caused much controversy. In April 2002 the OECD issued a report[10], in which it came to the result that no conclusive evidence exists for the fact that joint price fixing and rate discussion in liner shipping are overall beneficial. The Commission has recently started an enquiry with the purpose of establishing whether or not it should remain legal for liner shipping operators to co-operate on prices[11]. Such developments demonstrate that this study seeks to find an answer to one of the most pressing questions in liner shipping from a regulatory point of view.

---

[5] Bellamy/Child, (1993), p. 35.
[6] Pons, (1998), p. 4.
[7] For an overview over these factors see: WSC submission to the OECD, 2001,p. iii.
[8] OJ, (1986), L-378/4.
[9] OJ, (2000), L-100/24.
[10] OECD, (2002).
[11] Stragier, (2002), p. 9 ff.

The purpose of the first three chapters of this study is mainly to provide sufficient background information about the liner shipping industry. These chapters therefore cover the historical development of the liner shipping industry, the current state of the liner shipping industry and the development of a European perspective on liner shipping. Chapter four then turns to the economical analysis of liner shipping as a first analytical element of this study. Chapters five and six constitute the core of the legal analysis of European competition law in the field of maritime transport. Therein contained is an evaluation of the provisions of secondary law that regulate agreements in liner shipping as well as an evaluation of these provisions in the light of relevant Treaty law. The final chapter of this study concerns the U. S. approach towards regulation of the liner shipping industry. The purpose of this chapter is not only to explain the U. S. laws on agreements in liner shipping, but also to demonstrate that shipping is an international industry, a circumstance which needs to be taken into account by the European legislator.

Chapter one - The history of liner shipping

The state of the liner shipping industry today is the result of a continuous development over the last 200 years. In order to understand the current problems of this industry in relation to modern competition law, it is essential to sketch out the main steps of its development. As Britain was the main seafaring nation of the 19th century, the history of early liner shipping is largely a history of British shipping[1]. Crucial for the development of the shipping industry in the 19th century was the introduction of the steamship. The second important technological development that changed the liner shipping industry occurred in the 20th century with the switch from breakbulk to containerised shipping.

1. The development of the first liner services

After the Middle Ages there was only limited need for international seaborne transport. Ships did not sail on a regular schedule, even if they sailed on regular routes. Instead, they waited at port until there was enough cargo to fill the holds of the ship[2] and then they took to sea. This pattern of sailing was to change in the 19th century with the increase in international trade. After the British economy had been transformed by the process of industrialisation, it became necessary to transport large amounts of raw materials from the dominions and colonies to Britain. In return, the goods manufactured there, had to be carried in the opposite direction[3]. As a consequence, the volume of international trade increased considerably[4]. This increased volume of trade made it possible for carriers to offer the first scheduled sailings. The chief risk connected with the provision of such a service was that ships might have to sail partly empty and thus with less or no profit, especially in the winter time when business was poor. This danger was counterbalanced by the chance to charge higher rates for offering fast and scheduled sailings[5]. Only shippers of high value cargoes could afford such higher rates. With the general increase in cargo the amount of high valued cargoes also rose, making the just described risk bearable for the carriers. The financial risk for carriers connected to the provision of scheduled sailings was also offset by the fact that the port time of ships decreased, since they did not have to wait in port until they acquired sufficient cargo. The level of utilisation of the vessels engaged in liner services was 50 per cent higher

---

[1] For dates on the net tonnage of British mercantile vessels in comparison to merchant fleets of other nations see: Davies (1985), p. 46; Deakin, (1973), p. 13.

[2] Davies, (1985), p. 54; Marx, (1953), 45.

[3] Deakin, (1973), p. 13.

[4] Erdmenger, FS Raisch, (1995), p. 391.

[5] Davies, (1985), p. 55.

than that of vessels operating under traditional conditions. As a result, the 1820s and 1830s witnessed the emergence of the first scheduled sailing services[6].

The first liner services were operated by sailing vessels[7], nevertheless the newly invented steamship soon began to dominate liner shipping[8]. From the 1850s onwards the steamship rapidly replaced the older sailing vessels and by the 1870s carriers offered steamship operated liner services on most of the major trade routes of the time[9]. Steamships were better suited for the provision of liner services, as these new vessels could sail independently of the weather. It was only with the steamship that a schedule with precise times of departure and arrival could be kept[10].

2. Changes in the industry structure

The arrival of the steamship and subsequent technological innovations did not only improve the punctuality of liner services, but they also influenced the structure of the shipping industry. Originally, traders operated their own vessels, which they filled up to a large extent with their own cargoes[11]. Only the remaining spare capacity was chartered out to other merchants[12].

This business structure changed in the wake of colonisation. Not only did shipping become an independent activity from trading[13], but also new shipping lines were typically operated by a company[14] and not by a single owner. Such changes were prompted by the increased capital demand of carriers that wanted to establish and maintain modern steamship-operated liner services[15]. One reason for the mounting capital needs of carriers was the fact that the price of new vessels had risen substantially. New steamships were not only bigger in size than the traditional sailing vessels, they were also more expensive[16]. The initialisation of a steam liner service on a new route was also very costly due to the fact that it was not possible to operate a liner service on a deep sea route with just one vessel, it was rather necessary to commission several ships for the op-

---

[6] Davies, (1985), p. 55.

[7] Davies, (1985), p. 54.

[8] The gross tonnage of steamships had overtaken that of sailing ships by 1885; per: Deakin, (1973), p. 15.

[9] Davies, (1985), p. 56.

[10] Herman, (1983), p. 7; Marx, (1953), p. 45.

[11] Kühne, (1996), p. 19.

[12] Davies, (1985), p. 54.

[13] Herman, (1983), p. 7; Jacobs, (1991), p. 16, who states that this process could be witnessed in England from the year 1800 onwards.

[14] Davies, (1985), p. 54.

[15] Jacobs, (1991), p. 16.

[16] Kühne, (1996), p. 20.

eration on one route[17]. Finally, the provision of a modern liner service meant that the land side operations of the shipping service had to be reorganised. As the ships grew bigger, the number of dock workers had to be increased to handle the larger amounts of freight. In order to match the now fixed sailing schedule of these larger vessels with the demands of cargo shippers and passengers, increased administrative efforts became necessary as well[18].

As a result of the introduction of the steamship and the changes associated therewith, shipping became a complex and expensive business that could not be conducted merely as a side activity to regular trading, but demanded the full attention of specialists. The large amounts of money that were now necessary for the operation of scheduled shipping services were beyond the resources of a single person[19]. As a consequence, the major shipping lines of the 19th century were created as companies, thereby providing for the possibility to generate capital through investment of the public[20].

3. The development of liner conferences

Although the demand for shipping capacity rose steadily during the 19th century, the supply of shipping space grew even faster[21]. This lead to a situation in the 1870s, where the shipping industry was characterised by a large surplus of shipping capacity[22].

The technological advances connected with the introduction of the steamship were one reason for the rapid increase of cargo capacity. The absolute size of a steamship was bigger than that of a traditional sailing vessel[23]. With the invention of new types of engines, steamships became more fuel efficient and needed less coal per voyage, which resulted in a further growth of shipping capacity[24]. The available transport capacity also increased due to the fact that steamships were faster than sailing vessels and could perform more voyages per year[25]. Another important event that suddenly lead to a rise in cargo capacity was the opening of the Suez-Canal in 1869. The reduced length of the Europe-Asia

---

[17] Jacobs, (1991), p. 17.
[18] Davies, (1985), p. 51.
[19] Davies, (1985), p. 54; Jacobs, (1991), p. 16.
[20] Davies, (1985), p. 54.
[21] Deakin, (1973), p. 21.
[22] Kühne, (1996), p. 22; Marx, (1953), p. 46.
[23] Herman, (1983), p. 8 states that the goods that had to be transported with four sailing ships at the beginning of the 19th century could be transported with one steamship at the end of the 19th century.
[24] Deakin, (1973), p. 15.
[25] Deakin, (1973), p. 15.

route resulted in substantial excess capacities[26] because the vessels on this route could now perform more sailings per year. The already existing problem of overtonnage was worsened by a recession in 1873. Now the shipping industry not only had to face an ever growing supply of shipping space, but it also experienced a sudden drop in demand for shipping services[27].

The resulting difference between supply and demand on the markets for liner shipping services lead to a deterioration of freight rates[28]. Competition became so severe that it had been called "cut-throat competition". This situation induced the carriers to enter into the first conference agreements[29]. The first conference ever to be established was a conference on the United Kingdom - Calcutta (India) route, which started its operation in 1875[30]. The aim of this conference, as of subsequent agreements of this type, was to control competition amongst its members and to reduce competition from outsiders. It did so with the establishment of a common tariff and by distributing the available sailings to the different vessels of the participating carriers[31]. In order to increase the loyalty of shippers to the members of the conference, it introduced a system of deferred rebates in 1877[32]. Under such a system the shipper does not profit from a direct discount, but he has the opportunity to get a partial refund. The first prerequisite for such a refund is that the shipper remains loyal to the conference during the initial rebate period. As a second requirement, the shipper must then prove his continued loyalty to the conference in an additional loyalty period[33]. If the shipper commissions any cargo to a non-conference carrier in either period, he then will forfeit the right to claim payment of any rebates that have accumulated so far.

This system, by which shipowners organised themselves into conferences, quickly spread throughout the world and still characterises the shipping industry today[34]. Yet, shippers and shipowners, who were not admitted to the conferences, soon started to complain about the business practices of the conferences[35]. It was especially the system of deferred rebates that caused such complaints.

---

[26] Report by the Australian Productivity Commission on Liner Shipping, (1999), p. 41.
[27] Jacobs, (1991), p. 17.
[28] Deakin, (1973), p. 21; Kühne, (1996), p. 22; Marx, (1953), p. 46.
[29] Kühne, (1996), p. 22.
[30] Davies, (1985), p. 59; Kühne, (1996), p. 22; Marx, (1953), p. 47.
[31] Herman, (1983), p. 8.
[32] Davies, (1985), p. 59; Marx, (1953), p. 47.
[33] Jacobs, (1991), p. 26.
[34] Davies, (1985), p. 59; Kühne, (1996), p. 24.
[35] Herman, (1983), p. 8.

4. The first official reactions

The complaints from shippers and non-conference carriers prompted the British as well as the American government to investigate into the effects of shipping conferences. The arguments used in these first evaluations still feature prominently in current discussions about agreements among liner shipping carriers[36]. In 1906 the *Royal Commission on Shipping Rings* was appointed in Britain and in 1912 a congressional committee, called the *Alexander Committee*[37], was charged in the United States with the enquiry into the practises of liner conferences. The following account focuses on the *Royal Commission on Shipping Rings*. The dealings of the *Alexander Committee* will be scrutinised in more detail in the last chapter of this study, which is dedicated to the American approach towards liner conferences and like agreements[38].

The *Royal Commission on Shipping Rings* sat for three years and delivered its report in 1909[39]. Members of the commission were representatives of the British shipping industry, as well as representatives of shippers from Britain, the colonies and dominions. As a result of the different interests that were represented by the individual members of the commission, the 16 members could not agree on a common position. Instead, the commission submitted a majority report signed by 11 members and a minority report signed by 5 members.

a) The majority report

The majority took a generally positive attitude towards liner conferences. It did not have the view that conferences concentrated market power excessively, as there were limits to the power of conferences. These were identified as competition from existing outsiders and new shipping lines, competition among the members of a conference themselves and as common action by the shippers. The majority was of the opinion that liner conferences proved positive for the shipping industry in several ways. A first benefit of the conferences system was seen in the fact that the formation of liner conferences lead to an improvement in service as a result of the higher regularity of sailings and due to a better vessel standard. Another positive aspect according to the majority of the commission was the circumstance that the organisation of carriers into conferences pacified the market and lead to a greater stability of rates. The majority saw a further advantage of conferences in the reduction of so-called *wasteful* competition between individual carriers through a co-ordination of sailing times. Fi-

---

[36] See for example: ESC submission to the OECD, (2001), p. 8 ff.

[37] Named after the chairman of the House of Representatives Merchant Marine and Fisheries Committee, Joshua Alexander.

[38] See below, p. 167 ff.

[39] Report of the *Royal Commisssion on Shipping Rings*, London, (1909), Cd. 4668-70, 4685 - 86.

nally, it was also considered an advantage of liner conferences that they could establish tariffs, which took into account the value of the shipped cargo.

On the other hand the majority report did not fail to notice that conferences might earn excess profits and cause overtonnage. As far as the above described deferred rebates were concerned, the majority was of the opinion that they were a necessary device to ensure the loyalty of the shippers to the conferences. The majority also qualified its positive view on liner conferences by stating that the formation of liner conferences may result in the just described advantages, but that these merits did not necessarily follow the creation of any conference.

Coherent with its positive attitude towards liner conferences, the majority only suggested marginal variations to the existing system. Its report emphasised the use of collective bargaining power on the side of the shippers, as adequate means to ensure that their position be duly taken into account in the price building process. Consequently, it was advocated to grant associations of shippers the possibility to receive official recognition by the Board of Trade[40] as representatives of all shippers in a certain trade. The majority also recommended to deposit information on tariffs and conference agreements of those conferences, which made use of deferred rebates with the Board of Trade in order to ensure more transparency in the shipping industry. A third proposition of the majority was that the same body should be given the power to conduct an investigation in cases of alleged wrongdoing on the part of liner conferences, where important national interests were at stake.

b) The minority report

The minority report was more critical in its assessment of liner conferences. It stressed the circumstance that conferences were able to stabilise the freight rates but at a higher level than that, which would prevail in a competitive market. The minority also emphasised that the conference system, as a monopoly, hindered rationalisation of the shipping industry, as there was no pressure on the carriers to operate as cost efficiently as possible. Finally, the minority could not find sufficient evidence for the fact that conferences lead to a greater regularity of sailings or an improved quality of vessels used.

Although the minority did not judge conferences as positively as the majority, it did not advise to abolish the conference system or to legislate restrictively on the matter. Instead of developing a separate coherent strategy, the minority followed the majority in its suggestions in principle and only opted for detailed changes where it considered the majority's opinion to unduly neglect the shippers interests. Consequently, the minority suggested that the Board of Trade

[40] The Board of Trade was what is now the British Department of Trade.

should also be empowered to recognise associations of shippers that only represent parts of the shippers in one trade as suitable partners in the collective bargaining process. A second variation recommended by the minority was that the power of the Board of Trade to conduct an enquiry should not be restricted to cases where vital national interests were at stake, but that such enquiries should always be possible when a colonial government made a request to that effect. The minority also suggested that Parliament be informed yearly on all conference agreements.

5. Containerisation

After the introduction of the steamship had triggered a first revolution in the shipping industry, a second revolution in maritime transport occurred from 1966 onwards, with the invention of containerised shipping. This type of shipping originated in the United States - Europe trade and soon spread to the routes from those two destinations to the Far East. Transport on these routes became containerised quickly. In 1980, 73 per cent of United States trade with Europe and 81 per cent of the United States trade with the Far East were conducted via container[41]. Containerised transport remains the most important mode of transport in liner shipping until today, especially for industrialised countries. By the mid-1990s containerised cargoes made up about 75 per cent of their total liner cargoes (by volume)[42].

Both the introduction of the steamship and containerisation had a similar impact on the shipping industry, as the switch from breakbulk to containers also resulted in an enlargement of transport capacity because containerised ships were able to carry larger loads than breakbulk carriers. A second similarity between the introduction of the steamship and the advent of containerised shipping can be seen in the circumstance that sea travel was sped up by containerised vessels due to the fact that these ships were newer and therefore faster than the existing breakbulk vessels. In 1970, the average containership was 36 per cent faster than the average non-container general cargo freighter[43]. One of the main effects of containerisation, affecting both the shippers and the carriers, is the possibility of engaging in door-to-door transport. This so-called *intermodal* or *multimodal* transport is a combination of sea and land transport, which is offered to the customer by the same carrier. The legal problems connected to this kind of transport will be evaluated in chapter five[44]. They centre around the

---

[41] Hummels, (1999), p. 8.

[42] OECD, (2002), p. 67; this figure relates to statistics from Australia, Canada, Japan, Korea, the Netherlands, New Zealand and the United Kingdom.

[43] Hummels, (1999), p. 9.

[44] See below, p. 112.

question of whether the legal regime which governs sea transport, is also applicable to the land leg of an intermodal transport operation.

For the carriers containerisation proved positive in several ways. They could reduce the costs for stevedoring, as containers are loaded and unloaded mechanically on board[45]. Another advantage for the carriers was that the port time of ships could be shortened substantially and that the ships also sailed faster. Whereas a breakbulk carrier spends around 60 per cent of a year in port, a container vessel only has to spend 25 per cent of a year in port[46]. As a consequence, a container vessel can spend more time at sea, thereby generating profits, and the transport costs decline since expensive port time is reduced in relation to the amount of freight carried. However, the process of containerisation also provided challenges to the carriers, mainly because the purchase of new and expensive vessels was necessary, since the conventional breakbulk carriers were not equipped to carry containers. The carriers had to incur further expenses because they had to provide the containers[47]. It has been stated that the costs for the containers during the total live-span of a ship may be as high as the price for the vessel itself[48].

The chief aspect of containerisation that constitutes an advantage to shippers is the availability of multimodal transport. The fact that one operator organises the transport from one end of the journey to the other greatly facilitates trade[49]. The customer also profits from the circumstance that, due to containerisation, his packaging costs are likely to be reduced, since the carrier regularly provides the containers free of charge[50]. Another positive aspect for the customer is that the goods transported in a container are less susceptible to damage and pilferage. Finally, the customer benefits from the speedier port handling procedure and reduced sailing times as a consequence of containerisation[51], as described in the preceding paragraph.

The steamship revolution and containerisation are also similar insofar as both developments lead to structural changes in the maritime transport industry. Whereas liner conferences developed in the wake of the introduction of the steamship, containerisation triggered the emergence of a new form of agreement

---

[45] Herman, (1983), p. 136.
[46] Herman, (1983), p. 135, similar numbers are presented by Hummels, (1999), p. 8.
[47] Erdmenger, FS Raisch, (1995), p. 397.
[48] TACA submission to the OECD, (2001), p. 7.
[49] Shashikumar, (1999), p. 4.
[50] Herman, (1983), p. 139.
[51] Herman, (1983), p. 139.

called *consortium*[52]. The majority of existing liner companies was no longer able to raise the large amounts of capital necessary to purchase new container vessels. The shipping companies reacted to this problem with the formation of consortia. As a result, consortia differ from traditional liner conferences in that they do not focus primarily on price fixing. A consortium is rather a form of co-operation with the aim of sharing the high costs connected to the operation of a modern container fleet[53] while, at the same time, improving the quality of shipping services[54]. They take such diverse forms as joint scheduling, slot and space exchanges, equipment pools, joint offices, joint terminal operations, cargo sharing, revenue sharing agreements and shared inland operations[55]. The most sophisticated consortia agreements that exist in liner shipping today are often called *alliances*. This type of agreement first appeared in the liner shipping industry in the middle of the 1990s. Whereas traditional consortia agreements typically foresaw the co-operation of its members in just one trade lane, the operational area of modern alliances extends much further. They constitute a form of co-operation that covers at least two out of three of the major trade lanes[56] and seeks to give the individual carrier the possibility to offer world wide shipping services to its customers. It has been stated that consortia are the most important form of co-operation in the field of maritime transport today[57].

6. New types of agreements

A recent development in the shipping industry is the emergence of yet another type of agreement distinct from the traditional liner conference, which is called *talking* or *discussion agreement*[58]. This trend started in the 1980s when agreements emerged that included both conference and non-conference lines operating in the same trades[59]. Talking agreements provide a forum within which conference and rivalling non-conference lines can co-ordinate their behaviour by acting together on such issues as capacity management, rates and various other charges and fees[60] without the restriction of a joint tariff structure. It has been suggested that this new type of agreement emerged because the traditional conferences were not able to attract the participation of the new independent lines. These new carriers were offering a service with a quality comparable to

---

[52] Braakman, ETL (1996), p. 265 ff, p. 270; Green, ETL (1993), p. 477 ff, p. 477; Ruttley, ETL (1993), p. 487 ff, p. 488; Williams, (2000), p. 44.

[53] Green, ETL (1993), p. 477 ff, p. 477; Williams, (2000), p. 44.

[54] Faull/Nikpay, (1999), p. 901.

[55] Green, ETL (1993), p. 477 ff, p. 477.

[56] The three major trades are the north - north trade routes between North America, Europe and Asia.

[57] Commission working document on Regulation 870/95, rec. 140; Williams, (2000), p. 44.

[58] Francois/Wooton, (2000), p. 3.

[59] FMC OSRA Report, (2001), p. 24 f.

[60] FMC, OSRA Report, (2001), p. 24.

that of liner conferences[61]. Yet, they were not willing to join a conference, because they did not want to give up their pricing freedom[62]. It was this need for a broader and sufficiently flexible type of arrangement between conference and non-conference carriers that lead to the formation of discussion agreements.

7. Conclusion

The liner shipping industry has experienced two important technological revolutions during the last 200 years. From the 1850s onwards the traditional sailing vessels were replaced by steamships, and from 1966 onwards containerised ships replaced breakbulk carriers. Both of these changes were similar insofar, as they resulted in enlarged transport capacities, reduced sailing times and higher costs for the purchase of new vessels.

Both events also triggered changes in the structure of the liner shipping industry. In order to cope with rate deterioration that occurred after the introduction of the steamship, due to overcapacities in the liner shipping markets, the carriers formed the first liner conferences. A key feature of a liner conference is that the member carriers agree on a common tariff for their shipping services. Such agreements still exist in the liner shipping markets today and are exempted from the regular cartel prohibitions in the legal orders of all major trading nations, including the European Community[63]. The basis for such a favourable treatment of liner shipping conferences throughout the world was laid in the first two official investigations, the British *Royal Commission on Shipping Rings* and the American *Alexander Committee.* Both these enquiries accepted the existence of liner conferences as necessary to stabilise the liner shipping markets. The second technological revolution that affected shipping in the last 200 years was the introduction of containerised shipping. Again, this technological change had effects on the organisation of the liner shipping industry, as the carriers now started to enter into agreements called consortia.

The liner shipping industry has a rich tradition of carriers entering into collective arrangements. Subjects that are covered by the different types of agreements are divers and sometimes very sensitive from a competition law point of view, such as the fixing of prices, capacity reduction agreements and the prohibition of individual service contracts. The question that remains and which this study seeks to answer is whether or not the reasons that have been forwarded by the carriers to justify such an industry structure are still valid today and whether or not European competition law should allow carriers to enter into the different kinds of agreements today and in the future.

---

[61] Shashikumar, (1999), p. 8.

[62] FMC OSRA Report, (2001), p. 25.

[63] Art. 3 Regulation 4056/86.

Chapter two - Liner Shipping today

This chapter has the aim to provide information on the current state of liner shipping. In order to analyse possible competitive problems in this industry, it is necessary to have some knowledge on such matters as the development of the world liner fleet, the markets for liner shipping and on the structure of the liner shipping industry.

1. World fleet development

Liner Shipping markets can be divided into two main parts, routes on the East/West axis (North America - Europe, Europe - Far East, Far East - North America) and the North/South trades [1]. The carrying capacity of fully containerised vessels and the demand for such shipping services in the East/West direction clearly outnumbers that of the North/South routes. In the year 2001 the top three East/West trades had a combined carrying capacity of about 72 per cent of the world's fully containerised shipping fleet. The strongest trade was the transpacific route with 33 per cent, followed by the Asia/Europe route with 25 per cent and the transatlantic route with 13 per cent[2]. Over the last years containerised trade has grown continuously at high rates. From 1985 until 1995, the demand for container transport grew at an average of 7.1 per cent a year. From 1995 until 2005, growth is expected to average at 6.4 per cent per year[3]. This growth in demand for containerised transport coincided with an increase of world-wide container capacity, which quadrupled from 1.25 million TEU in 1991 to 4.99 million TEU in the year 2001[4]. Capacity growth was strongest on the Europe/Asia route (13.1 per cent from 1990 to 1995), followed by the transpacific route (5.6 per cent) and the transatlantic route (1.5 per cent)[5]. In the year 2000, approximately 54 per cent of all general cargo was transported by container. Since it is estimated that up to 65 per cent of world trade are suitable for containerised transport, there remains considerable room for future growth in the container shipping markets, both because of growth by substitution from other forms of shipping and because of an overall increase in trade volume[6].

The world shipping fleet is not only characterised by an overall increase in carrying capacity, but also by a growing average vessel size. In 1990, vessels that could carry more than 3.000 TEU made up one fifth of all vessels in the nine

[1] Mercer Study, (1997), p. 20.
[2] OECD, (2002), p. 16
[3] Mercer Study, (1997), p. 28
[4] OECD, (2002), p. 15.
[5] Mercer Study, (1997), p. 92.
[6] Brooks, (2000), p. 15; OECD, (2002), p. 17.

major world trades, whereas by 1995, this number increased to one third[7]. The average vessel size has grown from 955 TEU in 1980 to more than 1.600 TEU in 1996[8]. Today, the largest containerised ships have a size of 7.000 TEU and it is planned to build ships with a total carrying capacity of 10.000 TEU[9].

Another characteristic of modern shipping is the growing imbalance of cargo between the outbound and inbound legs of a journey. All three major trades have experienced such a growing imbalance in the 1990s. The worst imbalance exists on the transpacific route, where the trade in the eastern direction (Asia to U.S.) outnumbered the trade in the opposite direction by 73 per cent in 1999. In 1995, the difference amounted only to 15.5 per cent. The trade imbalance in the Asia/Europe trade rose from 22.8 per cent in 1995 to 38.6 per cent in 1999 and the imbalance in the transatlantic trade grew from 19.9 per cent in 1995 to 30.1 per cent in 1999[10]. The exceptional high imbalance in the transpacific trade can partially be explained by the crisis that hit the Asian economies in 1996/97, whereas the U.S. economy remained strong during that time. The problem that arises out of such trade imbalances is that vessels have to sail partly empty in the direction where trade is weaker. Secondly, carriers must incur costs for the repositioning of empty containers to the origin of the stronger leg.

2. Concentration in the liner shipping industry

One of the most prominent trends in liner shipping in the recent past has been the process of continuous concentration among carriers. The 20 largest carriers controlled 26 per cent of world-wide TEU capacity in 1980[11], this number rose to 38.8 per cent in 1990[12] and to 72 per cent in the year 2001[13]. The movement to ever bigger and bigger units of production is not unique to liner shipping. Rather, the process of concentration is linked to the globalisation of the economy. International producers and suppliers have a growing demand for global transport services because they increasingly purchase their raw materials and component parts all over the world and ,similarly, because they need to send

[7] Mercer, (1997), p. 105.

[8] Hoffman, (1998), p. 68.

[9] OECD, (2002), p. 15. The largest of these ships are called Post-Panamax vessels. Due to their size, they cannot travel through the Panama Canal anymore. Such Post-Panamax vessels have a carrying capacity, which is bigger than 4.442 TEU, and they are currently employed on the transpacific and the Europe/Asia route; per: Hoffmann, (1998), p. 68 ff.

[10] OECD, (2002), p. 15.

[11] Brooks, (1998), p. 151.

[12] Brooks, (2000), p. 2.

[13] OECD, (2002), p. 14; a recent estimate suggests that the process of concentration in liner shipping is not at an end yet, but that the largest 20 carriers may in the future control up to 80 per cent of the total global TEU capacity, per: Meyrick, (1999), p. 10.

their manufactured goods to all parts of the globe as well[14]. Since maritime transport is the chief mode of international transport, it is particularly affected by the economic globalisation[15]. Only large carriers can offer such worldwide logistics. Until 1996 growth in the liner shipping industry mainly occurred in the form of internal growth. Then carriers realised that they could no longer grow exclusively through organic means and, as a consequence, the pattern of growth now focused more on the formation of global alliances and, in the late 1990s, also on mergers [16].

Liner shipping companies started to enter into the first alliance agreements in the early 1990s, but it was not until 1995 that the process of alliance building gained substantial momentum. By August of that year, four alliances of carriers had been announced[17]. This new type of agreement in the liner shipping industry is different from conference agreements insofar as it does not include a common policy on prices. Furthermore, the members of an alliance normally do not agree on a system of cargo quotas or on the pooling of revenues, nor do they engage in joint management and sales[18]. Even though alliances seek to increase efficiency and cost reductions through co-operation at the operational level, and thus share this approach with the more traditional consortia agreements, they do differ from these agreements on several grounds[19]. One crucial difference between traditional consortia and alliances is their geographical scope. A consortium typically covers only one trade route, whereas the members of an alliance essentially agree on a world-wide co-operation. In the beginning, alliances covered only two of the three major East/West trades, but after a substantial regrouping among the alliance members in the first years of their existence, all alliances now operate services on all three major trade routes, and they have done so since 1998.

Secondly, the depth of co-operation in consortia agreements is often limited to the relatively riskless pooling of resources. Up until the formation of alliances, the co-operation in the form of traditional consortia often consisted only of limited vessel and/or slot chartering agreements[20]. On the other hand, the members of alliances agree on very far reaching forms of co-operation. These agreements

---

[14] Brooks, (2000), p. 1.

[15] Hoffmann, (1998), p. 68.

[16] Meyrick, (1999), p. 9.

[17] Brooks, (1998), p. 154; for a listing of the members of the different alliances see: OECD, (2001), p. 27.

[18] OECD, (2002), p. 26.

[19] Under the legal regime of Regulation 823/2000 alliances may be considered as consortia, but since they constitute an entirely new form of co-operation in comparison to the traditional small-scale consortia, they are in fact a distinguishable type of agreement.

[20] Brooks, (2000), p. 14.

cover all aspects of vessel management, such as vessel size, vessel type, port coverage, sailing schedules and capacity management on a global basis. The members of an alliance also agree on such matters as slot chartering, the joint use of terminal facilities, the joint management of containers and common feeder services for their long-haul routes. From the scope of these activities it becomes clear that alliances go far beyond the level of co-operation that was typical for consortia up until that time, since they aim for the operational integration of each participant's service into one single service[21]. Through the formation of alliances it became possible for carriers to reap some of the benefits typically associated with mergers, without having to give up their individual identities. In the late 1990s, some carriers decided to proceed one step further. As a consequence, the process of concentration through the formation of alliances was superseded by a wave of mergers[22], the most prominent of which was the merger between *Maersk* and *Sealand*, creating the world's biggest carrier[23].

In spite of this concentration process, the liner shipping industry is not as concentrated as other industries. A study undertaken for the European Commission in 1997 concluded that there are still no dominant players in liner shipping, since the largest joint service controls a maximum of 16 per cent of all available capacity in any of the three major East/West trades. Secondly, there are up to 30 carriers that compete for cargoes in the major trade lanes[24]. The count of competing suppliers increases even further if the number of NVOCC, that offer their services on these routes, is added. In this context it is also important to note that the number of competitors in the different trades has increased over the last years and not decreased, as might be feared in a more concentrated industry. Carriers that have entered into global co-operations now extend their services to markets that they did not cover before. As a consequence, the number of competitors in many markets has risen[25], offering a potential gain for shippers, since competition generally increases the pressure on prices.

---

[21] On the other hand, alliances clearly do not constitute mergers according to Art. 3 I Regulation 4064/89. This is mainly so because, according to the European law position, a merger requires the establishment of a permanent link between two or more economic entities. The alliance agreements typically fail such a permanence test, since they contain clauses with respect to their possible termination; per: Brooks, (1998), p. 160 f.

[22] Other important mergers in liner shipping were the joint venture of *P&O* and *Nedloyd*, *Hanjins* acquisition of the *DSR-Senator Linie* and the *Neptune Orient Lines* acquisition of *American President Lines*.

[23] For a thorough description of the development of this merger see: Brooks, (2000), p. 9 ff.

[24] Mercer, (1997), p. 61.

[25] Statement of the chairman of the FMC, Harold Creel, before the Committee on the Judiciary of the House of Representatives, May 5, 1999, p. 11 f; Hoffmann, (1998), p. 73.

Carriers decided to enter into global alliances or to merge because they were eager to reduce their costs and increase their profits[26]. They wanted to achieve this goal through the employment of bigger and more cost efficient vessels. Larger ships are more cost effective because they require proportionately less steel per unit of carrying capacity in their construction. Similarly crewing and fuel costs per TEU mile are also lower on bigger vessels[27]. The continuous use of ever bigger vessels in liner shipping required a reorganisation of shipping services.

Estimates agree that for every increase of carrying capacity of ten per cent, transport costs per unit will decrease by three to four per cent[28]. As described above, the largest container vessels now have a size of 7.000 TEU, a number, which is expected to rise to 10.000 TEU in the near future[29]. The use of such vessels is only efficient on routes with a very high cargo volume. As a consequence, liner transport changed from the traditional pattern, whereby a ship called at several ports at each end of a deep sea route, to a hub and spoke system, a system often employed by international airlines. Post-Panamax vessels operate on the intercontinental leg of a liner service and smaller feeder vessels distribute and collect the containers from the major hub ports to the smaller ports in the region[30]. The development of such a transport pattern increased the necessity for carriers to work together on a global scale. In order to fill large Post-Panamax vessels on intercontinental routes, they had to instate continent-wide cargo collection systems, so as to amass enough cargo for such large vessels, without substantially reducing the frequency of sailings. Secondly, they had to raise sufficient funds for the purchase of such expensive new ships, which furthered the need for co-operation on a financial level.

Another incentive for carriers to enter into alliance agreements or even to merge completely, is the chance to exploit economics of fleet size. Large alliances that operate vessels in many trade lanes are in a position to react more flexibly to fluctuations in capacity demand through a re-deployment of their vessels from routes where demand is currently low onto more frequented routes, that are also part of the alliance sailing schedule[31]. Similarly, it is easier for a global alliance to operate round-the-world services, which can be used to battle overcapacities

---

[26] Meyrick, (1999), p. 10.
[27] Meyrick, (1999), p. 6 f.
[28] Meyrick, (1999), p. 7 f.
[29] See above, p. 29.
[30] Indication for the rising popularity of hub and spoke transport patterns is the continuous increase of transhipped cargoes. For example, estimates for the port of Singapore state that about 80 per cent of the cargoes shipped through that port are being transhipped.
[31] Meyrick, (1999), p. 9.

in trades where one leg is chronically weak[32]. Carriers that enter into a global alliance agreement can also profit from the fact that they are in a better position to satisfy the needs of shippers that have increased global shipping needs. Furthermore, carriers may increase their market power through the formation of large alliances and mergers in relationship to their suppliers such as inland transport providers or port operators[33]. The exercise of their market power may reduce their costs for the purchase of land transport services[34] or port handling operations.

3. Financial aspects of liner shipping

The following part will address three issues of a financial nature: the cost structure of liner shipping operators, their profitability and the development of freight rates in the past.

a) Profitability

Analysts of the liner shipping industry came to the conclusion early on that liner shipping is not a particularly profitable business[35]. The findings of more recent evaluations of liner shipping point in the same direction[36]. While the actual numbers in these studies differ somewhat from each other, they nevertheless show that liner shipping is less profitable than many other non-transport industries[37]. On the other hand, the available data suggest that the profitability in liner shipping is not below average in comparison with other transport industries. A study undertaken by the OECD in 2001/2002 states that the average return on equity[38] of 84 different companies involved in road, rail or freight transport is 9.16 per cent, whereas the average return on equity for 16 different liner carriers is 10.55 per cent. The same study also provided data for both groups of undertakings on their net profit margin. The 16 carriers had an average net profit margin of 3.95 per cent and the average net profit of the other transport companies amounted to 2.07 per cent[39]. These data indicate that the profitability of liner carriers is low, but that they share this characteristic with other branches of the transport industry.

---

[32] See above, p. 30 .

[33] Meyrick, (1999), p. 10.

[34] A liner carrier may need to purchase such services, if it wants to provide door-to-door transport to its customers.

[35] Deakin, (1973), p. 182; Marx, (1953), p. 250.

[36] Mercer, (1996), p. 217; OECD, (2002), p. 45; Report by the Australian Productivity Commission on Liner Shipping, (1999), p. 16.

[37] Mercer, (1996), p. 217.

[38] Return on equity is defined as earnings before tax and interest divided by interest bearing debt and equity.

[39] OECD, (2002), p. 46.

b) Freight rate development

Carriers repeatedly pointed out that the freight rates in liner shipping have continuously declined throughout the 1990s[40]. This finding is backed by results from recent official investigations of the liner shipping industry[41]. In the transpacific trade, rates in 2001 were twelve per cent lower than in 1993 on the eastbound leg and 46 per cent lower on the westbound leg. In the same time, rates in the transatlantic trade decreased by 42 per cent on the eastbound leg and by twelve per cent on the westbound leg. The numbers for the Europe/Asia trade indicate a decrease of 35 per cent in the eastbound direction and a 23 per cent decrease on the westbound journey[42].

However, the decline in freight rates throughout the 1990s must be considered in light of the fact that freight rates reached an all-time high in 1985. Data from the German liner price index show that relative freight rates were rather stable until the first oil price shock in 1973. From that time on, freight rates increased at great speed until 1985, after which the level of relative freight rates started to decline continuously[43]. In relationship to these data it is interesting to note that the level of freight rates for 1998 was still above the level of 1973, the last year before the period of yearly strong increases in freight rates, if the prices were deflated by the German consumer price index. If however, the prices were deflated by the US GDP deflator, then the 1998 level of freight rates would be just slightly below the level of freight rates in the base year of 1954. This long-term analysis of indexed freight rates demonstrates that, although average rates have dropped continuously over the last years, the situation is not as dramatic as these short-term freight rate decreases might indicate.

c) Cost structure

Traditionally, the costs for shipping, as for other business operations, are divided into fixed and variable costs. Fixed costs make up about 70 per cent of the total costs for liner shipping[44]. Capital costs constitute the first substantial part of fixed costs, since liner shipping is one of the most capital intensive industries in the world[45]. Liner shipping operators require large amounts of capital for the purchase of new vessels. A new Post-Panamax vessel with a carrying capacity of 6.000 TEU might cost up to $ 80 million. During the whole life span of such a vessel a similar sum must be spent for the sufficient supply of

---

[40] See for example: TSA submission to the OECD, (2001), p. 3; WSC submission to the OECD, (2001), p. 13.

[41] OECD, (2002), p. 30; Report by the Australian Productivity Commission on Liner Shipping, (1999), p. 15.

[42] OECD, (2002), p. 31.

[43] For the relevant data see: Hummels, (1999), p. 28, figure 2.

[44] Herman, (1983), p. 30.

[45] Sletmo/Williams, (1981), p. 136 ff.

containers[46]. The capital need of liner carriers is aggravated by the fact that they often cannot purchase just one ship at a time; instead they need to buy several ships at once, in order to establish a service on a new route.

A second component of fixed costs are the costs that have to be incurred to keep the vessels running. These so-called operational costs make up about 30 per cent of total costs[47] and they include the costs for fuel, crewing, general insurance, maintenance and repair as well as port and canal fees. Apart from the fuel costs, the operational costs are constant, irrespective of whether or not the ship sails with a full load. It has been said that the carrier has only very limited influence over such costs[48]. This statement needs to be qualified on two accounts. A first possibility for carriers to reduce their operational costs is by registering their vessels under a flag of convenience[49]. In the year 1995, 47 per cent of all European Community owned container vessels were registered under a flag of convenience[50], and the paramount reason for such a move was the desire of vessel operators to reduce their crewing costs[51]. The reduction in crewing costs for a 4.000 TEU container vessel that results from the switch to an open registry from a regular EC flag amounts from $ 0.38 to $ 0.63 million per year[52]. Carriers see also a significant potential for cost savings in the formation of larger and hence more powerful buying groups, with the aim to negotiate lower port fees[53].

A third component of fixed costs are the costs for landside operations, such as administration and sales offices. This area of fixed costs has also been identified as an area, where potential cost savings can still be realised in the future[54]. Variable costs make up for about 30 per cent of total costs[55]. They consist mainly of the costs for handling and loading of cargoes and also cargo specific insurance premiums.

4. The markets for liner shipping

An analysis of competition in the liner shipping industry, and of possible restraints thereto, necessitates a definition of the relevant markets for liner ship-

---

[46] TACA submission to the OECD, (2002), p. 7.
[47] Mercer, (1996), p. 76.
[48] Kühne, (1996), p. 30.
[49] The five most popular open registries for shipping operators from the European Community are Cyprus, Panama, Malta, Liberia and the Bahamas; per: Mercer, (1996), p. 54.
[50] Mercer, (1996), p. 20.
[51] Mercer, (1996), p. 76 f.
[52] Mercer, (1996), p. 59.
[53] Mercer, (1997). p. 115.
[54] Mercer, (1997), p. 112 f.
[55] Herman, (1983), p. 30; Mercer, (1997), p. 76.

ping services as a basis for such an evaluation. The relevant market has to be defined in qualitative, as well as in geographical terms.

a) Qualitative market assessment

In order to determine the boundaries of a market, the ECJ[56] as well as the Commission[57] have chosen an approach that focuses on the substitutability or interchangeability of the relevant products[58]. The principle tool in the assessment of the substitutability of two or more different products is the cross price elasticity of demand[59], which measures how much the quantity demanded for good A changes as a response to a change in price for good B[60]. If the cross price elasticity for two products is low, then the demand for product A does not change much, if the price for product B changes, and thus the markets for the two products are separate entities.

As simple as the concept of cross price elasticity of demand may be in theory, it is not always possible to gather reliable data on this matter in practice. In such situations the ECJ has resorted to an analysis of objective characteristics of the products in question[61]. An illustrative example of this strategy is the ECJ's approach in the *United Brands* case[62], where the Court had to assess whether or not the market for bananas is separate from that of other fruits. In its evaluation, the Court considered the appearance, taste, softness and seedlessness of bananas and came to the conclusion that, due to these special characteristics, the market for bananas is separate from that of other table fruits[63].

The Commission adopted a somewhat different stance on the consideration of objective product characteristics in the definition process of the relevant market[64]. In 1997, the Commission issued a notice with the purpose of clarifying its own approach towards matters of market definition[65]. In this document the

---

56 Case 322/81, *Nederlandsche Banden-Industrie Michelin NV v Commission,* (1983) ECR, p. 3461 ff, p. 3504 f, rec. 37.

57 Commission notice on the definition of relevant market for the purposes of Community competition law, rec. 7, OJ, (1997), C-372/5.

58 Craig/de Burca, (1998), p. 942; Jacobs, (1991), p. 59.

59 Craig/de Burca, (1998), p. 942.

60 Baumol/Blinder, (1999), p. 128; Eaton/Eaton/Allen, (1999), p. 106, Mankiw, (2001), p. 104.

61 Craig/de Burca, (1998), p. 943.

62 Case 27/76, *United Brands Co. & United Brands Continentaal BV v Commission,* (1978), ECR, p. 207 ff.

63 Case 27/76, *United Brands Co. and United Brands Continentaal BV v Commission,* (1978), ECR, p. 207 ff, p. 282 f, rec. 23/33.

64 Craig/de Burca, (1998), p. 949.

65 Commission notice on the definition of relevant market for the purposes of Community competition law, OJ, (1997), C-372/5.

Commission stated that objective product characteristics or the intended use of products do not constitute sufficient indicators for the substitutability of these products. Instead, the Commission emphasised *inter alia* the importance of: evidence of substitution from the recent past, the opinion of consumers and competitors as well as barriers and costs associated with substitution[66]. Due to the role of the European Commission as the principal administrator of EC competition law, this notice clearly cannot be dismissed in practical terms. It is necessary, however, to keep in mind that the Commission's notice does not have any legal quality[67]. Since the therein stated position of the Commission deviates from the standpoint of the ECJ, as far as the definition of the relevant market under consideration of objective product characteristics is concerned, it would be necessary for the latter to recognise this new approach for it to become good law. Until the present day, the Court has not done so and, as a consequence, the following evaluation of the markets for liner shipping focuses on the more product oriented approach of the ECJ.

aa) Conference carriers and non-conference competition

Non-conference lines have historically provided a service of lower quality at rates below the relevant conference rate[68]. The service of non-conference carriers often suffered from a lower frequency of sailings, a lower vessel standard and from the fact that the commitment of an independent carrier to a certain route was often deemed as unstable in comparison to the conference service. To compensate the shippers for these qualitative shortcomings the non-conference carriers charged freight rates that were typically ten per cent below the conference rate level[69]. In some instances the difference in rates between conference and independent carriers could amount up to 25 per cent[70].

In the last 25 years this traditional picture of the liner shipping industry has changed. New independent carriers have emerged whose quality of service matches that of conference carriers[71]. Their size[72] allows them to operate a sailing schedule that covers many parts of the globe and they are also in a position to offer intermodal transport services to their customers[73]. These carriers

---

[66] Commission notice on the definition of relevant market for the purposes of Community competition law, rec. 37 f, OJ, (1997), C-372/5.

[67] Jones/Sufrin, (2001), p. 42.

[68] Meyrick, (1999), p. 18.

[69] Herman, (1983), p. 84; Marx, (1953), p. 189.

[70] Jacobs, (1991), p. 36.

[71] FMC, OSRA Report, (2001), p. 24.

[72] For example, *Evergreen*, the 5th largest carrier in the world, had a fleet with a total capacity of 211.883 TEU in 2001 and *Hanjin*, the 7th largest carrier worldwide, had a fleet capacity of 179.424 TEU in the same year; per: OECD, (2002), p. 14.

[73] Meyrick, (1999), p. 18.

operate outside the conference system because they deliberately choose to do so for the sake of their own managerial independence and not because they have no other option. Another development that blurred the clear distinction between a high quality conference service and a low quality non-conference service is the decision of some of the traditional conference carriers to leave the conferences at least on some routes and to provide their services as independent operators instead[74]. Today the question of conference membership is often a question of business tactics and not a requirement for the provision of a high quality shipping service. As liner operators inside and outside a conference provide shipping services of similar quality and frequency, they also operate within the same markets.

bb) Competition from tramp shipping

Tramp services are typically employed for the transport of bulks[75]. In tramp shipping, the vessel does not follow a set schedule, but the shipper normally charters the whole vessel for a certain period of time or a certain voyage[76]. The rates are not set in accordance with a fixed tariff, as in liner shipping, but they are negotiated individually between the tramp carrier and the shipper[77] through several large shipping exchanges[78]. Traditionally, some competition arose between liner shipping and tramp shipping, when the tramp was looking for cargoes that it could transport on the back-haul of its journey, in order to avoid having to sail in ballast[79]. Since the tramp shipping rates already remunerate the carrier for an empty back-haul, the tramp carriers could offer very low rates on these journeys, which made them an attractive alternative to liner shipping[80]. The actual competition that arose from tramps for the liners was restricted, because tramps often did not sail on a scheduled service, which rendered them unattractive for shippers that required a regular delivery of their goods[81]. Tramps also constituted only limited competition to liner transport because they operate typically on port-to-port routes[82]. They do not call at several ports at either end

---

[74] Meyrick, (1999), p. 18 f.

[75] The major bulk commodities can be differentiated from general cargo by the fact that bulks, such as oil, iron ore, coal, bauxite, phosphate rock and grain do not have to be packed for shipment; per: Jansson/Shneerson, (1987), p. 21.

[76] A time charter is a contractual transport arrangement by which the charterer is responsible for the vessel and has it at his disposal for a defined period of time. Under a voyage charter, on the other hand, the shipowner remains responsible for the vessel and leaves it at the disposal of the customer for one or more voyages; per: Sletmo/Williams, (1981), p. 8.

[77] Herman, (1983), p. 85.

[78] For example: London, New York, Hong Kong.

[79] Herman, (1983), p. 85.

[80] Jacobs, (1991), p. 39.

[81] Herman, (1983), p. 85.

[82] Herman, (1983), p. 87.

of the journey, like the liners, and consequently they could only pick up cargo at one port at each end of the voyage.

Today, the traditional competition between liners and tramps has greatly declined[83]. The main reason for this decline is the diversification of vessel types. Originally, tramps, as well as liners, employed the same kind of all-purpose ships for their transport operations. In modern shipping, liner carriers use containerised vessels that are not common in tramp shipping[84]. Tramp shipping carriers rather employ ships that are specially fitted for the transport of bulks, such as, for example, tankers or grain ships. The use of such special ships makes it difficult or even impossible to switch from the transport of bulks to the transport of containerised general cargo. Consequently, the competition between tramps and liners is limited.

Yet, some competition between liners and tramps may arise if tramps employ vessels that can carry bulk, as well as containers. Such ships allow competition between tramps and liners on the back-haul of a bulk transport in the manner described above. The importance of this type of competition is restricted, since the number of such vessels is small[85]. Another way in which tramps might successfully compete with liners is with cargo that can either be transported as general cargo or as so-called minor bulk[86]. With the continued growth in world trade, the amount of such cargoes may rise to a level where it becomes possible to move this cargo in quantities that are sufficient to fill a whole ship[87], with the result that these goods may also be carried as bulk by tramp carriers. In a similar way, liners and bulk carriers may compete for the carriage of refrigerated cargoes, since it is possible to transport them either in special ships or in containers that are equipped for the transport of refrigerated goods[88]. Although tramp carriers and liner operators may compete with each other occasionally, the two modes of shipping display substantial differences, which make them partial alternatives[89] at best. It is for this reason that the markets for tramp shipping and liner shipping have to be regarded as two separate markets.

cc) Competition with airborne transport

Air transport is characterised by the fact that even the largest aeroplanes have

[83] Jansson/Shneerson, (1987), p. 19.
[84] Herman, (1983), p. 87.
[85] Jansson/Shneerson, (1987), p. 19.
[86] Examples for such minor bulks are sugar and rice.
[87] Jansson/Shneerson, (1987), p. 19.
[88] So called *reefers*.
[89] Jansson/Shneerson, (1987), p. 19; Herman, (1983), p. 88.

only a small carrying capacity in comparison to liner vessels[90]. An advantage of airborne transport is its speed and the fact that planes can deliver their freight directly to airports inland, which may be far away from the nearest seaport. These qualities make air transport an alternative to maritime transport for the carriage of goods that are low in volume, high in value and that require speedy delivery, such as fruits, vegetables and flowers[91]. Although the overall capacity of airborne transport has remained small in comparison to the carrying capacity of maritime transport, the fact that air transport has taken over the transport of high value cargoes (for which carriers could charge high rates) has lead to a disproportionately high loss of revenue for the providers of maritime transport services[92]. Since the ton per mile costs of air freight are still considerably higher than the costs of maritime transport, it is not to be expected that air transport will replace maritime transport on a large scale in the future[93]. Those freights that make up much of the general cargo of liner conferences[94] are simply too heavy for transport by air at reasonable costs. As a consequence, many shippers do not have a choice between air and maritime transport for their goods, and both modes of transport constitute separate markets.

dd) Competition with land transport

A land bridge is the connection between two ports via land. There are two main railroad connections that serve as land bridges today, the Trans-Sibirian Railway and transcontinental railroad connections in the U.S.. Railroad transport is relatively cheap, well-suited for the transport of containers and it can also be faster than maritime transport[95]. Another advantage of railroad transport is that conference loyalty agreements do not punish the use of railroad transport and ,consequently, shippers that use such services do not have to fear hostile conference behaviour[96]. As a result, land bridges do constitute competition to liner shipping[97]. The impact of this competition should not be overestimated though, because on many shipping routes it is not possible to substitute maritime trans-

---

[90] An aeroplane of the Boing 747 type can only carry five FEU; per: Jacobs, (1991), p. 41. Although a plane can make several return trips in the time, it takes a ship to complete just one round trip, the overall carrying capacity of air transport is still considerably smaller than that of maritime transport.

[91] Herman, (1983), p. 98; Jacobs, (1991), p. 41 f.

[92] Herman, (1983), p. 97; Jacobs, (1991), p. 41.

[93] Herman, (1983), p. 98.

[94] For example: machinery, textiles, tools, chemicals, steel products, paper and wood.

[95] Herman, (1983), p. 150; Jacobs, (1991), p. 42.

[96] Kühne, (1996), p. 64.

[97] For example: 50 per cent of all freight from Asia to New York was carried by rail from the West Coast to the New York area and not by ship through the Panama Canal in the early 1990s; per: Kühne, (1996), p. 64.

port with land transport. Secondly, difficulties in railroad operations may render such a service less attractive in spite of the advantages mentioned above[98].

b) Geographical market assessment

A second aspect of importance to the evaluation of a relevant market is the definition of the geographical boundaries of a market. The fact that liner shipping is a global business does not mean that there is only one global market for liner shipping services. Neither is every shipping route between two ports a separate market. The solution lies somewhere in between, and it is again the substitutability of routes and ports that is the chief indicator of the geographical markets boundaries. Shippers often do have the possibility to choose between different carriers that operate different routes. For example, it may be possible that carrier A offers a transatlantic service from New York to Hamburg, whereas carrier B offers a service from Baltimore to Rotterdam. The fact that origin and destination of these two routes differ from each other does not necessarily mean that they are two separate markets. An important factor for the assessment of the substitutability of different shipping routes is the possibility of accessing the different ports from the hinterland[99]. Shippers that often demand door-to-door delivery of their freights are not so much concerned with the origin and end of the sea leg of such a transport operation, but rather with the speed and punctuality with which the transported goods reach their final inland destination. If two ports, that could serve as possible endpoints of a sea voyage, have similar access to the hinterland, it is likely that inland shippers will consider them as equal alternatives. As a result, services that start or terminate in these ports constitute only one market.

However, accessability from the hinterland is not the only criterion in the evaluation of the substitutability of different shipping routes. Other factors, such as the speed of customs services in the different ports or the likelihood of adverse weather conditions that affect either port operations or the possibility of reaching a certain port, do play a role in the analysis of port and hence route substitutability[100]. For these reasons, it is not possible to define the geographical boundaries of shipping markets in a general manner. They need to be assessed on an individual basis. The geographical closeness of two ports might be a first indicator of the substitutability of shipping services that begin or terminate at these ports, but it is by far not the only aspect that is of relevance in assessing of the geographical boundaries of the markets for liner shipping.

---

[98] This applies especially to the Trans-Siberian railroad; see: Herman, (1983), p. 151 f.
[99] OECD, (2002), p. 20.
[100] OECD, (2002), p. 20.

5. The typical liner conference

Approximately 150 conferences exist in liner shipping today. Membership in most conferences is below ten, but some have up to 50 members[101]. Analysts of liner shipping have stated that the days of conferences as a crucial element of liner shipping are over[102], since their share of TEU capacity has declined from a high of 80 to 90 per cent in the 1970s[103] to about 60 per cent in the three major trades in the 1990s[104]. Yet, conferences still control a considerable part of the available transport capacity. An understanding of the main features of a typical liner conference is an essential prerequisite for the evaluation of liner conferences in the context of European Community competition law. Since liner conferences may differ considerably from each other in their organisation and in their scope of activities[105], the following description is not necessarily applicable to every single conference, but it is a presentation of the most common features of liner conferences.

a) The legal quality, structure and membership of liner conferences

Most legal writers who evaluate the conference system agree that liner conferences do not have legal personality[106]. They emphasise that the conference members do not give up their managerial autonomy, and that it is solely the responsibility of the carriers to provide maritime transport services to the shippers[107]. This position is doubtful at least. One point of criticism is that conference agreements may contain clauses that do limit the independence of the individual member line considerably. Examples of such provisions would be cargo and revenue pooling arrangements or clauses that relate to the quality of service. Such forms of co-operation effectively limit the business choices of the individual conference member. In consideration of the long existence of some conferences, the fact that they have their own institutions and some capital at their disposal, as well as the fact that they often have a purpose that goes beyond the mere economic co-operation of different carriers[108], it is sound to say that liner conferences have many of the characteristics that are typical for a legal person and as a consequence they should be considered as such.

The members of a conference typically appoint a secretary as chairman of the conference. Some conferences have a system by which the chairmanship rotates

---

101 Kang/Findlay, (2000), p. 155.

102 Brooks, (1998), p. 142; Kang/Findlay, (2000), p. 159.

103 Report by the Australian Productivity Commission on Liner Shipping, (1999), p. 10.

104 Mercer, (1997), p. 64 f; OECD, (2002), p. 20.

105 Jansson/Shneerson, (1987), p. 35.

106 Herman, (1983), p. 15; Jacobs, (1991), p. 18; Marx, (1953), p. 137.

107 Herman, (1983), p. 18; Jacobs, (1991), p. 18.

108 For example: to ensure a stable provision of liner shipping services; per: Würdinger, WuW (1969), p. 655.

between the different member lines, others appoint an independent person as secretary, who is not connected to any of the conference members[109]. The conference secretary is in charge of the routine administration of the conference; one of his most important duties is to direct and co-ordinate the establishment of the common conference tariff[110]. The more important institution in a conference is the owners committee, which is composed of representatives of the member lines. This body decides in regularly scheduled meetings on all matters of general importance for the conference policy[111]. Normally, the votes of all conference members carry equal weight, irrespective of the size and importance of the individual carriers[112]. The voting requirements vary from conference to conference, depending on the subject matter. In some affairs, a simple majority is sufficient, whereas other decisions require unanimity. Apart from these two institutions, a conference may have further committees that are in charge of special subjects, such as the relationship to the shippers or the continuous adjustment of the conference tariff to the current economic situation. Sometimes, conferences also employ regional co-ordinators who represent the conference at the different conference ports.

Conferences are divided into open and closed conferences[113]. Since the passage of the Shipping Act of 1916, U. S. legislation requires conferences, that cover trades to and from the U. S., to be open. In an open conference, there are no formal restrictions to entry into the conference. Any carrier may join the conference, as long as it offers a service that fulfils the qualitative requirements of the conference. In reality, entry is often hindered by the fact that potential new entrants find it difficult to secure enough cargo for themselves. Carriers that want to join a conference need sufficient cargo in order to be able to provide a service that matches conference standards, while, at the same time, operating at a profitable level. The reason for the often encountered difficulty of newcomers to a trade in obtaining a sufficient amount of freight, is the fact that the conferences tie many of the shippers to the established conference carriers through loyalty rebates. As shippers do not want to loose their rebate benefits, they are not inclined to shift their cargo to a potential new competitor[114].

Closed conferences, which dominated all non-U. S. trades, are not accessible to potential newcomers at free will. A newcomer's entry is dependant on the ap-

---

[109] Herman, (1983), p. 15; Jacobs, (1991), p. 20; Kühne, (1996), p. 40.
[110] Herman, (1983), p. 15 f.
[111] Herman, (1983), p. 16; Jacobs, (1991), p. 20; Kühne, (1996), p. 40.
[112] Herman, (1983), p. 16.
[113] Deakin, (1973), p. 56; Herman, (1983), p. 17; Jacobs, (1991), p. 19; Jansson/Shneerson, (1987), p. 41; Kühne, (1996), p. 38.
[114] Herman, (1983), p. 18; Jacobs, (1991), p. 19; Kühne, (1996), p. 38 f.

proval of the conference. The decision on the admission of a new member to the conference is one that typically requires unanimity in the owners committee[115]. The clear distinction between open and closed conferences has eroded over the past, because closed conferences are nowadays more willing to admit new members into their ranks.

In a conference, there are typically two kinds of members: full and associated members. The latter often have reduced sailing rights and often they may not participate in conference voting either. Sometimes they are not even allowed to take part in the meetings of the owners committee. On the other hand, the associated members are subjected to all rules and regulations of the conferences. The creation of such a second class conference membership has several reasons. Occasionally, a carrier has only a limited interest in the affairs of a conference, for example because its engagement on the conference route is only marginal. In other instances, the status of an associated member is given to a new conference member for a certain period of time. In this period, the new conference member must prove its good faith and its ability to operate adequately as a common conference carrier[116].

b) The operational area of a liner conference

One major issue of any conference agreement is the geographical definition of the conference route. Since traffic on inbound and outbound routes often constitutes two separate trades, due to the differences in the kind and quantity of the carried freights, a conference typically covers only one direction of a trade lane[117]. Conferences also seek to ensure that their operational area does not overlap with the sphere of another conference. The conference agreement lays down a stretch of coast line at each end of the trade route as its area of operation, known as conference- or service range. The service range is either defined as the seaboard between two ports (e. g.: Hamburg - Dunkirk) or as a naturally delimited part of the seaboard of a country or continent (e. g.: Atlantic coast of North America)[118]. In the conference range the conference classifies the different ports according to their importance. Ports of major importance for conference trade are called base ports. The conference lines call regularly and frequently at these ports[119] because of the amount of cargo that is loaded and unloaded at such ports. Normally, conference tariffs cover the transport between two base ports. Ports of lesser importance are called direct ports. These ports are not part of the regular conference schedule and they are only served by con-

[115] Herman, (1983), p. 16.
[116] Herman, (1983), p. 19 f; Jacobs, (1991), p. 18 f; Kühne, (1996), p. 39 f.
[117] Herman, (1983), p. 21; Jacobs, (1991), p. 21; Marx, (1953), p. 137.
[118] Jansson/Shneerson, (1987), p. 157.
[119] Deakin, (1973), p. 54.

ference lines if there is sufficient cargo that necessitates a stop at such a port[120]. Transport to direct ports is conducted at the regular conference tariff, but occasionally a small additional charge has to be paid[121]. A third category of conference ports are outports. These ports are normally not serviced directly by conference members. In order to provide full coverage within their geographical range, conference carriers do service these ports by transhipment, for which the shipper is required to pay an additional fee that covers the costs of the transhipment service[122]. Finally, the conference carriers may also provide transport services to way ports. Such ports are not situated at either end of the conference route, but they lie *en route*. If there is sufficient cargo to be dropped or loaded at such a port, the conference vessel will stop there to do so[123].

c) The pricing policy of a conference

Based on the common conference tariff, which specifies the price of shipping services between two conference base ports, the final price for the transport of the shippers cargo is determined by taking into account all applicable rebates and surcharges.

aa) The common conference tariff

The most important decision of a conference is the establishment and the continuous adjustment of a common conference tariff. Such a tariff either catalogues the different commodities in detail or it groups them into several classes[124]. For cargoes that do not match any of the listings in the tariff, a special tariff called NOS (Not Otherwise Specified) is applicable. In the European Community, the EFTA and in Japan, commodities are grouped according to the Brussels Tariff Nomenclature (BTN). Under this system, the conferences are not free anymore to decide how to group the different commodities together, but they retain full authority over the pricing decision for each commodity group. Typically, conferences base their decision on the price for the transport of goods from a certain group on the value of these commodities. Sometimes, they also take into account the weight of a commodity.

In some instances, the common conference tariff is not applicable, although a shipper chooses to transport its goods with a conference line. One example of such a situation is where the service quality of an individual carrier deviates

---

[120] Deakin, (1973), p. 54; Jacobs, (1991), p. 22.
[121] Deakin, (1973), p. 54.
[122] Deakin, (1973), p. 55.
[123] Deakin, (1973), p. 55 f.
[124] Herman, (1983), p. 34.

substantially from the common conference standard[125]. The conference then sets special rates for the services of that carrier. A conference may also declare the rates for certain commodities or groups of commodities to be open[126]. If the conference decides to do so, then the conference members are allowed to determine the rates for these commodities individually. Conferences usually declare rates open when the conference carriers face substantial competition from outsiders, especially from tramp shippers. In such situations, conferences cannot successfully enforce their high tariffs, and in order to be able to provide a more competitive service, conferences may choose to declare the rates open[127].

bb) Rebates

The conference agreement lays down certain rebates that the carriers have to deduct from the common conference tariffs. These rebates all have the purpose of increasing the shippers' loyalty to the conference lines.

aaa) The deferred rebate

The first rebate system that conferences developed was the system of deferred rebates. Under this system, the shippers could benefit from a rebate of five per cent up to 20 per cent of the tariff price, the usual amount being ten per cent. In order to receive such a favourable treatment, shippers had to agree to send their cargoes exclusively with the conference members for a fixed period of time. The shipper was then obliged to remain loyal to the conference for an additional period of time, the period of deferment. Only at the end of this second period was the shipper eligible for a partial refund of the rates he paid during the initial rebate period. If the shipper at any point became disloyal, he would forfeit any claims for a refund[128]. This system was very effective in securing the shippers' loyalty and, as a consequence, it spread from the first conference on the UK - Calcutta route to most other conferences in the late 19th century. The U. S. Shipping Act of 1916 explicitly prohibited conferences that served the U. S trades to use deferred rebates, and since that time, deferred rebates were only used on non-U. S. routes[129].

bbb) The dual rate system

As a consequence of the prohibition of deferred rebates in U. S. trades, conferences serving the U. S. developed another rebate system to increase the loyalty

---

125 Herman, (1983), p. 35, an example would be if a single carrier employs older and slower vessels, or if its vessels operate on a longer route.

126 Herman, (1983), p. 36; Jansson/Shneerson, (1987), p. 37; Kühne, (1996), p. 55.

127 Herman, (1983), p. 36 gives further examples for situations where conferences might be inclined to declare the rates for certain commodities to be open.

128 Herman, (1983), p. 59; Jacobs, (1991), p. 26; Kühne, (1996), p. 56

129 Section 14 of the U. S. Shipping Act of 1916.

of shippers called the dual rate system. Rebates under this system could amount up to 25 per cent of the relevant common conference tariff[130]. This rebating system consists of two different tariff rates, a higher rate for shippers, who do not want to submit themselves to a loyalty obligation, and a lower rate for shippers who agree to send their cargoes exclusively with conference carriers over a certain period of time[131]. The crucial difference to the system of deferred rebates is that, under the dual rate system, the shipper benefits from the rebate in the form of an immediate rate reduction, and he does not have to wait an additional period of time after having paid the full tariff rate in the first place[132].

ccc) Conclusion

Both types of rebates have lost some of their virtue as devices in effectively securing the shippers' loyalty to conference lines. One reason for this development must be seen in the fact that conferences are not so strict anymore on punishing shippers for their infidelity. Conferences fear that such a behaviour would induce shippers to switch to other suppliers of maritime transport services[133]. It is also more difficult, nowadays, for conferences to detect disloyalty on the part of the shippers. They might decide to hand their cargoes over to a freight intermediary, such as a NVOCC. The conference carriers then can no longer determine whose freights they actually carry on their vessels[134] and, as a consequence, they cannot punish anyone for possible disloyalty. In spite of the reduced effectiveness of these two kinds of rebates, they still constitute the most commonly employed rebates in liner shipping[135]. Yet, sometimes shippers that transport large amounts of cargo with a conference are able to negotiate special rates for the transport of their goods. Such individually negotiated reductions may amount up to 30 per cent in comparison to the common conference tariff.

cc) Surcharges

Whereas rebates lead to a reduction of the common freight rate, conference agreements typically also contain provisions on the levying of additional surcharges that increase the price of liner transport services. Surcharges have the purpose of passing on to the shippers such cost increases that are not a consequence of a general increase in carriers costs, but rather are caused by singular events that increase the costs for the provision of liner shipping services. Usually, they are only imposed on those shippers whose cargoes are directly af-

---

[130] Kühne, (1996), p. 58.
[131] Herman, (1983), p. 62; Jacobs, (1991), p. 27; Kühne, (1996), p. 57.
[132] Herman, (1983), p. 62.
[133] Jacobs, (1991), p. 28.
[134] Jacobs, (1991), p. 28.
[135] Herman, (1983), p. 59.

fected by the cost increase[136]. Surcharges that are common features of conference agreements include the already mentioned special charge for transhipment services[137], port congestion surcharges in case a vessel loses time due to a delay of port operations, and bunker surcharges, which cover the risk of a sudden increase in fuel prices.

Surcharges constitute a problematic aspect of the conference's pricing policy insofar, as they are counterproductive to rate stability, which, in turn, is one of the main justifications for the existence of liner conferences. If a carrier has the possibility of passing increases of operational costs on to the shippers, the latter then face the danger that rates might change at short notice, according to the current cost situation of the carriers[138]. Another problem connected with the practice of charging various surcharges is the fact that such a system is not very transparent as to the causes of such surcharges[139] and also that carriers often consider surcharges to be non-negotiable[140].

A special surcharge is the currency adjustment factor, a device to reduce the consequences that the floating of the different currencies against each other has on the common freight rates. If a carrier and a shipper agree on the payment in a certain currency, and then this currency experiences a devaluation, the carrier will receive less for its services which it still has to render in equal quality. In the opposite situation, where the currency appreciates, it is the shipper who has to pay more, even though the objective value of the transport service does not increase. In order to mitigate the possible dangers that could arise out of currency fluctuations for carriers, as well as for shippers, both groups agreed on a system of surcharges and rate reductions that seeks to equalise the effects of such insecurities[141].

d) Pooling arrangements

A final aspect of conference agreements that needs to be considered for the purposes of their evaluation in the light of EC competition law, is the fact that these agreements occasionally provide for forms of co-operation that go beyond the establishment of a common tariff. Some conferences not only have a common pricing policy, but their members have agreed on further co-operation in the

---

[136] Herman, (1983), p. 52.

[137] See above, p. 48.

[138] OECD, (2002), p. 44.

[139] An example would be the practise of some carriers to raise the so-called terminal handling charges in a situation, where the port in question did not even raise its charges; per: OECD, (2001), p. 43.

[140] OECD, (2002), p. 44.

[141] Herman, (1983), p. 55; Jacobs, (1991), p. 58 f.

form of cargo or even of revenue pooling. The purpose of both types of pools is to reduce intra-conference competition[142].

aa) Cargo pools

Already the first conference on the UK - Calcutta route limited the amount of cargo that each member of the conference was allowed to carry through the allocation of the available sailings to the different conference lines[143]. This method of cargo distribution is not very effective, since carriers can still increase their carrying capacity through the use of bigger vessels. Today, the distribution of sailings is rarely used as a device to share the cargo among the different conference lines[144]. A more common form of cargo pooling is the establishment of a cargo quota system. Under such a system, each carrier is allowed to carry only a certain percentage of the total conference cargo in any given period of time. Cargo quotas can exist for certain commodities only, or they can also cover all conference cargoes. The cargo share of each member line is fixed on the basis of its performance in the time prior to the establishment of such a system[145]. If a carrier transports more cargo than he is allowed to, under the quota system, then the profit from these surplus cargoes will have to be handed over to the conference administration, which will distribute these funds among those carriers, who could not transport as much cargo as they would have been allowed to.

The rationale behind a cargo pooling arrangement is to avoid competition among conference lines for a bigger share of conference cargo. If all conference carriers are allowed to transport only a certain cargo volume, then they do not have an incentive anymore to exceed this amount, since they would have to hand over any profits that arose out of such behaviour. Yet, carriers might be tempted to exceed their allocated cargo share in spite of the fact that they do not have an immediate financial gain from such a practice. During the reallocation of cargo quotas, it will be taken into account that a conference line carried more than its allocated share of cargo in the past and as a result, the cargo quota of that carrier is likely to be increased. To avoid such behaviour of the conference members, some pooling agreements provide for heavy fines, if carriers exceed their cargo share[146]. Even if such a system of fines achieves a reduction of the intra-conference competition for cargo between the different conference members, they still compete for the most remunerative cargoes. Since the conference members are not allowed to increase their profits by simply transporting

---

[142] Jansson/Shneerson, (1987), p. 41.
[143] See above, p. 22.
[144] Deakin, (1973), p. 64.
[145] Deakin, (1973), p. 66; Herman, (1983), p. 24.
[146] Jacobs, (1991), p. 29; Herman, (1983), p. 24 f.

more cargo, they might consider increasing their gains through the transport of more profitable cargoes.

bb) Revenue pools

The revenue pool constitutes one of the strongest possible limitations on competition of a conference agreement. The purpose of such an arrangement is the elimination of competition among the conference lines for lucrative loads. If a conference establishes a revenue pool, then the profits will be shared among the members according to fixed quotas[147]. The revenue pool can simply include the revenue from some commodities, but it may also include all revenue[148]. Consequence of a revenue sharing arrangement is that there is no need for a carrier to transport especially lucrative cargoes, since this would not increase his overall profits[149]. Again, a conference line might still try to generate more revenue than is its due part according to the quota system, in order to ameliorate its position in future reassessments of the revenue quotas[150].

---

[147] Jacobs, (1991), p. 29.

[148] Jansson/Shneerson, (1987), p. 42.

[149] Herman, (1983), p. 25.

[150] Deakin, (1973), p. 67.

Chapter three - The development of a European legal order for maritime transport

The whole transport sector had largely been characterised by inaction of the Community as far as the development of a common transport policy was concerned[1]. This was particularly true for the field of maritime transport, as the Community was to a large extent inactive in the field of maritime transport until the middle of the 1980s[2]. Two main reasons have been put forward for this initial reluctance of the European Community to legislate in this area.

First, it has been argued that maritime transport only played a minor role in the Community of the six original Member States, since they were all connected by land[3]. Only with the accession of the United Kingdom, Ireland and Denmark on the 1st of January 1973[4] and later Greece on the 1st of January 1981 did the importance of maritime transport increase. Before 1973, 90 per cent of the intra-Community transport were landbound, whereas after 1973, transport to the new Member States was more than 90 per cent maritime transport, without the possibility of an alternative[5]. More recent numbers indicate that 33 per cent of intra-Community trade are carried by ship, as well as 90 per cent of the trade between the Community and third countries[6]. These figures display the importance of the maritime transport industry for the Community today. Another reason that has been advanced to explain the initial lack of legislative action of the European Community in the field of maritime transport is that Art. 80 II (ex 84 II) EC, the legal basis provision in this area, originally required unanimity in the Council[7]. It was only after the passage of the SEA that the Council could adopt measures based on this provision by a qualified majority[8]. As long as unanimity was required, progress was only possible if all Member States agreed on a common position in the Council[9]. It was this requirement of unanimity that hindered the development of a common maritime transport policy[10].

---

[1] Clough/Randolph, (1991), p. 41.
[2] Prieß, EuR (1989), p. 369 ff, p. 369.
[3] Clough/Randolph, (1991), p. 48; Basedow, TR (1994), p. 85 ff, p. 85; Schwarze, (2000), Art. 80, rec. 4; Lenz, (1999), Art. 80, rec. 1.
[4] Erdmenger, (1983), p. 81.
[5] Kreis, ETL (1988), p. 562 ff, p. 563; Kreis, ETL (1992), p. 155 ff, p. 156 f; Power, (1992), p. 136.
[6] Sir Leon Brittain, ETL (1993), p. 337 ff, p. 338; Erdmenger, ETL (1988), p. 543 ff, p. 543; Power, (1992), p. 3.
[7] Basedow, TR (1994), p. 85 ff, p. 85.
[8] Schwarze, (2000), Art. 80, rec. 1; Prieß EuR, (1989), p. 369 ff, p. 369.
[9] Basedow, TR (1994), p. 85 ff, p. 85.
[10] Erdmenger, ETL (1988), p. 543 ff, p. 546.

1. Applicable Treaty provisions

The rules on transport are contained in Title V (ex IV) of the Treaty. As far as maritime transport is concerned, the relevant provision is Art. 80 II (ex 84 II) EC, which states that the Council may adopt the necessary measures in the field of maritime transport with a qualified majority. Therefore, Art. 80 II (ex 84 II) EC is the legal basis provision in the field of maritime transport[11]. The main question during the early days of the Community in relation to maritime transport was whether or not the provisions contained in Title V (ex IV) EC and especially Art. 80 II (ex 84 II) EC allow for the application of other general Treaty provisions, including the rules on competition contained in Title VI (ex V) of the Treaty, to the field of maritime transport[12].

This question first came to the attention of the ECJ in the case of *Commission v France*[13]. The Commission had initiated proceedings against France, because it considered the French *Code du Travail,* that required a certain percentage of sailors on French vessels to be of French nationality, a violation of EC law, namely of Art. 39 (ex 48) EC and Arts. 1, 4, and 7 of Regulation 1612/68 which cover the free movement of workers[14]. In its ruling, the ECJ enquired in a first step as to whether or not the provisions of Title V (ex IV) EC preclude the application of general Treaty rules to the transportation sector, and, in a second step, the Court scrutinised the application of such general rules to the fields of air and maritime transport in the light of Art 80 II (ex 84 II) EC, which stipulates that "*The Council may (...........) decide whether, to what extend and by what procedure appropriate provisions may be laid down for sea and air transport.*".

The ECJ took the position that the fundamental rules of the Treaty are applicable to the sector of transport in general and that this is also true for the fields of air and maritime transport. The Court started out by stating that Art. 70 (ex 74) EC refers to the general aims of the Treaty enshrined in Arts. 2 and 3 EC. As a consequence, the provisions on transport do not have the purpose to restrict the application of general Treaty provisions in that area[15], instead they aim to give effect to the general rules of the Treaty. The ECJ then went on to say that the general Treaty provisions are of such paramount importance that their application may only be precluded or restricted, if the Treaty contains an explicit

[11] Grabitz/Hilf Vol. 1, (2002), Frohnmeyer, Art. 80, rec. 1; G/T/E Vol. 1, (1997), Erdmenger, Art. 84, rec. 1.

[12] Erdmenger, FS Raisch, (1995), p. 387, p. 389.

[13] Case 167/73, *Commission v France*, (1974) ECR, p. 359 ff.

[14] Case 167/73, *Commission v France*, (1974) ECR, p. 359 ff, p. 362.

[15] Case 167/73, *Commission v France*, (1974) ECR, p. 359 ff, p. 370, rec. 24/26.

statement to that effect[16]. Art. 36 (ex 42) EC explicitly precludes the application of EC competition rules to the field of agriculture. From the absence of an equivalent provision in Title V (ex IV) of the Treaty, the conclusion must be drawn that no such exclusion of general rules exists in the field of transport. Based on this position, the ECJ then proceeded with its analysis of Art 80 II (ex 84 II) EC. According to the position of the Court, it only restricts the application of the provisions contained in Title V (ex IV) EC to the fields of air and maritime transport, since Art. 80 II (ex (80 II) EC does not explicitly exclude the application of general Treaty rules to the sectors of air and maritime transport[17].

The position of the ECJ has not remained unchallenged. In favour of a broader interpretation of Art. 80 II (ex 84 II) EC, it has been argued that, at the time of the adoption of the Treaty, some Member States considered Title V (ex IV) to be the only part of the Treaty that should regulate the transport industry[18]. It has also been brought forward that the Title on the free movement of workers and the Title on transport are both contained in the same Part of the Treaty, and as a consequence it is not justified to construct the former as a set of paramount rules at the expense of the latter[19].

In the *Nouvelles Frontières*[20] decision, the ECJ had the possibility to rule on the interpretation of Art 80 II (ex 84 II) EC again, and it therein confirmed its earlier ruling on this issue. Since that case dealt with the application of competition rules to the sector of air transport, it is now also established through case law that the narrow interpretation of Art. 80 II (ex 84) EC also covers the provisions of Title VI (ex V) EC[21]. Consequently, the general Treaty provisions and especially the rules on competition are applicable in the field of maritime transport[22].

In its ruling in *Ahmed Saeed*[23], the ECJ held that Art. 82 (ex 86) EC is applicable without the necessity of secondary procedural provisions[24]. However, the

---

16 Case 167/73, *Commission v France*, (1974) ECR, p. 359 ff, p. 370, rec. 17/23.
17 Case 167/73, *Commission v France*, (1974) ECR, p. 359 ff, p. 370 f, rec. 29/33.
18 Necker, FS Luther, (1976), p. 113 ff, p. 114.
19 Necker, FS Luther, (1976), p. 113 ff, p. 121.
20 Joint Cases 209 - 213/84, *Nouvelles Frontières*, (1986) ECR, p. 1425 ff.
21 Joint Cases 209 - 213/84, *Nouvelles Frontières*, (1986) ECR, p. 1425 ff, p. 1464, rec. 32.
22 Joint Cases 209 - 213/84, *Nouvelles Frontières*, (1986) ECR, p. 1425 ff, p. 1466, rec. 42; Confavreux, RMC (1996), p. 367 ff, p. 371; G/T/E Vol. 1, (1997), Erdmenger, Art. 84, rec. 21; Rabe,TR (1994), p. 1 ff, p. 1; Werner, WuW (1987), p. 796 ff, p. 797.
23 Case 66/86, *Ahmed Saeed*, (1989), ECR, p. 803 ff.
24 Case 66/86, *Ahmed Saeed*, (1989), ECR, p. 803 ff, p. 848, rec. 32; Pernice, FS Deringer, (1993), p. 135 ff, p. 136.

situation is different for Art. 81 I (ex 85 I) EC, as this provision is only applicable to maritime transport if such secondary legislation exists. The reason for this differentiation is that the applicability of Art. 81 I (ex 85 I) EC is subject to a possible exemption from its scope based on Art. 81 III (ex 85 III) EC. The interaction between these two provisions necessitates detailed secondary legislation. Until such secondary law does not exist, Art. 81 I (ex 85 I) EC is only applicable if a decision over a possible exemption based on Art. 81 III has been made[25].

2. Secondary law

It has just been demonstrated how the application of Treaty provisions in relation to maritime transport has been clarified by the ECJ in its case law. However, the Council has also passed secondary legislation in the field of maritime transport.

a) Conservative first moves

The first pieces of secondary legislation regulating the field of maritime transport have been called to be of a preserving nature[26]. Regulation 17/62[27] is the basic piece of legislation which provides detailed rules for the application of the Treaty provisions on competition. However, Regulation 141/62[28] excludes air and maritime transport for an unlimited time from the field of application of Regulation 17/62. Yet, not all restrictions to competition in these two sectors are excluded from the field of application of Regulation 17/62 by virtue of Regulation 141/62. Those restrictions mentioned in Art. 81 I lit. a and c (ex 85 I lit. a and c) EC and Art. 82 (ex 86) EC are excluded from the scope of Regulation 17/62. In contrast, the restrictions mentioned in Art. 81 I lit. d and e (ex 85 I lit. d and e) EC are not exempted from the application of Regulation17/62[29]. Both Regulations entered into force on the 13th of April 1962.

The air and maritime transport industries experienced special treatment again under Regulation 1017/68[30]. As it has been explained in the preceding paragraph Regulation 141/62 exempts the transport sector from the scope of Regulation 17/62. The exemption is unlimited in time for air and maritime transport, but for transport by rail, road and inland waterway it was limited until the 30th of June 1968[31]. From that time onwards, additional legislation became neces-

[25] Immenga/Mestmäcker Vol. 2, (1997), Ritter, p. 1469 f, rec. 2.
[26] Erdmenger, FS Raisch, (1995), p. 387 ff, p. 390.
[27] OJ, (1962), p. 202; OJ Special Edition, (1959–62), p. 57.
[28] OJ, (1962), 124/2751.
[29] Immenga/Mestmäcker Vol. 2, (1997), Basedow, p. 1999, rec. 13.
[30] OJ, (1968), L-175/1.
[31] Art. 3 of Regulation 141/62.

sary if it was to be avoided that the general rules embodied in Regulation 17/62 would become applicable to these modes of transport. Consequently, Regulation 1017/68, which took effect on the 1st of June 1968, was passed. This Regulation contains special rules for the application of EC competition law in the field of transport by rail, road and inland waterway[32]. The areas of air and maritime transport were however excluded again from the scope of this Regulation[33].

As a result, there were no provisions on the level of secondary law dealing with the application of Arts. 81 and 82 (ex 85 and 86) EC to maritime transport. EC competition law could only be enforced in these areas by means of Arts. 84 and 85 (ex 88 and 89) EC, which provide transitional rules for the application of EC competition law until the adoption of more detailed secondary legislation.

b) The UNCTAD-code and the *Brussels package*

The first major step of the Community, with the purpose to regulate the field of maritime transport, was the adoption of Regulation 954/79[34], which enabled the Member States to ratify or accede to the UN Convention on a Code of Conduct for Liner Conferences as individual Member States of the Community[35]. This Regulation is also known under the name of *Brussels package.*

aa) The legislative history and objective of the UNCTAD-code

The UNCTAD-code has been worked out by the United Nations Conference of Plenipotentiaries in two sessions between the 12th of November 1973 and the 6th of April 1974[36]. It was based on a draft code issued by the UNCTAD III meeting in 1972. The UNCTAD-code was signed in Geneva on the 6th of April 1974[37]. According to Art. 49 UNCTAD, it was to come into force 6 months after at least 24 countries carrying 25 percent of the world's tonnage (in 1973[38]) had become contracting parties to the code. The importance of Regulation 954/79 can be seen by the fact that the UNCTAD-code only entered into force on October 6th 1983, after it had been ratified by two Member States, namely Germany and the Netherlands, on the 6th of April 1983[39]. Only after the acces-

---

32 Erdmenger, FS Raisch, (1995), p. 387 ff, p. 390.

33 Art. 1 of Regulation 1017/68.

34 OJ, (1979), L-121/1.

35 Clough/Randolph, (1991), p. 16; Vermote, ETL (1988), p. 571 ff, p. 572.

36 Grewlich, ZaöR (1975), p. 743 ff.

37 Clough/Randolph, (1991), p. 6 ff; Power, (1992), p. 274.

38 The tonnage of bulk carriers, typically for tramp shipping, is not taken into account in this respect, since the UNCTAD code only regulates liner shipping;per: Grewlich, ZaöR (1975), p. 746.

39 Vermote, ETL (1988), p. 571 ff, annex on p. 588.

sion of these two Member States was the combined tonnage of the signatory states large enough to fulfil the tonnage criterion.

The purpose of the UNCTAD-code was to give the developing countries a chance to realise their ambitions of having an own fleet. For some of the African countries, having just gained their independence, this ambition largely sprang from a feeling that a national fleet is a sign of independence[40]. Some South American countries were interested in developing their own fleet because, in a situation of crisis, they wanted to be independent from foreign ships. Secondly, they felt that carriers from the industrialised countries charged prices that were too high, and, as a consequence, many developing countries were eager to build up their own merchant fleets, as a device to save foreign currency[41].

Before the passage of the UNCTAD-code, 85-90% per cent of maritime transport was carried out by conference members[42]. During the 1960s the conference system dominated international liner shipping with a rigidity that made it difficult for new competitors to successfully engage in maritime transport activities[43]. As a result, the developing countries faced the difficulty of finding sufficient goods to be transported by their own national shipping lines[44]. Governments from the developing countries often saw the only solution in the establishment of cargo reservation schemes, which reserved cargo from and to their countries for ships bearing their own national flag[45]. From a Community perspective it was hoped that such practices, which were potentially harmful to European carriers engaged in crosstrading, could be avoided if the Member States could become parties of the Convention containing the UNCTAD-code[46].

bb) The contents of the UNCTAD-code

In the context of competition law, the main feature of the UNCTAD-code is the so-called 40:40:20 rule. Art. 2 IV UNCTAD provides that those shipping lines, which are the national lines of the countries between which the trade in question is conducted, shall obtain equal shares in the freight and volume of the trade. In addition, third country shipping lines are entitled to carry a significant part of the trade. Art. 2 IV UNCTAD gives the example of 20 per cent as an amount that would be considered adequate to constitute a significant part of the trade. This provision has consequently been interpreted in such a way as to contain the

---

[40] Erdmenger, FS Raisch, (1995), p. 387 ff, p. 393.
[41] Heldring, ETL (1988), p. 600 ff, p. 601.
[42] Vermote, ETL (1988), p. 571 ff, p. 572.
[43] Heldring, ETL (1988), p. 600 ff, p. 602.
[44] Erdmenger, FS Raisch, (1995), p. 387 ff, p. 393.
[45] Heldring, ETL (1988), p. 600 ff, p. 602.
[46] Vermote ETL (1986), p. 3 ff, p. 7; Vermote, ETL (1988), p. 571 ff, p. 573.

allocation of trade in the 40:40:20 pattern, although such a pattern is nowhere mentioned explicitly in the UNCTAD-code[47]. The allocation of cargo in the 40:40:20 pattern is not binding, since national shipping lines are free to agree on a different distribution of cargo. They may also decide that there shall be no quotas for the distribution of cargo at all. A necessary condition for such an agreement to be valid is the assent of all national lines from the affected countries. As soon as one carrier does not give its consent, in practise, nothing but the 40:40:20 rule can apply[48].

On the matter of freight rates, Art. 12 UNCTAD stipulates that the conferences should set their rates at the lowest possible level from a commercial point of view, at which the conference members may still generate a reasonable profit. Such an approach is positive in principle since it constitutes an attempt to outlaw excessive conference rates, but as Art. 12 UNCTAD does not define the term *reasonable profit*, it will be difficult to police conference rates on the basis of this provision[49]. The UNCTAD-code is also important for EC competition law insofar, as it contains a definition of the term *liner conference* that was later employed in Regulation 4056/86[50]. Finally, the UNCTAD-code also contains provisions that are important in relation to the freedom to provide services and the freedom of establishment. No detailed analysis of these provisions can be provided at this point, as this study is concerned primarily with competition law aspects of liner shipping[51].

cc) Regulation 954/79, the *Brussels package*

The Commission feared that the UNCTAD-code was *inter alia* contradictory to Arts. 81 and 82 (ex 85 and 86) EC. Between July 1974 and June 1975, the Commission put forth three legislative proposals with the aim of preventing Member States from becoming party to the convention containing the UNCTAD-code before a common position of the Community towards the UNCTAD-code had been developed[52]. Nevertheless, on June 30th 1975 the governments of Belgium, France and Germany signed the convention, which contained the UNCTAD-code, as this was the last day that the Convention was open for signature. Their signatures were accompanied by a declaration stating that ratification could only take place under the condition that their obligations arising out of the Treaty of Rome would not be violated[53].

---

47 Clough/Randolph, (1991), p. 11.
48 Grewlich, ZaöR, (1975), p. 749.
49 Clough/Randolph, (1991), p. 14.
50 Compare Art. 1 III lit. b Regulation 4056/86 and UNCTAD-code, Chapter One, Definition One.
51 For details see: Vermote, ETL (1988), p. 571 ff, p. 576 ff.
52 Vermote, ETL (1986), p. 3 ff, p. 5.
53 Vermote, ETL (1986), p. 3 ff, p. 5.

The Commission then replaced its first three proposals by a fourth proposal, which suggested that the Member States may accede to the Convention containing the UNCTAD-code under the condition that the principle of free trade will prevail within the Community and in relationship to all OECD countries[54]. After further discussions, the Council passed a measure to this effect on May 15th 1979, which became Regulation 954/79[55].

This Regulation seeks to ensure that a possible accession of a Member State to the convention containing the UNCTAD-code does not conflict with obligations arising out of the Treaty of Rome. It does so through the establishment of several modifications of the UNCTAD-code, which the Member States have to respect if they want to become party to the convention containing the UNCTAD-code. First, Regulation 954/79 contains two modifications of the above-explained 40:40:20 rule. Art. 3 Regulation 954/79 is concerned with intra-Community cargo allocation. It lays down that the cargo share allocated to Community national shipping lines and to Community third country shipping lines are not distributed according to the 40:40:20 rule, but with a view to all these lines carrying a fair share of the conference trade. The second reservation in relation to cargo allocation states that the 40:40:20 rule shall not apply to trade within the Community and to trade with other OECD countries, the latter only being true if agreed upon reciprocally[56].

Regulation 954/79 is a compromise. On the one hand, the support of the UNCTAD-code through the Community constitutes a concession to the developing countries and their proclaimed need to establish their own fleets[57]. On the other hand, it protects the fundamental principles of EC competition law[58] as the cargo distribution formula of the UNCTAD-code will not be applied within the Community and in trades between Member States and other OECD countries. Another important aspect from a competition law point of view is that, as a consequence of the Brussels package, it has been accepted at EC law level that international liner transport should be provided on the basis of the conference system[59].

---

[54] Vermote, ETL (1986), p. 3 ff, p. 5.
[55] Erdmenger, (1983), p. 88.
[56] Clough/Randolph, (1991), p. 20.
[57] Erdmenger, (1983), p. 89 f; Vermote, ETL (1988), p. 571 ff, p. 573.
[58] Vermote, ETL (1988), p. 571 ff, p. 586.
[59] Erdmenger, (1983), p. 90 f; Faull/Nikpay, (1999), p. 875; Werner, NJW (1988), p. 2159 ff, p. 2159, (see also note No. 9); Van Miert, ETL (1999), p. 3 ff, p. 5.

c) The legislation of 1986

The next and, until this date, the largest step in the development of an European maritime transport policy came about in the year 1986 when the Council adopted four Regulations that are at the centre of today's EC maritime transport policy[60].

aa) Legislative history

The last recital of the Preamble to Regulation 954/79 stated that, although the stabilising effect of liner conferences is being recognised, such agreements may still conflict with the fundamental Treaty provisions on competition. European Community legislation that covers the application of competition law to maritime transport was therefore deemed necessary for the future[61]. On October 16th 1981, the Commission submitted a first proposal to the Council for a Regulation laying down detailed rules on the application of Arts. 81 and 82 (ex 85 and 86) EC to the maritime transport sector[62], yet no decision was taken in the Council on this matter.

In 1983, the European Parliament started proceedings against the Council before the ECJ, based on the accusation that the inaction of the Council in respect to the development of a common transport policy constituted a breach of the Treaty[63]. The Court found that the Council was in breach of the Treaty insofar, as it did not adequately ensure the freedom to provide services in the transport sector[64]. This ruling of the ECJ triggered Commission action *inter alia* in the field of maritime transport[65]. In March 1985, the Commission issued a report entitled "*Progress Towards a Common Maritime Policy: Maritime Transport*"[66] which constituted the first attempt of the Commission to develop the Community shipping policy in a systematic way[67]. This report also contained several specific proposals for Regulations to be adopted in the sphere of maritime transport. *Inter alia* the Commission forwarded the following proposals:

First, the Commission submitted a revised proposal for a Regulation on the application of competition law to maritime transport[68]. Second, a proposal for a Regulation ensuring the freedom to provide services was put forward[69]. A third

[60] Erdmenger, ETL (1988), p. 543 ff, p. 548.
[61] Recital 9 of the Preamble to Regulation 954/79.
[62] OJ, (1981), C-282/4.
[63] Case 13/83, *Parliament v Council*, (1985) ECR, p. 1513.
[64] Case 13/83, *Parliament v Council*, (1985) ECR, p. 1513, p. 1601, rec. 70.
[65] Power, (1992), p. 147.
[66] Com (85) 90 final, March 6th 1985.
[67] Power, (1992), p. 148.
[68] OJ (1985), C-282/9.
[69] OJ (1985), C-282/4.

proposal was concerned with the issue of EC action against cargo reservation practices by third countries which prove harmful to Community interests[70]. The final suggestion of the Commission was the proposal for a Regulation with the aim of ensuring that Community carriers could compete with liner shipping operators from third countries and that the European Community is competent to act against unfair and non-commercial pricing practises in case they threaten or cause harm to Community carriers[71]. Based on these four proposals, the Council adopted four Regulations on December 22nd 1986. These four Regulations are briefly presented below.

bb) Contents

The four Regulations have the following content:

aaa) Regulation 4055/86[72]

This Regulation was based on Art. 80 II (ex 84 II) EC and came into force on the 1st of January 1987. It covers the application of the freedom to provide services in the maritime transport sector. Since that date the Treaty provisions on the freedom to provide services as well as those on the freedom of establishment are applicable in the field of maritime transport, be it transport between Member States or transport to third countries[73]. Any existing restrictions had to be lifted by January 1st 1993. Now the principle of freedom of the seas is part of the codified EC law, and undertakings, to which this Regulation is applicable, can directly rely on this principle[74].

As a consequence of the enactment of Regulation 4055/86, the only requirement for providing maritime transport services in the EC may be that the carrier is seated in a Member State other than that of the person for whom the service is intended or that the relevant vessels are registered under the flag of a Member State[75]. National rules that give preferential treatment to ships running under the own flag of that Member State are no longer permissible. Furthermore, existing agreements with third countries containing freight allocation rules had to be eradicated, unless they were non-discriminatory[76]. The conclusion of new agreements of this type became illegal in principle[77].

---

[70] OJ (1985), C-282/2.
[71] OJ (1985), C-282/12.
[72] OJ (1986), L-378/1.
[73] Grabitz/Hilf Vol. 1, (2002), Frohnmeyer, Art. 80, rec. 46.
[74] Calliess/Ruffert, (2002), Jung, Art. 80, rec. 11, G/T/E Vol. 1, (1997), Erdmenger, Art. 84, rec. 47.
[75] Calliess/Ruffert, (2002), Jung, Art. 80, rec. 11; Erdmenger, ETL (1988), p. 543 ff, p. 549.
[76] Calliess/Ruffert, (2002), Jung, Art. 80, rec. 11.
[77] Prieß, EuR (1989), p. 369. p. 374.

bbb) Regulation 4058/86[78]

The regime of Regulation 4055/86 was complemented by Regulation 4058/86, which was also based on Art. 80 II (84 II) EC and entered into force on July 1st 1987. Its objective is to ensure that European carriers have the same access to trade on routes to third countries as foreign carriers[79], by allowing the Member States to co-ordinate their efforts against third country measures aimed at protecting their fleet[80]. Upon application of a Member State, the Council may decide on measures such as import quotas, import charges or the requirement to obtain permission to load, unload and transport freight[81].

ccc) Regulation 4057/86[82]

This Regulation is based on Art. 80 II (ex 84 II) EC and entered into force on the 1st of July 1987. It seeks to level the playing field for European carriers in relation to third country carriers. The emphasis is placed on unfair pricing practices of third country carriers[83]. The Community may impose a redressive duty on third country carriers, if they have been found to cut rates due to state intervention and thus distort the market. The Community may only proceed in such a way if the distortion due to state intervention results in substantial damage on the part of the Community carriers and interests of the Community[84].

ddd) Regulation 4056/86[85]

Regulation 4056/86 was based on Arts. 80 II and 83 (ex 84 II and 87) EC and entered into force on July 1st 1987. For the purposes of community competition law Regulation 4056/86 constitutes the centrepiece of EC legislation in relation to maritime transport. It contains rules in two main areas. First, it provides procedural rules for the application of the Treaty provisions on competition in the field of maritime transport. Second, it contains a block exemption for liner conferences from the application of Art. 81 I (ex 85 I) EC[86].

It has been noted above that neither Regulation 17/62 nor Regulation 1017/68 established procedural rules for the application of Arts. 81 and 82 (ex 85 and

---

[78] OJ, (1986), L-378/21.
[79] Grabitz/Hilf I, (2002), Frohnmeyer, Art. 80, rec. 49.
[80] G/T/E Vol. 1, (1997), Erdmenger, Art. 84, rec. 55.
[81] Calliess/Ruffert, (2002), Jung, Art. 80, rec. 12.
[82] OJ, (1986), L-378/14.
[83] Grabitz/Hilf Vol. 1, (2002), Jung, Art. 80, rec. 48.
[84] Calliess/Ruffert, (2002), Jung, Art. 80, rec. 15.
[85] OJ, (1986), L-378/4.
[86] Calliess/Ruffert, (2002), Jung, Art. 80, rec. 13; Clough/Randolph, (1991), p. 151; Grabitz/Hilf Vol. 1, (2002), Frohnmeyer, Art. 80, rec. 47; G/T/E Vol. 1, (1997), Erdmenger, Art. 84, rec. 49.

86) EC to the maritime transport industry[87]. Without such rules the above mentioned judgements of the ECJ, laying down that the Treaty rules on competition are applicable to maritime transport[88], are of limited effectiveness, as the Commission was lacking the powers to administer Arts. 81 and 82 (ex 85 and 86) EC to maritime transport[89]. Although the Commission could in theory have acted on basis of Art. 85 (ex 89) EC it has not done so. The procedure contained therein has proved to be too complicated[90], thus necessitating more detailed secondary legislation. This lack was remedied by Regulation 4056/86 insofar, as it provides procedural rules for the application of EC competition law to liner shipping. Finally, it should be noted that Regulation 4056/86 is only applicable to liner shipping and not to tramp services. The latter are subject to Art. 1 Regulation 141/62, meaning that, for this type of shipping, competition law must be administered based on Arts. 84 and 85 (ex 88 and 89) EC[91]. This procedure, however, is impractical insofar, as the Commission cannot act independently, but must rely on the co-operation of the appropriate national authorities[92].

The second main element of Regulation 4056/86 is the block exemption for liner conferences. The intention of this block exemption was mainly to coordinate Community law with the UNCTAD-code[93]. It was stated already in the Preamble to Regulation 954/79 that there existed further need to ensure that behaviour of liner conferences, which is in line with the rules of the UNCTAD-code, also conforms to the EC Treaty provisions on competition[94]. By exempting liner conferences from the application of EC competition law such a conflict of laws is being avoided.

The block exemption for liner conferences contained in Art. 3 Regulation 4056/86 is special in several ways. First, it is unlimited in time, whereas normally block exemptions have to be renewed after a certain period of time[95]. Second, Art. 3 Regulation 4056/86 allows joint price fixing, which is a concession not found in any other block exemption. Regulation 4056/86 is also different from other block exemptions insofar, as it is passed in the form of a Council

---

[87] See above, p. 56 f.
[88] See above, p. 54 f.
[89] Werner, WuW (1987), p. 796 ff, p. 797.
[90] Werner, WuW (1987), p. 796 ff, p. 798.
[91] G/T/E Vol. 1, (1997), Erdmenger, Art. 84, rec. 49.
[92] Power, (1992), p. 273.
[93] G/T/E Vol. 1, (1997), Erdmenger, Art. 84, rec. 49; Calliess/Ruffert, (2002), Jung, Art. 80, rec. 13.
[94] Clough/Randolph, (1991), p. 17.
[95] Ginderachter/Durande, ETL (1996), p. 241 ff, p. 245.

Regulation and not as a Commission Regulation on the basis of a Council enabling Regulation.

d) The rules on consortia

It has been noted above that consortia are an important form of co-operation between carriers today[96]. The Community reacted to this situation with the passage of Regulation 870/95[97], which, after its expiry, was succeeded by Regulation 823/2000[98].

aa) Legislative history

Already at the time of the adoption of Regulation 4056/86, the Council asked the Commission to enquire as to whether there is a possibility to grant a group exemption to consortia[99]. In June 1990, the Commission presented a report to the Council in which it expressed its support for such a block exemption[100]. This report already contained a first draft of a Commission proposal for an enabling Council Regulation[101]. According to the Commission, consortia could help to increase productivity and capacity utilisation. The Commission further emphasised that consortia could produce economies of scale leading to reduced costs, as well as increase reliability and improve quality of liner shipping services[102]. After the European Parliament[103] and the ECOSOC[104] had given their opinion, the Commission altered its initial proposal and the Council then adopted Regulation 479/92[105] on the 25th of February 1992. This Regulation is, with some minor changes, identical to the altered Commission proposal[106]. It entered into force on the 1st of March 1992.

During the adoption process, two aspects caused disagreement between the different EC institutions. The first disagreement broke out over the question of who should adopt the Regulation containing the consortia block exemption. One possibility was that the Council passes the detailed Regulation, which contains the block exemption. The other solution was that the Council only passes an enabling Regulation, which works as a framework and empowers the Commission to pass a more detailed Regulation, which then contains the block

---

[96] See above, p. 27.
[97] OJ, (1995), L-95/7.
[98] OJ, (2000), L-100/24.
[99] Ginderachter/Durande, ETL (1996), p. 241 ff, p. 242; Faull/Nikpay, (1999), p. 900.
[100] COM 90 (260) final, June 18th 1990.
[101] OJ, (1990), C-167/9.
[102] Bellamy/Child, (1993), p. 848, rec. 15-027.
[103] OJ, (1991), C-305/35.
[104] OJ, (1991), C-69/16.
[105] OJ, (1992), L-95/3.
[106] Ginderachter/Durande, ETL (1996), p. 241 ff, p. 243.

exemption. This dispute is not so much concerned with aspects of competition law, but rather centres around the question of which institution should have how much power in the legislative process. Therefore, a more detailed analysis will be omitted at this point[107].

The second struggle during the passage of Regulation 479/92 concerned the question of what would be the correct legal basis for a Regulation containing a block exemption for consortia agreements. The Council based its Regulation only on Art. 83 (ex 87) EC. Art. 80 II (ex 84 II) EC was not mentioned as a legal basis provision. Already in its proposal the Commission took the view that Regulation 475/92 was an instrument of competition policy and, therefore, did not necessitate reference to Art. 80 II (ex 84 II) EC[108]. However, some Member States were of the opinion that Art. 80 II (ex 84 II) EC should be mentioned as the legal basis for Regulation 479/92, as well. This view can be supported by the fact that Regulation 4056/86, which contains the liner conference block exemption, was based also on a dual legal basis[109]. Consequently, it would be logical to proceed in the same way in relationship to a consortia block exemption.

The different treatment of the two block exemptions has been justified by saying that the regulation of liner shipping as an international activity could result in international legal disputes with third countries. The negotiations with third countries that may become necessary in the wake of such a disagreement are not part of EC competition policy anymore and, therefore, Regulation 4056/86 also required a legal basis in the field of shipping policy[110]. An example would be that negotiations might become necessary in consideration of the application of the UNCTAD-code. Valid as this reasoning might be, it does not support a different treatment of consortia though, as it could also be possible that EC legislation in the field of consortia gives rise to an international legal conflict, which necessitates negotiations between the EC and third countries[111]. It was also put forward that Regulation 479/92 should be adopted under a dual legal basis because of the importance of the consortia block exemption in the light of the development of a European maritime transport policy, since it constitutes a part of the positive measures package for the maritime transport industry[112]. As a con-

[107] For a more detailed analysis see: Green ETL (1993), p. 477 ff, p. 482 f; Ruttley, ETL (1993), p. 487 ff, p. 492.

[108] Green, ETL (1993), p. 477 ff, p. 483.

[109] Green, ETL (1993), p. 477 ff, p. 484.

[110] Green, ETL (1993), p. 477 ff, p. 484.

[111] Green, ETL (1993), p. 477 ff, p. 489.

[112] The positive measures package is a combination of different actions, adopted at EC level in order to stop the continuing crisis of the Community shipping industry.

sequence, Art. 80 II (ex 84 II) EC would constitute the correct legal basis for such a measure[113].

In conclusion, it must be stated that it seems doubtful whether or not it was correct to adopt Regulation 479/92 solely on the basis of Art. 83 (ex 87) EC. However, the consequences might be small, as an action based on Art. 230 (ex 173) EC is, nevertheless, unlikely to be successful. Art. 230 IV (ex 173 IV) EC according to the interpretation of the ECJ only provides very limited *locus standi* to individuals[114], thus reducing the possibility of a successful action from a non-privileged applicant. As far as the so-called privileged applicants are concerned, it should be borne in mind that Art. 230 V (ex 173 V) EC stipulates that actions can only be brought before the ECJ in a two month time period, which also severely limits the possibility of a successful action for annulment. It may be possible, however, that action against Regulation 479/92 might be taken on the basis of Art. 241 (ex 184) EC[115].

After the Council empowered the Commission to legislate on a block exemption for consortia, the latter issued a draft Regulation, which was published on the 1st of March 1994[116]. The European Parliament and the ECOSOC then commented on this first draft, which prompted the Commission to adopt some significant changes to the original version[117]. The Commission finally passed Regulation 870/95 on April 20th 1995. It entered into force on April 22nd 1995, after its publication in the Official Journal. Art. 13 Regulation 870/95 limited the life span of Regulation 870/95 to a period of five years, with the result that it expired on April 21st 2000. In a working document on Regulation 870/95 the Commission stated that the block exemption for consortia worked well in practice[118] and that this regime should be continued only with some minor changes[119]. In line with this opinion the Commission passed Regulation 823/2000 on April 19th 2000, which now contains the current block exemption for consortia. Regulation 832/2000 is in large part identical to its predecessor. It entered into force on the 26th of April 2000 and will be valid until April 25th 2005.

---

113 ECOSOC statement as cited in: Ruttley, ETL (1993), p. 487 ff, p. 492.
114 Craig/de Burca, (1998), p. 479 f; Ruttley, ETL (1993), p. 484 ff, p. 492.
115 Ruttley, ETL (1993), p. 484 ff, p. 492.
116 OJ, (1994), C-63/8; for a good summary of the contents of this draft see: Commission working document on Regulation 870/95, (1999), rec. 32 ff.
117 Ginderachter/Durande, ETL (1996), p. 241 ff, p. 244.
118 Commission working document on Regulation 870/95, (1999), rec. 144.
119 Commission working document on Regulation 870/95, (1999), rec. 145.

bb) Objective and contents

Recital two of the Preamble to Regulation 823/2000, as well as of Regulation 870/95, gives evidence to the fact that the Commission is of the opinion that consortia typically conform to the requirements of Art. 81 III (ex 85 III) EC and thus should be exempted by means of a group exemption from the prohibition of Art. 81 I (ex 85 I) EC[120]. The Council, however, emphasised in the Preamble to Regulation 479/92 that a block exemption for consortia should be granted because it could improve the competitiveness of EC liner shipping[121]. To date, there is no visible consequence of this difference in defining the aim of the consortia block exemption.

Although Regulation 870/95 and Regulation 823/2000 came into existence following the two-step approach, typical for the granting of a block exemption, the structure of these Regulations is not consistent with that of other block exemptions. Normally a block exemption contains a black list of forbidden clauses and a white list of permissible clauses. Regulation 870/95 and later Regulation 823/2000 are different insofar, as they do not contain such lists but rather exempt all co-operations between shipowners, with the purpose of providing a joint liner service, as long as the agreements in question conform to the obligations and conditions laid down in these Regulations[122]. To this end, Art. 2 No. 1 Regulation 823/2000 contains a broad definition of the term consortium and Art. 3 II Regulation 823/2000 contains a list of exempted activities[123]. In contrast to Regulation 4056/86, the Regulations containing the consortia block exemption are only valid for a five-year period. Regulation 870/95 and Regulation 823/2000 also differ from Regulation 4056/86 insofar, as that they contain only very limited procedural provisions.

e) European Liner shipping policy in the 1990s and beyond

Apart from the initial passage of the consortia block exemption in 1995 and its consecutive renewal in the year 2000, the Community did not take any major legislative action in the field of maritime transport during the last decade. Activity on the part of the Commission in the form of several important decisions has, however, served as a useful tool for the refinement of the European position on such important matters as conference pricing for multimodal transport, legality of individual service contracts and capacity withdrawal programmes. Only recently has the Court of First Instance ruled in three judgements that the

---

[120] Immenga/Mestmäcker Vol. 2, (1997), Basedow, p. 2081, rec. 3.

[121] Recital 6 of the Preamble to Regulation 479/92.

[122] Commission working document on Regulation 870/95, (1999), rec. 31.

[123] Ginderachter/Durande, ETL (1996), p. 241 ff, p. 247.

Commission was right in its legal analysis on these subjects[124]. There are indications that the EC might take a more active legislative position on liner conferences in the future. On April 16, 2002 the OECD published a report in which it voiced its criticism of the fact that liner conferences are exempted from the regular mechanisms of competition law virtually all over the world. As a consequence of this report, the Commission started a three stage review process of Regulation 4056/86. The Commission has the intention to publish its policy conclusions on the future development of European legislation on the issue of liner shipping in a Green or a White Paper, and if the conclusions made therein require such a move, then the Commission will proceed to formulate a proposal for an amendment to the existing EC liner shipping legislation[125].

[124] Case T-395/94, *Atlantic Container Line and others v Commission*, (2002), ECR II, p. 875 ff; Case T-86/95, *Compagnie Générale Maritime and others v Commission*, (2002), ECR II, p. 1011 and Case T-18/97, *Atlantic Container Line and others v Commission*, (2002), ECR II, p. 1125 ff.

[125] Stragier, (2002), p. 9 ff.

Chapter four - Liner shipping economics

Liner shipping conferences have not only triggered an ongoing debate over their legal treatment, but they have also caused discussion amongst economists. The controversy centres around the possible explanations for the existence of liner conferences and on the question of the actual effects of liner conferences on the markets for liner shipping services. This chapter has the purpose of presenting and evaluating the different positions that have been brought forward by economists on these issues. As this is predominantly a work of legal writing, this chapter does not aim to develop a new economic model of liner shipping. The economic analysis of liner shipping provides the necessary background knowledge for the formulation of a modern EC policy towards agreements in the liner shipping industry in general, and liner conferences in particular.

The traditional explanation for the existence and effects of liner conferences by economists is that they constitute a *monopoly*[1] or an *oligopoly*[2]. During the 1980s a new approach was developed to explain the existence of liner conferences, called the *theory of the empty core*[3]. Whereas those judging liner conferences to be monopolists or oligopolists regard their existence with some scepticism because of possible negative effects of such a market structure, the proponents of the theory of the empty core view liner conferences more positive as they consider them to be a necessary form of collusion to stabilise the otherwise chaotic markets for liner shipping services. Liner shipping carriers have argued, without a clear indication of what economic model they follow, that they consider liner shipping to be a special industry and that it is this unique character of liner shipping that requires an exemption of liner shipping from the traditional cartel prohibitions of competition law[4]. This approach will be considered towards the end of this chapter.

1. Liner conferences as monopolies

One group of economists argues that liner shipping conferences are essentially a monopoly and that their existence and effects can best be explained by the rules on monopoly behaviour.

a) The economics of a monopoly

Before turning to the question of whether or not a liner conference is a monopolist, it is necessary to give a short account of the main economic principles that govern the creation and the behaviour of a monopoly.

---

[1] Meyrick, (1999), p. 30.
[2] Fox, (1994), p. 343 ff.
[3] Sjoström, (1989), p. 1160 ff.
[4] WSC submission to the OECD, (2001), p. iii.

aa) Definition of the term *monopoly*

A *monopoly* exists under the following conditions[5]:

First, the monopolist must be the only supplier in the market. Second, prerequisite for the existence of a monopoly is that there must be no close substitutes[6] for the monopolists product. The consumer in a market with a supply-side monopoly, therefore, faces the decision either to buy from the monopolist, or not to purchase anything at all. The third requirement for the existence of a monopoly is that, for some reason, it is unlikely that other suppliers can successfully enter the market and remain therein. Such barriers to entry can be *inter alia* legal restrictions, such as patents or licences, or the existence of large sunk costs[7]. A monopoly may also exist if there are no external barriers that keep rivals out of the market, but if a single producer can supply a good or service to the entire market at lower costs, due to the advantages of large scale production, than could two or more producers[8]. Since such barriers result naturally out of the employed technology of production, this type of monopoly is also called a natural monopoly[9].

bb) A monopolist's influence on the price

The crucial difference between a monopoly and an undertaking in a competitive market is the fact that the monopolist can influence the price of the good or service it sells, whereas the producer in a competitive market is not able to do so[10]. A monopolist is said to be a *price maker*, while, in contrast, a supplier in a competitive market is a *price taker*. In a competitive market the individual producer is so small that it does not have any influence over the market price. In contrast, the monopolist, as the sole producer of a good or service, is at liberty to decide the price for its good or service. For any price that the monopolist decides to charge, it will find a certain number of buyers. The buyers on the demand side of the market act like buyers in a competitive market[11] and remain sensitive to price changes; the higher the price the less customers can afford the product and vice versa. Consequently, the monopolist is free to fix either the price or the quantity of output of a product, but it is not possible for a monopolist to determine both the quantity of output and the price at its free will[12].

---

[5] Baumol/Blinder, (1999), p. 230; Mankiw, (200)1, p. 316, Ruffin/Gregory, (2001), p. 206.

[6] A substitute is a good that can be used as an equal alternative; per: Mankiw, (2001), p. 68.

[7] In this context sunk costs denote such costs that are necessary as an initial investment for entering the market and that cannot be recovered in a short period of time; per: Baumol/Blinder, (1999), p. 231.

[8] Baumol/Blinder, (1999), p. 232; Mankiw, (2001), p. 316; Ruffin/Gregory, (2001), p. 206.

[9] Nicholson, (2000), p. 291.

[10] Baumol/Blinder, (1999), p. 233; Mankiw, (2001), p. 320.

[11] O'Sullivan/Sheffrin, (2001), p. 212.

[12] Baumol/Blinder, (1999), p. 233; Mankiw, (2001), p. 321.

cc) The monopolist's supply decision

Under the assumption that a monopolist has the aim of maximising profits, like a supplier in a competitive market, the monopolist will use its power to influence the price of a good to achieve the goal of profit maximisation. The profit of a monopolist equals its total revenue minus its total costs. The total revenue in turn equals the quantity sold multiplied with the price. When the monopolist decides what quantity/price combination will lead to a maximum profit, it has to take into account that for each additional unit it wants to sell, it must reduce the price (for all units sold) in order to find a customer for that additional unit[13]. Therefore, the monopolist will sell additional units as long as the benefit from selling an additional unit of output outweighs the disadvantage from having to reduce the price for all units in order to sell that additional unit. In economic terms this means that the optimal price/quantity combination for a monopolist is reached at the quantity where marginal costs equal marginal revenue[14].

In a competitive market the optimal price/quantity combination is also reached at the point where marginal revenue equals marginal costs[15]. The difference between a competitive market and a monopoly is, however, that in a competitive market the price also equals the marginal costs (and the marginal revenue), whereas the price which a monopolist charges is always higher than the marginal revenue and the marginal costs at the profit maximising price/quantity combination. In opposite terms this means that the marginal revenue of a monopolist is always lower than the price. This is so because in order to attract an additional customer for an additional unit of output the monopolist must lower its price for all units of output. Thus, the additional revenue that the monopolist receives when it sells one more unit of output (i.e. the marginal revenue) is the price the monopolist gets from the marginal customer minus the revenue it loses by cutting the price paid by all of its old customers. As a result, the marginal revenue is by definition smaller than the price[16]. The crucial consequence is that a monopolist charges a higher price than could a supplier in a competitive market, in order to maximise profits.

dd) Market distortions of a monopoly

A monopoly sells fewer units of output at a higher price than would all suppliers together in a competitive market[17]. This situation leads to several negative consequences for the performance of the market. First, due to the increased

[13] Mankiw, (2001), p. 322.

[14] Baumol/Blinder, (1999), p. 234; Eaton/Eaton/Allen, 1999, p. 332; Mankiw, 2001, p. 324; O'Sullivan Sheffrin, (2001), p. 217.

[15] Mankiw, (2001), p. 324.

[16] Baumol/Blinder, (1999), p. 234.

[17] Baumol/Blinder, (1999), p. 236.

price, there is an additional producer surplus[18]. As there is only one supplier in the market, the producer surplus belongs to the monopolist completely. It is therefore also called the monopoly's profit. This additional profit is gained at the expense of the consumers[19], because they have to pay a higher price.

A second consequence of the monopoly is that fewer consumers will buy the product, because of the higher price. In a monopolistic market fewer transactions take place than in a competitive market. The monopoly is said to create a deadweight loss[20]. This deadweight loss is the potential total surplus that remains unrealised at the monopoly price level. As resource allocation is efficient at the price level of a competitive market, the deadweight loss of a monopoly represents an inefficient market outcome and hence an inefficient resource allocation of a monopoly[21].

A third negative aspect about monopolies is that they might produce at higher costs than a producer in a competitive market would. Several reasons have been suggested for this effect. One explanation is that monopolists put considerable effort in attaining and later in keeping their position through such measures as intensive lobbying and advertising[22]. This effort to reach and keep the position of a monopolist is called *rent-seeking*[23]. Another cost increasing impact of monopolies is discussed under the term *plush carpet theorem*[24]. In a competitive market there is a high pressure on each individual producer to work as cost efficiently as possible, as there is always the threat that a more efficient producer lowers the market price and eventually forces the less efficient producer out of the market. Such a pressure does not exist for a monopolist. Therefore, the monopolist might allow itself a more cost inefficient way of production, without any consequences for its market position[25].

ee) Price discrimination

One last point worthy to note in the description of a monopoly is the fact that a monopolist is not obliged to charge all customers the same price. As the mo-

---

[18] Producer surplus is defined as the amount a seller is paid for a good minus the seller's costs. The concept of producer surplus denotes the net gain a seller has from making a sale.

[19] Nicholson, (2000), p. 298.

[20] Eaton/Eaton/Allen, (1999), p. 336; Mankiw, (2001), p. 329; Nicholson, (2000), p. 298.

[21] Baumol/Blinder, (1999), p. 237; Eaton/Eaton/Allen, (1999), p. 336; Mankiw, (2001), p. 329; Nicholson, (2000), p. 297.

[22] Baumol/Blinder, (1999), p. 238; Nicholson, (2000), p. 300.

[23] Nicholson, (1998), p. 774.

[24] Eaton/Eaton/Allen, (1999), p. 345.

[25] Studies have shown that this effect may even lead to a discriminatory employment policy, as a monopolist is under no pressure to hire only the most efficient workers; see: Eaton, Eaton/Allen,(1999), p, 346.

nopolist is the sole supplier in a market, it has the power to charge a different price for the same good to different customers. A seller in a competitive market could not engage in such a practise, as there would always be one of its competitors who would sell the product at the regular market price. Consequently, the strategy of such a differentiation of prices is closely related to the existence of a monopoly. The process of charging different prices to different customers for the same product is called price discrimination. Through such a behaviour a monopolist may increase its profits because it can charge each customer a price closer to its willingness to pay[26].

ff) Summary

This brief account on the economic rules governing the creation and the behaviour of a monopoly provides the basis for an analysis of liner conferences. For this purpose it is important to realise that a monopoly can only exist if there is just one supplier in the market, if there are no close substitutes for the product and if there are barriers that hinder other suppliers from entering and remaining in the market. As far as the behaviour of a monopolist is concerned, it is necessary to keep in mind that it sells fewer units of output at a higher price in comparison to a competitive market situation. This results in an increased producer surplus or monopoly profit at the expense of the consumers. Another consequence is that some gains from trade remain unrealised, as not all possible transactions take place. A monopoly, therefore, leads to an inefficient resource allocation. A final aspect of the behaviour of a monopolist that needs to be remembered is that it can use its market power to charge different prices to different customers, according to their individual willingness to pay.

b) Evaluation of the monopoly theory

A first step in the evaluation of liner shipping conferences as monopolies is to scrutinise whether or not the definition of a monopoly is applicable to liner conferences. In a second step, the analysis will focus on the merits of the classification of liner conferences as monopolies.

aa) Liner conferences and the definition of the term *monopoly*

It is only possible to explain the behaviour of liner conferences on the basis of monopoly theory, if they actually do constitute a monopoly in accordance with the definition supplied above[27]. Yet, it is not necessary to demonstrate that liner conferences match the definition of a monopoly 100 per cent. Instead the following analysis will focus on the question of whether or not liner conferences come sufficiently close to the ideal definition of a monopoly.

---

[26] Mankiw, (2001), p. 337.

[27] See above, p. 72 f.

The first part of the monopoly definition is that the monopolist must be the only supplier in its market. This requirement is not met by liner conferences. They do face competition *inter alia* from independent carriers and from conference carriers that do not operate within the conference tariffs[28]. Still, conferences had an approximate market share of 60 per cent in the major trades in the late 1990s[29]. This figure indicates that the rules of monopolistic behaviour may still be applicable to liner shipping since they carry a substantial part of all transported freights. Although liner conferences do not meet the strict criterion of complete market dominance, their market share is still large enough to explain their behaviour by the rules developed for the monopoly.

A second aspect of a monopoly is that there are barriers that hinder potential competitors from entering the market successfully. Conferences might exclude shipping lines from membership, but they cannot exclude carriers from operating independently in a certain trade. It is relatively easy for a carrier to transfer one or more vessels from one trade lane to another . Consequently, it is an often repeated statement that there are no restrictions to entry in the liner shipping industry[30]. This assertion must be qualified in two ways. First, even if it is possible for a carrier to enter a trade temporarily through a different allocation of its vessels, a long term commitment to a new trade route implies that the carrier commissions one or more of its ships to that route permanently. Under the assumption that the carrier does not want to leave another trade, this means that the carrier has to purchase new vessels, in order to enter a new trade permanently. He can do so only at considerable costs, which he cannot recover in the short run. The existence of such costs that resemble sunk costs, have been identified as one possible barrier to entry[31]. Another way in which conferences might successfully impede the entry of new competitors in a trade is through the conclusion of loyalty agreements or service contracts with the shippers[32]. These contracts bind the shippers to the conference carriers for a longer period of time[33]. It is, therefore, not possible for new entrants to simply offer their transport services in a new trade, as many of the shippers, especially those with a large transport volume, are bound to established carriers through long-term contractual obligations.

---

[28] See above, p. 38.

[29] Meyrick, (1999), p. 16; OECD, (2002), p. 20.

[30] CENSA submission to the OECD, (2001), p. 1; TACA submission to the OECD, (2001), p. 1.

[31] Creel, (1999), p. 8; see above, p. 72.

[32] Kühne, (1996), p. 39.

[33] See above, p. 47.

The third condition under which a monopoly is said to arise is that there must be no close substitutes for the product. In the context of liner shipping this requirement relates to competition from other types of transport, such as tramp shipping as well as air and land transport. The evaluation of all these modes of transport in chapter two has demonstrated that they do not constitute a workable alternative for shippers in most cases[34] and, consequently, they cannot be considered as close substitutes.

This analysis of liner conferences in the light of the textbook definition of a monopoly shows that shipping conferences do not conform to this definition completely, but that they do come close enough to this ideal definition. For this reason, it is sound to apply the rules of monopolistc behaviour to liner conferences.

bb) Merits of the monopoly approach

Supporters of the view that liner conferences are monopolies argue that they behave as monopolist insofar, as they engage in price discrimination[35]. Conferences traditionally charge *ad valorem* prices, meaning that they charge different prices for the transport of otherwise identical containers, depending on the value of the shipped goods[36]. Those who do not consider liner conferences to be monopolists have put forward that the differences in freight rates for the different commodities are not a product of price discrimination, but rather the result of the higher costs associated with the transport of high-value cargoes[37]. According to this view transport costs for these freights are often higher because they need special (and costly) treatment, such as special storage (e.g. for refrigerated good or liquids), and because the higher value of such cargoes requires the carriers to pay higher insurance premiums.

In liner shipping fixed costs account for about 80 per cent of total costs[38]. These costs associated with the operation of a containership remain constant irrespective of the value of the shipped goods. The above mentioned differences in handling costs for valuable goods affect only the variable costs. As these make up only the remaining 20 per cent of the total costs, the cost structure of liner shipping would suggest that the differences in handling and the resulting differences in handling costs cannot affect the freight rate by more than 20 per cent. The actual numbers show, however, that the differences in the per ton

[34] See above, p. 39 ff.
[35] Clyde/Reitzes, (1995), p. 6; Jansson/Shneerson, (1986), p. 94; Zerby/Colon, (1983), p. 394.
[36] Reitzes, (1993), p. 81.
[37] Butz, (1993), p. 75.
[38] Frank/Bunel, (1991), p. 143.

freight rate between the different commodities are much higher[39]. As a consequence, the hypothesis, that the differences in freight rates reflect higher variable costs for the transport of valuable cargoes, cannot be upheld, and the view, that the practice of price discrimination indicates that liner conferences are monopolies that wield market power, is more sound.

In opposition to the monopoly thesis, it has been suggested that price discrimination, according to the value of the shipped goods, is not a consequence of the conference system, but that such a pricing system has developed independently of the conference system[40], because of the high degree of market concentration[41]. The rationale for this argument is that in a concentrated market the individual supplier has market power because it controls such a large share of the market supply that the normal forces that subject him to be a price taker do not apply. As a result, the individual carrier is in a position to charge *ad valorm* prices. This line of argument looses much of its virtue if it is recalled that *ad valorem* freight tariffs have a long tradition in conference pricing practices, whereas today's market concentration is a relatively recent development. In this context it should also be borne in mind that concentration among carriers does not necessarily mean that the number of carriers that compete on a certain route decreases. The process of concentration through the building of alliances, mergers and acquisitions was triggered by the wish of carriers to develop a global presence. Their larger size gave them the possibility to extend their schedules to routes which they could not serve before. Concentration in the liner shipping industry did not lead to a situation where a few operators dominate certain trade routes; instead, more carriers were able to extend their services to other trades, which results in a bigger number of carriers competing on individual routes[42].

Although the existence of price discrimination on the part of liner conferences suggests that they are monopolists, critics of this approach have forwarded another argument in their favour, which cannot be dismissed easily. The monopoly thesis would suggest that liner conferences behave like typical monopolists by charging a higher price than suppliers would in a competitive market and by offering less transport capacity than would be offered under competitive cir-

---

[39] For an example see: Zerby/Colon, (1983), p. 392: The price for shipping one ton of grain from Australia to Europe in 1972/73 was A$ 11.96, whereas it cost A$ 156.48 to ship one ton of metal products and machinery on the same route in the same year.

[40] Clyde/Reitzes, (1995), p. 7.

[41] Market concentration has risen considerably during the last years. The data for the year 2001 indicate that the 5 largest carriers control 34 percent of the world's fleet, the 10 largest carriers control 50 percent of the world's fleet and the 20 largest carriers control 72 percent of the world's fleet; per: OECD, (2001), p. 14.

[42] Creel, (1999), p. 12.

cumstances. Reality does not support either of these predictions. The liner shipping industry is burdened with chronic excess capacity[43], and it is undisputed that carriers only generate moderate profits in comparison to other industries[44].

It is especially this last aspect that critics of the monopoly view have stressed. They argue that traditional monopoly analysis would predict comparatively high monopoly rents for the liner shipping industry, as the price elasticity of demand for liner shipping services is low[45]. The price elasticity of demand measures how much the quantity demanded changes as a consequence of a change in price[46]. A low price elasticity of demand describes a situation where the consumers will not stop to purchase the product as a consequence of only moderate price increases. In the liner shipping industry, this situation can easily be explained by the fact that shippers have no alternative to seaborne transport[47]. Since the consumers in a market with a low price elasticity of demand do not react to an increase in price with a substantial withdrawal of business, the classical monopoly analysis would suggest that the monopolist has the power to charge a price high above its marginal costs (and hence the competitive market price), without running the risk of losing much business. As a consequence, a monopolist is expected to generate substantial excess profits under such conditions.

The absence of such supernormal profits in the liner shipping industry indicates that liner conferences cannot simply be considered to be typical monopolists, as this finding does not conform to the predictions of classical monopoly theory, especially in a market with a low price elasticity of demand.

cc) Liner conferences as inefficient producers

One way to bring the absence of high profits and the existence of market power in line with the traditional monopoly analysis, is to argue that liner conferences produce inefficiently and consume potential monopoly rents through inefficient production[48]. Inefficiencies may arise because carriers that do not face the threat of competition disregard market demands and provide a service that is too luxurious and/or a quantity of shipping space that is above the quantity which they would provide under competitive circumstances. It has also been suggested that the conference system induces carriers to be inefficient because, in

[43] Meyrick, (1999), p. 37.
[44] OECD, (2002), p. 45.
[45] Franck/Bunel, (1991), p. 143.
[46] Baumol/Blinder, (1999), p. 119; Mankiw, (2001), p. 94.
[47] See above, p. 39 ff.
[48] Meyrick, (1999), p. 30.

the absence of competition, they can use up more resources than necessary in the production process and still remain in the market. This latter inefficiency has been described above as the *plush carpet theorem*. In economic terms the first kind of inefficiency arises because the conference carriers produce at a wrong point on the production frontier and the second inefficiency is caused by a production level inside the production frontier[49].

Opponents of this view have argued that liner shipping operators are also under considerable pressure to produce efficiently. In liner shipping, returns on investment are so low that efficient production is essential for the survival of any liner shipping operator[50]. The explanation for the absence of supernormal monopoly profits through the *plush carpet theorem* also loses credibility in consideration of the fact that conference carriers not only enter into conference agreements, but that they are also often members of consortia. It would not make sense for carriers to increase efficiency through the creation of complicated consortia agreements that restrict the capability of the single carrier to decide individually on its business operations, if the same effect could be reached through an increase in internal efficiency. For this reason, the explanation that potential monopoly profits are simply consumed by inefficient production appears too simple. It should be noted, however, that this finding does not necessarily mean that all carriers have similar cost structures. The cost structures of carriers may, for example, still differ because of exogenous effects which they cannot influence, such as ,for example, different tax and crewing requirements[51].

dd) Liner conferences as sales revenue maximisers

Another attempt that has been made to explain the absence of supernormal profits in the liner shipping industry is the proposition that liner conferences do not pursue the goal of profit maximisation, but that they aim to maximise of sales revenue[52]. The central notion of the theory of sales revenue maximisation is that, due to the separation of ownership from management in a modern enterprise, the managers might follow a strategy that suits their own interests better than those of the owners of such an undertaking, who would like their firm to generate maximal profits. For the managers, the maximisation of sales revenue has several positive effects. Managerial salaries are often related to the sales (and an increase thereof) of that firm and not to its rate of profitability. Often, an enterprise with large and increasing sales is treated favourably by the banks and other financial institutions, which is positive for the management, as it fa-

[49] Meyrick, (1999), p. 30.
[50] Meyrick, (1999), p. 31; Creel, (1999), p. 13.
[51] Clyde/Reitzes, (1995), p. 5.
[52] Meyrick, (1999), p. 38.

cilitates their work in situations of capital demand. A third positive aspect of revenue maximisation for managers is that it is simply more prestigious to work for a firm that increases its sales and possibly its market share.

The application of this theory to the liner shipping industry has faced criticism, some of a general nature, some of a liner shipping specific nature. One problem is that the application of this theory to liner shipping can only be tested if the data on demand and costs of each individual carrier were available[53]. However, since such data are not available, it is also difficult to verify this approach. A general problem of the theory of sales revenue maximisation is that it cannot explain, how a market reaches its equilibrium[54]. Through its focus on the decision-making process within the single firm, it neglects the impact that competitors, who are also deemed to pursue the goal of sales revenue maximisation, have on managerial decisions of the individual firm. Another criticism of the application of the theory of sales revenue maximisation to liner shipping is that even if it could be employed to explain the absence of supernormal profits in this industry, it still does not explain the subnormal profits that characterise many of the liner shipping operators[55]. If the owners of a firm would find out that its managers intentionally keep the profits at a very low level, it would become likely that they take steps to replace that management.

A final criticism of the application of the theory of sales revenue maximisation to liner shipping is that the absence of supernormal profits in the face of a low price elasticity of demand also contradicts the application of this theory to liner shipping[56]. If the price elasticity of demand is very low, the majority of the customers will continue to purchase the product after a price increase. In such a market the positive effect, which an increase in prices has on the total revenue, is larger than the parallel reduction in revenue, due to the loss of only a few customers. As a consequence, it would be a wise strategy for a carrier with the goal to maximise its revenue to raise the price, as such a behaviour would not only result in an increased profitability, but also in an increase of total sales revenue. The absence of supernormal profits, therefore, also contradicts the sales maximisation theory.

It is especially in consideration of this last aspect that the application of the theory of sales maximisation to liner shipping does not provide a coherent explanation for the absence of supernormal profits in this industry.

---

[53] Koutsoyiannis, (1979), p. 348.
[54] Koutsoyiannis, (1979), p. 348.
[55] Meyrick, (1999), p. 38.
[56] Meyrick, (1999), p. 38.

2. Liner conferences as oligopolies

Whereas those who judge liner conferences to be monopolists stress the fact that shipping conferences constitute a single entity, economists who consider liner conferences to be oligopolies, emphasise the fact that they are made up of individual carriers, a circumstance that needs to be reflected in the economic evaluation of the conference system. The following analysis will first focus on some general aspects of the rules governing the behaviour within an oligopoly. What follows, is the analysis of the open cartel model and an examination of liner shipping, in the light of traditional oligopoly theory.

a) The economics of a collusive oligopoly

An oligopoly is said to exist when there are only a few sellers in a market that offer similar, or even identical products[57]. Although the producers have some power to influence the market price, they must take into account the behaviour of their competitors[58]. In a collusive oligopoly (also called cartel) these few producers act together, in order to control the quantity of output and the price of their product or service. Collusion between the suppliers in an oligopoly is only effective, if the members of the cartel can agree on the overall quantity of output as well as on the distribution of that output among themselves[59]. The intended goal of such a collusive practise is to create a single entity on the supply side of the market[60], thereby creating the possibility to generate the same excess profits as a monopoly[61]. The expectation to earn supernormal profits like a monopolist is a clear incentive for the suppliers in an oligopoly to create a cartel[62], especially if it is not forbidden by law to do so.

The difference between a monopoly and an oligopoly is, however, that in a monopoly, there is only one supplier in the whole market, whereas in an oligopoly, there are several. It is this difference that has a decisive influence on the analysis of cartel behaviour. The problem is that a collusive strategy of all cartel members maximises the profits for the cartel as a whole, but not necessarily for each individual member. For an individual cartel member it might be more beneficial to undercut the common price in order to attract a larger share of business and in order to maximise its own profits. Thus, a second rule can be established for oligopoly behaviour. It might be the best strategy for an individual member of a collusive oligopoly to cheat on the common oligopoly pol-

[57] Mankiw, (2001), 350.
[58] Ruffin/Gregory, (2001), p. 238.
[59] Mankiw, (2001), p. 353.
[60] The market, thereby, becomes a monopoly and the rules on monopoly behaviour that have been developed above become fully applicable.
[61] Baumol/Blinder, (1999), p. 254; Koutsoyiannis, (1979), p. 237.
[62] Eaton/Eaton/Allen, (1999), p. 502; Mankiw, (2001), p. 353.

icy. This contradiction between the strategy to maximise profits for the cartel as a whole and the strategy to maximise individual profits can develop into a constant source of conflict in a cartel[63].

b) The open cartels model

One attempt to explain the exercise of market power by liner conferences and the simultaneous absence of supernormal profits in liner shipping with the help of the rules on oligopolistic behaviour is the open cartels model. The central aspect of this model is that conference carriers act as collusive oligopolists that initially restrict the available shipping capacity below the amount, that would exist under competitive conditions. At the same time, they set the freight rates at a level that is above the market equilibrium in a competitive market. As the collusive behaviour prohibits competition on prices, the individual carrier then tries to attract a larger share of conference business, at the expense of the other conference members, through an increased quality of service, especially through an increased number of sailings[64]. The consequence of such a behaviour is that the cost of shipping increases due to the increased quality/quantity of service, which in turn induces the liner conferences to raise the rates even further. Now, a vicious circle between further quality improvements or capacity enlargements and further rate increases develops, leading to ever more overcapacities and ever higher shipping rates[65].

The virtue of this model is evident. It can not only explain the phenomenon that conference carriers do not earn supernormal profits, due to the transformation of such potential profits into costs for excess service competition, but it can also explain the existence of overcapacity, which has been called a *chronic* feature of the liner shipping industry[66].

As inviting as this explanation for the behaviour of liner shipping conferences may be, there are some convincing arguments against the open cartels model. One criticism is that data from the shipping industry do not support the idea that carriers can increase shipping capacity and freight rates at the same time. In recent years the shipping industry rather witnessed an increase in capacity and a constant decline in freight rates[67]. Another argument against the open cartel model centres on the underlying assumption that conferences can only control freight rates. It is startling indeed that conferences are supposed to have strict

[63] Eaton/Eaton/Allen, (1999), p. 490.
[64] Fox, (1989), p. 41 f; Jansson/Shneerson, (1987), p. 275.
[65] Meyrick, (1999), p. 32; OECD, (2002), p. 53; Report by the Australian Productivity Commission on Liner Shipping, (1999), p. B7.
[66] Creel, (1999), p. 12.
[67] OECD, (2002), p. 53.

authority over freight rates, but no power over the kind of services that its members provide[68]. Already the first conferences allocated the different sailings to the individual member carriers[69]. The distribution of available sailings amongst its members has been a typical conference activity until today[70]. This challenges the assumption that liner conferences only exercise control over the freight rates but not over the quality of service and the tonnage of its members. To challenge this hypothesis at the same time questions the open cartels model.

A final argument against the open cartels model is that the system of conference behaviour, which it suggests is inherently unstable[71] but that it cannot realign this instability with the market outcome it suggests. According to the open cartels model, conference members raise the freight rates and increase the shipping capacity in a continuous circular movement. The problem with such a mechanism is that it increases the incentive for conference carriers to break ranks and for new competitors to enter the market. These market participants would provide shipping services in a more cost efficient way without the overcapacities that conference carriers have accumulated over time, and they could consequently offer their services at a lower price than the current conference price. As a result, the price of shipping and the shipping tonnage would fall to competitive levels. The open cartels model does not predict such a market outcome, which in turn offers a basis upon which to criticise the model.

For the above outlined reasons, it is not possible to accept the open cartels model as a coherent explanation for the behaviour of liner conferences and especially the absence of supernormal profits in the shipping industry. A virtue of he open cartels model, however, is that it highlights the conflict between individual and collusive strategies in its explanation of conference behaviour.

c) Liner conferences and the traditional oligopoly conflict

A further possibility to explain the absence of excessive profits in the liner shipping industry is to focus on the different preferences of a conference as a whole and of the single carriers, as far as the price level is concerned. To transfer the classical example of the *prisoners dilemma*[72] to liner shipping is to analyse whether it is wise for a carrier to demand the conference price or whether an individual carrier is better off deciding for itself the price it charges. A key

---

[68] Butz, (1993), p. 76.

[69] See above, p. 9.

[70] See above, p. 49 ff.

[71] Meyrick, (1999), p. 32; Report by the Australian Productivity Commission on Liner Shipping, (1999). p. B 8.

[72] For a description of the prisoners dilemma see: Baumol/Blinder, (1999), p. 262; Mankiw, (2001), p. 359 ff; Nicholson, (1998), p. 275.

aspect in such a situation is the heterogeneity of the different carriers. It has been noted above that carriers may well have different cost structures and consequently different average costs of production, even if they do not intentionally waste resources in the production process[73]. Typically, conferences set their common freight tariff at a level where even the least efficient member of a conference can still operate profitably[74]. Such a pricing policy creates an incentive for the more efficient carriers to undercut the agreed conference price and thereby attract a larger share of the business. This incentive grows as the differences in efficiency between the individual carriers become larger.

Another reason to deviate from the common conference tariff for the more efficient conference carriers may be their fear of competition from outsiders. In order to battle such competition they may choose to charge prices below the current conference rates. This model can only explain the behaviour of conference carriers in an environment where the individual carrier is allowed the right to independent action and where conference carriers face non-conference competition[75]. Independent action in the form of individual service contracting is a permissible conduct for conference carriers under EC law[76] and the possibility to depart from the conferences pricing policy without great difficulty is also given under U. S. laws[77]. Another characteristic of liner shipping is that conference carriers have faced increased competition from non-conference carriers since the early 1980s. At that time a group of new independent operators, which mainly originated in the Far East, appeared on the markets for liner shipping. Consequently, this model could provide a valid basis for the analysis of a carrier's decision on prices.

The argument that efficient carriers opt for cutting the high conference tariff, if they can do so without having to fear punishment from the conference, is supported by a study conducted by *Clyde* and *Reitzes* in 1995[78]. According to their findings, the level of freight rates was around 19 per cent lower in such trades, where it was possible for conference members to undercut conference prices on an individual basis without having to fear conference punishment[79]. The proposition that efficient conference carriers decide to deviate from the common conference tariff in the face of non-conference competition can be confirmed by

---

[73] See above, p 80.
[74] OECD, (2001), p. 59.
[75] OECD, (2002), p. 64.
[76] See below, p. 122 ff.
[77] The impact of OSRA (1998) on the shipping industry will be considered in detail in chapter seven.
[78] Clyde/Reitzes, (1995).
[79] Clyde/Reitzes, (1995), p. 33.

developments in the shipping industry[80]. The emergence of the new independent carriers at the beginning of the 1980s coincided with the beginning of a continuous process of rate deterioration. In both instances the tendency of the more efficient conference carriers to undercut the conference rate can be explained by the fact that deviation from the conference tariff and charging lower prices became the best strategy to maximise individual profits. They could engage in such a practise, as they could still operate profitably at a lower price level.

According to this line of reasoning, the interpretation of conference and, more importantly, carrier behaviour in the light of the classical conflict in a collusive oligopoly between the policy of the cartel as a whole and the strategy of its individual members can explain the absence of supernormal profits even though liner conferences are allowed to fix prices collectively. The main reason for this failure is the heterogeneity of the different carriers that make up each conference and the existence (or at least the threat) of non-conference competition. As the relevant data from the shipping industry support this view, it is so far the most convincing explanation for the current state of liner shipping.

3. The theory of the empty core

Another approach that has been developed by economists to explain the existence and behaviour of liner conferences is the theory of the empty core[81]. The crucial difference between this hypothesis and the aforementioned models is that proponents of the empty core theory do not consider liner conferences to be a typical monopoly or collusive oligopoly. As a consequence, the theory of the empty core is not an attempt to explain the absence of monopoly profits in an industry that displays the formation of monopolies. The supporters of this view see liner conferences as a necessary device to stabilise an otherwise inherently unstable industry and not as a means of extracting monopoly rents from the market[82].

A market has a core when there is one price/quantity combination that maximises the well being of all buyers and sellers in a market. At this market outcome no market participant or group of market participants has an incentive to move towards another price/quantity combination in order to increase their profits. In a market with an empty core, there is no such stable position and no matter what the current market outcome, there will always be some market par-

[80] OECD, (2002), p. 65.
[81] Pirrong, (1992); Sjoström, (1989).
[82] Pirrong, (1992), p. 89; Sjoström, (1989), p. 1061.

ticipants who want to get together to disrupt the original market outcome in order to maximise their individual profit[83].

It can easily be perceived, how the theory of the empty core might be applicable to liner shipping. Suppose, a particular trade route only generates enough traffic for two weekly services to be run at costs above average costs. Suppose also that three different carriers want to operate their vessels on that route. The one carrier that is currently left out has an incentive to make an agreement with some of the shippers in order to enter the market, thereby disrupting the original market solution. If the third carrier enters the market and the established competitors remain therein, then all three carriers operate at a loss, because their services do not cover the average costs of the provision of such a service. If, however, one of the established carriers leaves the market, the other two will operate profitably, with the result that the carrier that is outside is now eager to get back into the market. If this carrier decides to re-enter the market, the whole process starts over again. The consequence of such a market situation is a continuously unstable market[84].

Supporters of the empty core theory argue that the longevity of the conference system suggests that their explanation for the existence of liner conferences is correct[85]. They emphasise that the durability of liner conferences in an industry, where entry of new competitors in unrestricted, is evidence for the fact that liner conferences do not constitute cartels that have the purpose of extracting monopoly profits. As long as liner conferences raise the price for shipping services above the competitive market price, other carriers would enter the market and the level of freight rates would fall. The liner conference would eventually cease to exist, as it has failed in its purpose to extract monopoly profits. The possibility of unrestricted entry of new carriers rather implies that the members of a liner conference will only earn normal profits. The longevity of liner shipping conferences indicates that they serve some other purpose, and this purpose is to bring stability to the otherwise chaotic markets for liner shipping[86].

This line of reasoning can be criticised on several accounts. The first criticism concerns the assumption that the longevity of the conference system is strong evidence for the necessity of liner conferences as a means to bring order to the otherwise chaotic and unstable maritime transport industry. Although it is true that liner conferences have characterised the shipping industry for the last 120 years, this longevity only relates to the system of carriers forming liner confer-

[83] OECD, (2002). p. 61.
[84] OECD, (2002), p. 61.
[85] Pirrong, (1992), p. 118; Sjoström, (1989), p. 1161.
[86] Meyrick, (1999), p. 47, Pirrong, (1992), p. 124.

ences. It does not apply to individual conferences that may only exist for a few years, and it does not apply to the membership of a single carrier to a conference that fluctuates according to the individual carriers' business strategy[87]. A second criticism centres on the fact that the argumentation presented above is only correct, if the liner shipping industry is an industry, where entry of new competitors is truly unrestricted. The forgoing analysis in this chapter has shown that, although there are no legal barriers to entry into a certain trade[88], there are contractual barriers that obstruct the free entry of competitors into new trades[89]. This finding also weakens the argumentation of the supporters of the theory of the empty core.

The central problem concerning the application of the empty core theory to liner conferences is that it does not prove that liner conferences with their power to fix prices are a necessary device to bring order to otherwise unstable markets for liner shipping services. One way that the instability of liner shipping markets may be reduced without having to resort to price fixing arrangements, such as liner conferences, is by increasing loyalty of individual shippers to certain carriers by rebate systems[90]. It is also possible to employ the use of service contracts as a means to increase the stability of liner shipping markets. Such contracts are beneficial for the carriers insofar, as they can be concluded for a longer period of time, which in turn reduces the uncertainties of shipping for the carriers. Carriers could also stabilise the markets for liner shipping through an agreement on a fixed schedule and a computerised booking and reservation scheme, by which the single shipments are allocated to the different sailings. Such a system would make it impossible for new entrants to the market to steal business in a "hit-and-run" manner from carriers that already operate in the market. The consequence of such a system is a reduction of possible instabilities in the liner shipping market[91]. These last two suggestions have shown that, even if the empty core theory correctly explains the rationale behind the existence of liner shipping conferences, it does not prove that they are the only possibility to battle the alleged instabilities in the markets for liner shipping services. It is, therefore, not sound to deduct from the application of the empty core theory to liner shipping that liner conferences are a necessary means to stabilise liner shipping markets.

---

[87] OECD, (2002), p. 62;
[88] WSC submission to the OECD, (2001), p. ii.
[89] See above, p. 76.
[90] Sjoström, (1993), p. 423.
[91] OECD, (2002), p. 63.

4. Uniqueness of liner shipping

Representatives from the liner shipping industry often argue in a more factual way on the issue of retaining the exemption for price fixing arrangements in their industry. According to this position, liner shipping is a unique industry mainly because of the following factors[92]:

- lumpy supply, since it is only possible to add shipping capacity by adding a whole vessel, or even a complete string of vessels to a trade,
- uneven demand, both seasonally and directionally, leading to overcapacities in times of low trade volume and
- high fixed costs.

As a consequence of these special circumstances, it is proclaimed as necessary for the liner shipping industry to fix prices, in order to avoid a process of competition that would otherwise become destructive with detrimental effects for the carriers, as well as for the shippers, because of the decreased reliability and quality of liner shipping services[93]. Such a reasoning somewhat resembles the empty core approach, which has been discussed above. Since the carriers do not make explicit reference to that theory, their argumentation will be considered independently.

The problem with this view is that there is little knowledge about the behaviour of liner shipping operators in the absence of price fixing arrangements, because they have characterised the industry since the 1870s. However, the opinion that the uniqueness of the liner shipping industry warrants the right to fix prices can be challenged in two ways. First, even if liner conferences constitute a functioning device to battle feared destructive competition, this does not mean that there are no other, less restrictive, means to reduce unstable market conditions in the liner shipping industry. Some suggestions to that effect have already been made in the discussion of the theory of the empty core[94]. In addition to the already suggested measures to increase the stability of liner shipping markets it would also be possible for liner shipping operators to battle overcapacities through a more flexible deployment of their vessels. The adoption of a round-the-world schedule for some of their vessels permits carriers to avoid excess capacities on the weak leg of a trade. Another possibility to battle excess capacities is to engage in slot chartering agreements[95]. Through such an agreement, it is no longer necessary for every carrier that wants to offer its services in a certain trade, to operate one or more of its own vessels in that trade.

---

[92] Creel, (1999), p. 12; OECD, (2002), p. 54; WSC submission to the OECD, (2001), p. iii.

[93] WSC submission to the OECD, (2001), p. iii.

[94] See above; p. 86 ff.

[95] NITL submission to the OECD, (2001), p. 12.

A second line of argument against the carriers' reasoning is to challenge the assumption that liner shipping is a truly unique industry. High fixed costs and uneven demand are characteristics of any industry that provides a scheduled service[96]. Experience from other sectors of the transport industry (airline, road haulage and railways) that have undergone a process of liberalisation in the past, has shown that the deregulation of these markets, which included the prohibition to fix prices, has not lead to a collapse of these industries, as envisioned by the carriers[97]. For this reason, the proposition that liner shipping is a unique industry is correct in the sense that every industry has its unique character, but not in the sense that liner shipping is a business, which is more unique than other industries[98]. The position of the carriers must, therefore, be dismissed.

5. Conclusion

The analysis of the different positions that economists developed to explain cartel behaviour and especially the behaviour of liner conferences demonstrates that there is little agreement on this issue. Several of these views highlight a specific aspect of conference behaviour. Yet, they always stumble over some other aspect of conference behaviour, which they cannot explain. Consequently, they cannot provide a coherent explanation for the complex market mechanisms in liner shipping. An example would be the open cartels model, which emphasises the conflict between strategies that benefit the individual cartel member and such strategies that are beneficial for the cartel as a whole. This model suggests a vicious circle between ever increasing prices for shipping and a continuous increase in shipping capacity. The reality of liner shipping does not support this outcome, since the last decade has been characterised by a growth of shipping capacity (as predicted) and a decline of shipping rates (not as predicted).

It is, nevertheless, the classical conflict within an oligopoly that provides the key for an understanding of the market mechanisms in liner shipping. The often witnessed phenomenon that conferences cannot enforce their rates due to rebating practices of their members, results from the fact that such a practice is positive for the profits of the more efficient conference members[99]. Only when the rate level decreases so much that the profits of the more efficient carriers are endangered, can collusive strategies find the approval of the majority of the conference members and have a chance to be put into effect. An example for such a switch from individual to collusive strategy could be witnessed in the Asia - U. S. trades in the late 1990s. After the economic crisis hit Asia in

[96] OECD, (2002), p. 54.
[97] OECD, (2002), p. 54; ESC submission to the OECD, (2001), p. 11 ff.
[98] OECD, (2002), p. 55.
[99] OECD, (2002), p. 64.

1996/97, the volume of trade from the U. S. to Asia decreased in 1998, which in turn led to a severe trade imbalance, since U. S. imports from Asia grew 20 per cent in that year[100]. In this situation, the collusive strategy suddenly became more appealing, even to the more efficient carriers, since inbound rates were so low that even the more efficient carriers were no longer able to operate profitably. As a consequence, the carriers established a well functioning cartel, called the Transpacific Stabilisation Agreement (TSA), which successfully eliminated competition on the inbound leg[101].

The finding that the liner conferences function in accordance with classical oligopoly theory has several implications for the policy development on this issue. First, the often repeated statement that the liner shipping industry is special can be dismissed, since its functioning can be explained on the basis of a model that has not been developed specifically for this industry. A second implication is that conference agreements do not enhance the competitiveness of liner carriers. Rather the opposite is true, since the liner shipping industry is often competitive in spite of the existence of liner conferences. This finding leads to the third conclusion that is relevant for the purposes of the development of a modern policy toward liner conferences. Liner conferences constitute oligopolies and they, therefore, display negative effects on competition, typically associated with an oligopolistic market structure.

[100] Won, (1999), p. 17.
[101] Won, (1999), p. 17.

Chapter five - Regulation 4056/86 and Regulation 823/2000

The purpose of this chapter is the evaluation of the current secondary law in the field of maritime transport. Since the focus of this study is the analysis of restrictive practices among liner carriers, the emphasis will be put on the provisions that govern the different exemptions for collusive action in the liner shipping sector that exist at the level of secondary law; it is not intended to provide a complete commentary on all provisions contained in Regulations 4056/86 and 823/2000[1].

1. Regulation 4056/86

The examination of Regulation 4056/86 begins with some remarks on the relationship between the Treaty provisions on competition and Regulation 4056/86 and then continues with an evaluation of the scope of Regulation 4056/86. What follows, is an analysis of the different material provisions of Regulation 4056/86 that regulate collusive practices in liner shipping. The main emphasis will be put on the block exemption for liner conferences contained in Art. 3 Regulation 4056/86.

a) The position of Regulation 4056/86 in relationship to Arts. 81 and 82 (ex 85 and 86) EC

The ECJ has laid down in the rulings analysed above[2], that Arts. 81 and 82 (ex 85 and 86) EC are applicable to the maritime transport sector. The only problem was that there were no detailed procedural provisions governing their application in this field.

After the passage of Regulation 4056/86 it has been argued that, as a consequence, the application of Arts. 81 and 82 (ex 85 and 86) EC to maritime transport is restricted. According to this position, Regulation 4056/86 constitutes a closed system of rules that must not be interpreted in the light of the Treaty provisions on competition, but primarily from within[3]. Arts. 81 and 82 (ex 85 and 86) EC and especially Art. 81 III (ex Art. 85 III) EC must not be obeyed in all details, only such general Treaty provisions as Arts. 2 and 3 EC must be followed as a standard for interpreting Regulation 4056/86. Others argue that Arts. 81 and 82 (ex 85 and 86) EC constitute the standard for a correct interpretation of Regulation 4056/86 and that, as a consequence, it is necessary to

---

[1] For such a complete commentary see: Immenga/Mestmäcker, Vol. 2, (1997), Basedow, p. 2035 ff; Jacobs, (1991); Kühne, (1996).

[2] See above, 54 ff.

[3] Kröger, ETL (1993), p. 423 ff, p. 426.

pay special attention to Art. 81 III EC[4]. This dispute not only touches upon general aspects of the European legal structure, but it also centres on the question of whether the provisions relating to the liner conference block exemption contained in Regulation 4056/86 should be interpreted in a narrow, or rather in a more liberal way.

In favour of the first opinion it has been argued that Arts. 81 and 82 (ex 85 and 86) EC are mainly concerned with the functioning of the Internal Market, but as shipping is a world-wide activity, it is not possible to transfer these provisions to liner shipping on a one-to-one basis[5]. Another argument that has been brought forward in favour of a broader interpretation of Regulation 4056/86 is the fact that its very objective, which is to co-ordinate EC law and the provisions of the UNCTAD-code[6], cannot otherwise be achieved, since the UNCTAD-code does not restrict liner shipping as much as would a strict application of Art. 81 III (ex 85 III) EC[7].

Yet, there are severe doubts as to whether such an approach to Regulation 4056/86 is correct. Regulation 4056/86 is based not only on Art. 80 II (ex 84 II) EC but also on Art. 83 (ex 87) EC. Even the partial disapplication of Arts. 81 and 82 (ex 85 and 86) EC cannot be based on a provision which seeks to give "*effect to the principles set out in Articles 81 and 82*" (ex 85 and 86) EC. The conflict between the legal basis and the above-suggested interpretation of Regulation 4056/86 is evident. Serious doubts also arise from a constitutional point of view. Traditionally, there is a hierarchy of norms in EC law[8]. Primary law always prevails over secondary law. Consequently, a Regulation must conform to all Treaty provisions[9], as the former is part of secondary law and the latter are part of primary law. The above-stated opinion would also indicate that the Treaty provisions are of a different quality, as some must be obeyed (Arts. 2 and 3 EC) and some may be disregarded (Arts. 81 and 82 (ex 85 and 86) EC). Yet, there is no such difference, as all Treaty provisions are equal in rank and prevail as a whole over all provisions of secondary law[10], such as Regulations.

It also is a misguided assumption that the application of Regulation 4056/86 in conformity with Arts. 81 and 82 (ex 85 and 86) EC does not pay sufficient trib-

---

[4] Temple Lang, ETL (1993), p. 405 ff, p. 406.
[5] Kröger, ETL (1993), p. 423 ff, p. 425.
[6] Recital 3 and 4 of the Preamble to Regulation 4056/86.
[7] Kröger, ETL (1993), p. 423 ff, p. 426.
[8] Oppermann, (1999), p. 182.
[9] Temple Lang, ETL (1993), p. 405 ff, p. 406.
[10] Oppermann, (1999), p. 182.

ute to the specialties of maritime transport. Regulation 4056/86 contains a block exemption for price fixing arrangements of liner conferences, which is unlimited in time. This already constitutes a unique treatment of this sector[11], as such an exemption is granted nowhere else. For these reasons it is correct to state that Arts. 81 and 82 (ex 85 and 86) EC are the yardstick for the interpretation of Regulation 4056/86 and that, as a consequence, a careful evaluation of its provisions, in the light of the principles laid down in Art. 81 III (ex 85 III) EC, is necessary.

b) The scope of Regulation 4056/86

According to Art. 1 II Regulation 4056/86, Regulation 4056/86 is applicable to "*international maritime transport services from or to one or more Community ports, other than tramp vessel services*". The analysis of the scope of Regulation 4056/86 is divided into an evaluation of its territorial and its personal scope.

aa) The territorial scope of Regulation 4056/86

One aspect of the territorial scope of Regulation 4056/86 is that it is only applicable to *maritime* transport, a term which is not defined in that Regulation. Maritime transport typically means transport by sea[12]. What exactly constitutes maritime transport must be assessed on the basis of a number of factors, such as the general purpose of the employed vessel and the geographical range in which it is used[13]. The location of the port may also serve as a useful device for the definition of maritime transport, but it is not always possible to define the term maritime transport solely on an assessment of the location of the port. For example, if a port is not located directly on the seaboard, but further inland, a transport operation may still be considered maritime transport, if the vessel reaches this port after a long ocean crossing[14]. A special problem that is connected with the restriction of Regulation 4056/86 to maritime transport is the question of whether or not multimodal transport operations, which combine sea transport with a land leg, do fall within the scope of Regulation 4056/86 in their entirety. This question will be addressed later in this chapter[15].

Secondly, Regulation 4056/86 is only applicable to *international* transport operations. It has been argued that every transport operation is international, as long as the vessel crosses a border on its voyage, but that it is not required that

[11] Faull, ETL (1995), p. 3 ff, p. 5.
[12] Case T-86/95, *Compagnie générale maritime and Others v Commission*, (2002), ECR II, p. 1011 ff, rec. 234.
[13] Jacobs, (1991), p. 88.
[14] Jacobs, (1991), p. 89.
[15] See below, p. 112.

the ports of origin and destination be situated in different countries[16]. As a consequence, Regulation 4056/86 could be applicable to transport between two ports that are situated within the same Member State. Others argue that international transport is only such transport as takes place between ports of two different countries[17]. Proponents of the former claim that Art. 71 (ex 74) EC, which is the legal basis provision in the Title on transport in the Treaty, is also applicable to transport that merely passes across the territory of at least one of the Member States[18]. The latter opinion is supported by the wording of Regulation 4056/86. International literally translates into in-between states or nations. Therefore, international transport is such transport that takes place between ports of different countries. Another argument in support of this position is the fact that transport between two ports of the same Member State is unlikely to affect trade between Member States[19]. However, since this requirement is contained in Art. 81 I (ex 85 I) EC, which has to be obeyed in the interpretation of Regulation 4056/86[20], only the latter position provides a correct interpretation of Art. 1 II Regulation 4056/86.

A third element of the territorial scope of Regulation 4056/86 is that it is not applicable to transport between two ports outside the Community[21]. A problem might arise where the transport operation in question does not end or originate at a Community port, but where there is, nevertheless, an impact on Community shipping[22]. In the United States, relevant legislation is applicable in such situations, if there is a direct, substantial and reasonably foreseeable effect on the commerce of the United States. It has been suggested that Regulation 4056/86 should be interpreted similarly, thereby creating coherence with U. S. law[23]. However, the express wording of Art. 1 II Regulation 4056/86, which states that Regulation 4056/86 "*shall apply only to international maritime transport serv-*

---

[16] Jacobs, (1991), p. 90, the example given is that of a vessel sailing from Le Havre to Marseilles, which crosses Spanish waters during this voyage.

[17] Clough/Randolph, (1991), p. 169; Immenga/Mestmäcker, Vol. 2, (1997), Basedow, p. 2044, rec. 15; Pernice, FS Deringer, (1993), p. 135 ff, p. 150; Power, (1992), p. 300.

[18] Jacobs, (1991), p. 90.

[19] Clough/Randolph, (1991), p. 169, note 1; Munari, RabelsZ (1990), p. 627 ff; p. 636; Pernice, FS Deringer, (1993), p. 135 ff, p. 151.

[20] See above, p. 95.

[21] Clough/Randolph, (1991), p. 169; Kreis, ETL (1992), p. 155 ff, p. 169; Power, (1992), p. 300.

[22] Clough/Randolph, (1991), p. 170; the example given is that of a possible boycott of Community carriers on a route between third countries, with the aim of hindering EC feeder transport, see: p.171, note 1.

[23] Rycken, ETL (1987), p. 483 ff, p. 488.

ices from or to one or more Community ports", leaves no room for such a wide application of Regulation 4056/86[24].

bb) The personal scope of Regulation 4056/86

Regulation 4056/86 is only applicable to scheduled liner services and not to tramp vessel services by virtue of Arts. 1 II juncto 1 III lit. a Regulation 4056/86. As this restriction to the scope of Regulation 4056/86 is clear and unequivocal, there is no dispute on this point. Tramp shipping is defined in Art. 1 III lit. a Regulation 4056/86 through the enumeration of the following four cumulative criteria: transport of goods in bulk or break-bulk, on the basis of a voyage or time charter, without a fixed schedule and under a contract where the rates are the result of individual negotiations.

Disagreement exists, however, on the question of what happens if a tramp service does not fulfil the criteria set out in Art. 1 II lit. a Regulation 4056/86, the most important of which is the individual negotiation of prices. The argument primarily centres around the question of whether or not it must be shown in each individual case of tramp shipping that prices have been negotiated on an individual basis. According to one position, tramp vessel services are always excluded form the scope of Regulation 4056/86, even if they do not fully correspond to the definition of Art. 1 III lit. a Regulation 4056/86[25]. Others argue that Regulation 4056/86 becomes applicable to tramp shipping services as soon as they do not fulfil all the criteria laid down in Art. 1 III lit. a Regulation 4056/86[26].

Proponents of the first opinion rely on Recital 4 of the Preamble to Regulation 4056/86, which states that "*it appears preferable to exclude tramp vessel services from the scope of this Regulation*". They interpret this expression in such a way that tramp services should be generally excluded from Regulation 4056/86. According to their position, Art. 1 III lit. a Regulation 4056/86 only describes tramp services in a general way, but does not establish obligatory criteria that have to be met in each specific case[27]. It can be argued against this position that such a broad interpretation is unhelpful, as it subjects tramp services at large to the uncertainties of the cumbersome[28] procedure laid down in Arts. 84 and 85

---

[24] Clough/Randolph, (1991), p. 171; the dispute between the principle of territoriality and the doctrine of effects does not arise in relation to Regulation 4056/86. Since the wording of Art. 81 I (ex 85 I) EC is not as unequivocal as that of Art. 1 II Regulation 4056/86, this conflict does play a role in the interpretation of the former provision, see below, p. 140 ff.

[25] Pernice, FS Deringer, (1993), p. 135 ff, p. 151.

[26] Jacobs, (1991), p. 92; Kreis, ETL (1988), p. 562 ff, p. 573; G/T/E Vol. 2/1, (1999), Schröter, Art. 87 2nd part, rec. 32.

[27] Pernice, FS Deringer, (1993), p. 135 ff, p. 151.

[28] Wood, (1999), p. 5.

(ex 88 and 89) EC[29]. Secondly, even those who argue in favour of the first opinion concede that there is no apparent reason for the exclusion of tramp services from Regulation 4056/86[30]. A logical consequence would be to subject the exemption of tramp shipping from the scope of Regulation 4056/86 to the general rule that exemptions are to be interpreted narrowly, thereby giving preference to the second opinion.

The underlying reason for the exclusion of tramp vessel services from the scope of Regulation 4056/86 is that this sector of shipping typically operates according to competitive market principles[31]. Yet, if the free play of competition is not ensured, as for example in the case of joint price fixing, then the reason for exempting tramp services from the scope of Regulation 4056/86 has disappeared. As a consequence, they should be included in the scope of Regulation 4056/86 in such situations. The reasons just outlined above necessitate a narrow interpretation of the tramp service exclusion contained in Arts. 1 II juncto 1 III lit. a Regulation 4056/86. Finally, it should be noted that the Commission is likely to pursue a strict interpretation of the tramp shipping exemption as well[32]. Such an approach of the Commission may not seem surprising, as it thereby widens its own competences. Only Regulation 4056/86 provides the Commission with the necessary procedural powers to apply EC competition law to the sector of maritime transport.

c) Art. 2 Regulation 4056/86 - technical agreements

Art. 2 Regulation 4056/86 regulates technical agreements in a way similar to Art. 3 Regulation 1017/68. Both provisions establish that the prohibition of Art. 81 I (ex 85 I) EC shall not be applicable to the types of agreements listed therein.

aa) The legal quality of Art. 2 Regulation 4056/86

One of the principle disputes in relation to Art. 2 Regulation 4056/86 centres on the question of the legal nature of that provision. A first position on this issue is that Art. 2 Regulation 4056/86 constitutes a block exemption, comparable to Arts. 3 and 6 Regulation 4056/86[33]. The wording of Art. 2 Regulation 4056/86 in comparison to the wording of the latter provisions does not support such an approach. Arts. 3 and 6 Regulation 4056/86 explicitly *exempt* certain types of agreements from Art. 81 I (ex 85 I) EC, whereas Art. 2 Regulation 4056/86 states that the prohibition of Art. 81 I (ex 85 I) EC is *not applicable* to the types

---

29 Clough/Randolph, (1991), p. 183.
30 Pernice, FS Deringer, (1993), p. 135 ff, p. 151.
31 Recital 4 of the Preamble to Regulation 4056/86; Power, (1992), p. 301.
32 Clough/Randolph, (1991), p. 181.
33 Jacobs, (1991), p. 94.

of agreements that are enumerated in that provision. This choice of words indicates that Art. 2 Regulation 4056/86 does not constitute an exemption from Art. 81 I (ex 85 I) EC[34]. Furthermore, Art. 2 Regulation 4056/86 covers agreements that are technical in nature, as opposed to such agreements that restrict or distort competition in the sense of Art. 81 I (ex 85 I) EC. This finding is supported by Recital 7 of the Preamble to Regulation 4056/86, which states that technical agreements "*do not, as a general rule, restrict competition*". To exempt agreements from Art. 81 I (ex 85 I) EC that typically do not even fall under this provision, does not make sense[35]. For these reasons, Art. 2 Regulation 4056/86 does not constitute a block exemption like Arts. 3 and 6 Regulation 4056/86.

According to another view, Art. 2 Regulation 4056/86 constitutes a binding restriction of the scope of Art. 81 I (ex 85 I) EC[36]. This position has the virtue that it correctly considers Art. 2 Regulation 4056/86 in the context of Art. 81 I (ex 85 I) EC and not in connection to Art. 81 III (ex 85 III) EC. It is questionable, however, whether such a strict limitation of the scope of Art. 81 I (ex 85 I) EC through a provision of secondary law is permissible[37]. Art. 83 II lit. b (ex 87 II lit. b) EC allows any type of derogation from Art. 81 I (ex 85 I) EC through secondary law, as long as the principles set out in Art. 81 III (ex 85 III) EC are obeyed. Arts. 4 and 5 Regulation 4056/86, which create a system of conditions and obligations that are connected to the liner conference block exemption, have the purpose to ensure just that, as far as Art. 3 Regulation 4056/86 is concerned. They are, however, not applicable to Art. 2 Regulation 4056/86. For this reason, Art. 2 Regulation 4056/86 by itself guarantees only insufficiently that the principles laid down in Art. 81 III (ex 85 III) EC are duly protected[38]. The position that Art. 2 Regulation 4056/86 constitutes a binding restriction to the scope of Art. 81 (ex 85 I) EC thereby looses much of its appeal. It is also not possible to reconcile this position with the wording of Art. 83 II lit. c (ex 87 II lit. c) EC, which empowers the Council to *define* the scope of Art. 81 I (ex 85 I) EC, but not to *restrict* and thereby alter the scope of that provision[39]. For these reasons, it is misguided to assume that Art. 2 Regulation 4056/86 constitutes a binding restriction to the scope of Art. 81 I (ex 85 I) EC.

The most convincing position in the debate over the legal status of Art. 2 Regulation 4056/86 is to say that this provision constitutes a purely declaratory

[34] Jacobs, (1991), p. 94.
[35] Jacobs, (1991), p. 94.
[36] Kühne, (1996), p. 142; Rabe/Schütte, RIW (1988), p. 701 ff, p. 701 f.
[37] It has already been pointed out above that provisions of secondary law must be interpreted in accordance with relevant provisions of primary law and not vice versa; see above, p. 93 ff.
[38] Jacobs, (1991), p. 95.
[39] Pernice, FS Deringer, (1993), p. 149 ff, p. 152.

clarification of Art. 81 I (ex 85 I) EC, which is not binding and which does not restrict the application of the general principles embodied in that provision[40]. The types of agreements that are enumerated in Art. 2 Regulation 4056/86 typically do not constitute a restriction to competition in the sense of Art. 81 I (ex 85 I) EC. Yet, since Art. 2 Regulation 4056/86 does not have a binding character, it is possible for the Commission to decide in an individual case that a technical agreement violates Art. 81 I (ex 85 I), even though it corresponds to Art. 2 Regulation 4056/86. The Commission is only precluded to depart from the verdict of Art. 2 Regulation 4056/86 in an arbitrary manner[41]. Such an approach conforms to Recital 7 of the Preamble to Regulation 4056/86, which states that technical agreements "*as a general rule*" do not constitute a restriction to competition in the sense of Art. 81 I (ex 85 I) EC. This wording indicates that the creators of Regulation 4056/86 did not consider it impossible that technical agreements may occasionally violate Art. 81 I (ex 85 I) EC. Only the position just presented above, manages to reconcile Art. 2 Regulation 4056/86 with a strict coherence to the principles of Art. 81 I (ex 85 I) EC. For this reason, it provides the best interpretation of the legal nature of Art. 2 Regulation 4056/86.

bb) The contents of Art. 2 Regulation 4056/86

Art. 2 Regulation 4056/86 contains an exhaustive list of technical arrangements that regularly do not violate Art. 81 I (ex 85 I) EC. The enumeration of the different types of agreements under Art. 2 Regulation 4056/86 has not given rise to much legal controversy, which is not surprising in consideration of the fact that their wording is clear and unequivocal. Dispute does exist however in relation to another aspect of Art. 2 Regulation 4056/86, which is the condition that it only covers agreements "*whose sole object and effect is to achieve technical improvement or cooperation*". One first aspect in the analysis of this expression is a definition of the term *technical*. Technical agreements must be differentiated from economical agreements on the basis of their impact on the operation of liner shipping services[42]. The difference is that technical agreements do not have negative consequences for the competition within the Common Market.

A second matter for discussion is the interpretation of the word *sole*. It has been argued, in this respect, that technical agreements in the sense of Art. 2 Regulation 4056/86 are agreements that do not restrict competition beyond what is absolutely necessary, in order to attain the defined goal of technical improvement[43]. In a similar manner it has been suggested that agreements that are

[40] Pernice, FS Deringer, (1993), p. 149 ff, p. 152; Werner, WuW (1987), p. 796 ff, p. 800.
[41] Jacobs, (1991), p. 96.
[42] Green, ETL (1988), p. 612 ff, p. 620; Jacobs, (1991), p. 97.
[43] Kühne, (1996), p. 143.

not purely technical in nature may constitute technical agreements in the sense of Art. 2 Regulation 4056/86, as long as the economic impact is merely of an ancillary nature and at the same time an inseparable consequence of the technical agreement[44]. Both these positions, which consider the restriction of Art. 2 Regulation 4056/86 to technical agreements to be relative and not absolute, cannot be reconciled with the wording of Art. 2 Regulation 4056/86. The employment of the word *sole* indicates a restriction of that provision to agreements that are purely technical in nature. In the face of such an explicit expression there is no room for the application of any kind of derogation based on the principle of proportionality or necessity. Such a strict interpretation of Art. 2 Regulation 4056/86 also corresponds to the structure of Regulation 4056/86. Whereas Art. 2 Regulation 4056/86 covers all such agreements that do not have a negative influence on competition, Art. 3 Regulation 4056/86, on the other hand, covers agreements that have a negative impact on competition. As a consequence, Art. 2 Regulation 4056/86 only covers such agreements that are exclusively of a technical nature. As soon as an agreement has an economic impact as well, it does not correspond to the requirements of that provision anymore[45].

cc) Conclusion

The preceding analysis of Art. 2 Regulation 4056/86 has demonstrated that its practical importance is small. Since Art. 2 Regulation 4056/86 does not have any decisive impact on the interpretation of Art. 81 I (ex 85 I) EC it is possible that arrangements that fall within the scope of the former provision nevertheless constitute a restriction to competition according to the latter provision. It is equally possible that agreements that do not correspond to any of those listed in Art. 2 Regulation 4056/86 still do not violate Art. 81 I (ex 85 I) EC[46]. As far as consortia agreements are concerned, it is unlikely that such agreements may fall under Art. 2 Regulation 4056/86. Although consortia agreements emphasise the importance of technical aspects of co-operation, they often extend to technical matters that are not contained in the list of Art. 2 Regulation 4056/86[47]. Furthermore, the objects and effects of consortia agreements are typically not limited to purely technical aspects of liner shipping, but they also embrace forms of commercial co-operation[48]. As a result, they normally do not fall within the scope of Art. 2 Regulation 4056/86. What is true for consortia, equally applies to conference agreements that typically engage in concerted pricing activities.

---

44 Immenga/Mestmäcker, Vol. 2, (1997), Basedow, p. 2016, rec. 21.

45 Clough/Randolph, (1991), p. 204, note 1; Munari, RabelsZ (1990), p. 627 ff, p. 641; Power, (1992), p. 304.

46 Green, ETL (1988), p. 612 ff, p. 621; Werner, WuW (1987), p. 796 ff, p. 800.

47 Jacobs, (1991), p. 101.

48 Clough/Randolph, (1991), p. 206; Kreis, ETL (1992), p. 155 ff, p. 164.

Such a behaviour does not constitute technical co-operation and goes beyond the scope of Art. 2 Regulation 4056/86. It may be argued that such an interpretation of Art. 2 Regulation 4056/86 runs opposite its purpose, which is to increase legal security for the carriers[49] and to reduce the workload of the Commission, but the clear wording of Art. 2 Regulation 4056/86 does not leave room for a wider interpretation.

d) Arts. 3 to 5 Regulation 4056/86 - the liner conference block exemption

The liner conference block exemption constitutes the centrepiece of the material provisions of Regulation 4056/86. It consists of the actual block exemption in Art. 3 Regulation 4056/86; Art. 4 Regulation 4056/86 attaches compulsory conditions to the block exemption and Art. 5 Regulation 4056/86 contains several mandatory obligations that govern the liner conference block exemption.

aa) Art. 3 Regulation 4056/86

Art. 3 Regulation 4056/86 is the most important provision of that Regulation, since it contains the actual block exemption for liner conferences, a term which is defined in Art. 1 III lit. b Regulation 4056/86 as "*a group of two or more vessel-operating carriers which provides international liner services for the carriage of cargo on a particular route or routes within specified geographical limits and which has an agreement or arrangement, whatever its nature, within the framework of which they operate under uniform or common freight rates and any other agreed conditions with respect to the provision of liner services*". The most important aspect of this definition is that liner conferences are only such agreements between carriers that establish and operate uniform and common freight rates. Both the CFI[50] and the Commission[51] relied on this requirement when they refused to extend the liner conference block exemption to the TAA agreement.

Freight rates are common, if all conference carriers offer the transport of the same commodity for the same price. Freight rates are uniform if a shipper is offered the same freight rate by all conference members[52]. Any minimum, maximum or differentiated tariffs are not suitable for exemption under Art. 3 Regulation 4056/86[53], instead it is necessary that the same price be offered by all and to all. The *TAA* operated a two tier pricing structure, the purpose of which was

[49] Immenga/Mestmäcker, Vol. 2, (1997), Basedow, p. 2015, rec. 20; Werner, WuW (1987), p. 796 ff, p. 800.

[50] Case T-395/94, *Atlantic Container Line AB and Others v Commission*, (2002), ECR II, p. 875 ff, rec. 172 ff.

[51] "*TAA*", OJ, (1994), L-376/1, rec. 320 ff.

[52] "*TAA*", OJ, (1994), L-376/1, rec. 326.

[53] "*TAA*", OJ, (1994), L-376/1, rec. 321.

to bring formerly independent lines inside the agreement[54]. The formerly independent carriers enjoyed more freedoms to depart from the conference tariff than the traditional conference members. For example they did not have to inform their fellow carriers if they wanted to depart individually from the conference tariff[55], whereas the others had to give ten days notice of such a practise. Secondly, the formerly independent carriers were allowed to undercut the conference tariff by $ 100 per TEU[56] and they were also permitted to conclude independent service contracts. For these reasons neither the Commission nor the CFI extended the block exemption of Art. 3 Regulation 4056/86 to the *TAA* agreement. They thereby established that talking agreements cannot benefit from the liner conference block exemption.

aaa) The parties to agreements exempted under Art. 3 Regulation 4056/86
Art. 3 Regulation 4056/86 not only exempts agreements between all the member carriers of a conference, but it is sufficient, if only some of the conference carriers participate in the agreement. In addition, Art. 3 Regulation 4056/86 extends even further to agreements between some or all carriers of different conferences.

Only agreements between conference members and outsiders, so-called tolerated outsider agreements, are beyond the scope of Art. 3 Regulation 4056/86[57]. It has been suggested that this restriction does not make sense, since Art. 3 Regulation 4056/86 permits agreements between carriers of different conferences, a measure which may be more restrictive than the formation of an agreement between conference carriers and one or more independent carriers[58]. However, the wording of Art. 3 Regulation 4056/86 is unambiguous on this point and does not leave room for interpretation. Another argument to this effect focuses on the fact that it is the organisational structure of liner conferences that ensures stability in liner shipping[59]. Agreements with outsiders do not establish such stable institutional surroundings and are, therefore, not suitable for exemption under Art. 3 Regulation 4056/86. Finally, Recital 8 of the Preamble to Regulation 4056/86 stresses the importance of non-conference competition. It is not possible to exempt agreements with outsiders under Art. 3 Regulation 4056/86, since this would permit a reduction or elimination of competition from

[54] Hautau, (2002), p. 25 and 27.
[55] "*TAA*", OJ, (1994), L-376/1, rec.138.
[56] "*TAA*", OJ, (1994), L-376/1, rec. 140.
[57] Clough/Randolph, (1991), p. 211; G/T/E, Vol. 2/1, Art. 87 2nd part, (1999), Schröter, rec. 33; Immenga/Mestmäcker, Vol. 2, (1997), Basedow, p. 2051 f, rec. 33; Jacobs, (1991), p. 124; Kreis, ETL (1988), p. 562 ff, p. 566; Pernice, FS Deringer, (1993), p. 149 ff, p. 154; Temple Lang, ETL (1993), p. 405 ff,p. 417; Werner, WuW (1987), p. 796 ff, p. 604.
[58] Jacobs, (1991), p. 124.
[59] Pernice, FS Deringer, (1993), p. 149 ff, p. 154.

independent carriers. Such an exemption cannot be reconciled with Recital 8 of the Preamble to Regulation 4056/86, which states that non-conference competition is an indispensable feature of the markets for liner shipping. The only way by which a tolerated outsider agreement could gain acceptance of the Commission is through an application for individual exemption according to Art. 12 Regulation 4056/86[60]. The chances for success of such an application are however limited[61], because of the just-mentioned importance of non-conference competition.

Another controversial issue is the question of whether Art. 3 Regulation 4056/86 exempts conference agreements and agreements between conferences themselves[62] or whether it only covers consecutive agreements by the carriers on the basis of their initial agreement[63]. In favour of the first position, it has been argued that Art. 3 Regulation 4056/86 covers agreements among all members of one or more conferences and as such also the initial conference agreement or the initial agreement between conferences[64]. However, the latter position is preferable on several accounts. First, it should be taken into consideration that the initial conference agreement only establishes the institutional framework of a conference but typically does not in itself constitute a restriction to competition. Only later decisions adopted through the conference mechanisms may restrict competition contrary to Art. 81 I (ex 85 I) EC[65]. Second, it should be borne in mind that liner conferences themselves are not liable under EC competition law[66], a circumstance, which indicates that there is no need for an exemption of liner conferences themselves[67].

bbb) The contents of agreements exempted under Art. 3 Regulation 4056/86

Art. 3 Regulation 4056/86 only exempts agreements that contain provisions on collusive pricing activities and common conditions of carriage[68]. As far as the latter are concerned, a possible conflict with the requirements of Art. 81 III (ex 85 III) EC is not easily perceivable, since a system of common conditions of carriage is beneficial for the shippers insofar, as it facilitates international transport operations through the abolishment of a multitude of different carriage

60 Kreis, ETL (1992), p. 155 ff, p. 162.

61 Ginderachter/Durande, ETL (1996), p. 241 ff, p. 249; Kreis, ETL (1992), p. 155 ff, p. 162.

62 Jacobs, (1991), p. 124; Pernice, FS Deringer, (1993), p. 149 ff, p. 153; Werner, WuW (1987), p. 796 ff, p 800.

63 Immenga/Mestmäcker, Vol. 2, (1997), Basedow, p. 2050, rec. 29.

64 Jacobs, (1991), p. 124.

65 Immenga/Mestmäcker, Vol. 2, (1997), Basedow, p. 2050, rec. 29.

66 See below, p. 151 f.

67 Immenga/Mestmäcker, Vol. 2, (1997), Basedow, p. 2050 f, rec. 29.

68 Jacobs, (1991), p. 103 f, Werner, WuW (1987), p. 796 ff, p. 801.

systems[69]. The evaluation of price fixing in the light of Art. 81 (ex 85) EC is not as straightforward and requires a more detailed analysis, which will be provided in chapter six[70].

Apart from the two requirements mentioned above, Art. 3 Regulation 4056/86 also exempts further activities, such as the co-operation in the field of sailing schedules, including the frequency and dates of sailings or calls, the allocation of sailings or calls, the regulation of capacity and the pooling of cargo or revenue among the members of a liner conference. As far as the enumeration of objectives in Art. 3 lit. a to e Regulation 4056/86 is concerned, a dispute exists as to whether or not the pursuit of at least one of these objectives is a mandatory requirement for an exemption under Art. 3 Regulation 4056/86[71]. The wording of Art. 3 Regulation 4056/86 clearly supports the view that these objectives do not constitute an indispensable requirement of the block exemption for liner conferences, since their enumeration is introduced with the words "*and, as the case may be*". This expression indicates that conferences that collude on these matters can profit from the exemption in Art. 3 Regulation 4056/86, but that such co-operation does not constitute a *condicio sine qua non* for the applicabillity of Art. 3 Regulation 4056/86.

Disagreement also exists about the treatment of consortia under Art. 3 Regulation 4056/86. According to one position, consortia are exempted from Art. 81 I (ex 85 I) EC by virtue of Art. 3 Regulation 4056/86[72], a view that is opposed by most commentators on this problem[73], as well as by the Commission[74]. Those who argue against an exemption of consortia under Art. 3 Regulation 4056/86 emphasise the fact that Art. 3 Regulation 4056/86 is only applicable to agreements that have some close connection to the institutional framework of a traditional shipping conference and not to all types of agreements between carriers that were concluded coincidentally by members of one or more liner confer-

---

[69] Jacobs, (1991), p. 114.

[70] See below, p. 152 ff.

[71] Such a strict interpretation is supported by: Werner, WuW (1987), p. 796 ff, p. 801. Others consider the enumeration of objectives in Art. 3 lit. a to e Regulation 4056/86 as an exhaustive list of additional but non-compulsory objectives beside price fixing and the establishment of common conditions of carriage; see for example: Green, ETL (1988), p. 612 ff, p. 622; Munari, RablesZ (1990), p. 627 ff, p. 641.

[72] Erdmenger, FS Raisch, (1995), p. 387 ff, p. 400; Jacobs, (1991), p. 120 ff.

[73] Clough/Randolph, (1991), p. 217; G/T/E, Vol. 2/1, Art. 87 2nd part, (1999), Schröter, rec. 32; Immenga/Mestmäcker, Vol. 2, (1997), Basedow, p. 2052, rec. 33; Kreis. ETL (1992), p. 155 ff, p. 165; Pernice, FS Deringer, (1993), p. 149 ff, p. 156 f; Temple Lang, ETL (1993), p. 405 ff, p. 409 ff.

[74] 19th Competition Report, (1989), p. 45, rec. 26; 20th Competition Report (1991), p. 73, rec. 78.

ence[75]. Regulation 4056/86 seeks to reconcile the UNCTAD-code, on the one hand, and EC competition law on the other[76]. Evidence for this circumstance is the fact that the definition of liner conferences in Art. 1 III lit. b Regulation 4056/86 is identical to that embodied in Chapter 1, Definition 1 UNCTAD[77]. Although containerised shipping already existed in some trades when the UNCTAD-code was drafted in the early 1970s, liner shipping at that time was still in large parts conducted by breakbulk vessels that were operated by carriers organised in shipping conferences. Consortia did not yet constitute a key feature of the liner shipping industry. As a consequence, the definition of shipping conferences in the UNCTAD-code only embraces traditional liner conferences and it does not extend to consortia type agreements. This finding is equally true for Art. 3 Regulation 4056/86 considering the wording and the purpose of that provision.

In this respect, it is also important to note that conferences and consortia attempt to organise the liner shipping industry according to different objectives. Conferences seek to stabilise the markets for liner shipping mainly through price fixing, a circumstance that is reflected in Recital 8 to the Preamble of Regulation 4056/86. Consortia on the other side attempt to realise potential economies of scale and scope as a means to ameliorate the position of their member carriers in the markets for liner shipping[78]. This difference between conferences and consortia also precludes the exemption of the latter under Art. 3 Regulation 4056/86[79], which, as Recital 8 of the Preamble to Regulation 4056/86 indicates, is restricted to agreements that chiefly rely on price fixing as a tool to ensure stability in the markets for liner shipping.

Another argument is that the European legislator was also of the opinion that consortia agreements do not fall within the scope of Art. 3 Regulation 4056/86, since otherwise the creation of a separate block exemption for such agreements through the passage of Regulation 870/95 and later Regulation 823/2000 would not have been necessary. Finally, consortia often do not correspond to the requirements of Art. 3 Regulation 4056/86, because they pursue objectives other than those that are enumerated in Art. 3 lit. a to e Regulation 4056/86 and, therefore, they are beyond the scope of that provision[80]. For these reasons, Art.

---

[75] Temple Lang, ETL (1993), p. 405 ff, p. 409 f.

[76] See: Recital 3 and 4 of the Preamble to Regulation 4056/86.

[77] See above, p. 59.

[78] G/T/E, Vol. 2/1, (1999), Schröter, Art. 87 2nd part, rec. 49; Immenga/ Mestmäcker, Vol. 2, (1997), Basedow, p. 2052, rec. 33.

[79] Clough/Randolph, (1991), p. 217; Pernice, FS Deringer, (1993), p. 149 ff, p. 156

[80] Clough/Randolph, (1991), p. 217; Temple Lang, ETL (1993), p. 405 ff, p. 409.

3 Regulation 4056/86 does not exempt co-operation in the form of consortia from the prohibition contained in Art. 81 I (ex 85 I) EC.

bb) Art. 4 Regulation 4056/86

Art. 4 I Regulation 4056/86 contains the condition that a conference agreement must not be discriminatory. Therefore, Art. 4 I Regulation 4056/86 embodies the principle of non-discrimination, found in Art. 81 I lit. d (ex 85 I lit. d) EC[81]. Art 4 Regulation 4056/86 prohibits the application of different rates or conditions of carriage for the transport of the same goods to the detriment of ports, transport users or carriers within the EC[82], based on the fact that their port or country of origin or destination differs, unless such a difference in treatment is justified on economic grounds. Art. 4 I Regulation 4056/86 prohibits to treat like situations differently, but also to treat situations that differ from each other alike[83], since the economic impact of both types of behaviour is the same. As a consequence of the growing importance of intermodal transport, the shippers have lost their traditional power to decide on the route by which their cargoes are transported[84]. It is, therefore, even more important for the functioning of the Internal Market to ensure that carriers do not discriminate in the above-described manner.

A first problem in connection with Art. 4 I is the question of what goods constitute *same* goods in the sense of that provision. It has been suggested that this question shall be answered in reference to the conference tariffs, which classify the different goods in a large number of different categories[85]. An advantage of this position is that there is little room for uncertainty, since the conference tariffs provide a category for nearly all types of transportable cargoes. The problem that arises under such an approach is, however, that goods that are substitutes may, nevertheless, be classified in different categories and charged different rates accordingly, something which could lead to an allegation of discrimination[86]. A better solution is to judge the "*sameness*" of goods from the viewpoint of the carriers. As long as the actual costs of carriage of certain goods for a carrier do not differ from each other, these goods then constitute same goods according to Art. 4 I Regulation 4056/86[87]. This position corresponds to the

---

[81] G/T/E, Vol. 2/1, (1999), Schröter, Art. 87 2nd part, rec. 36.
[82] Green, ETL (1988), p. 612 ff, p. 623.
[83] G/T/E, Vol. 2/1, (1999), Schröter, Art. 87 2nd part, rec. 36; Immenga/Mestmäcker, Vol. 2, (1997), Basedow, p. 2052, rec. 34; opposing view: Rabe/Schütte, RIW (1988), p. 701, p. 702.
[84] Shashikumar, (1999), p. 4.
[85] Kühne, (1996), p. 155
[86] Green, ETL (1988), p. 612 ff, p. 623.
[87] Green, ETL (1988), p. 612 ff, p. 623; Jacobs, (1991), p. 129.

circumstance that the addressees of Art. 4 Regulation 4056/86 are the carriers[88]. They cannot be held accountable for the fact that shippers may want to transport goods that are uneconomical to transport because of their size or weight. Such a circumstance falls into the responsibility of the shippers and not into that of the carriers[89].

The crucial element of the non-discrimination clause in Art. 4 Regulation 4056/86 is the fact that a rate or condition of carriage is only discriminatory if it cannot be justified objectively on economic grounds[90]. The underlying rationale is that conference tariffs must reflect the actual costs of carriage of the different goods[91]. Art. 4 I Regulation 4056/86 does not contain a set of specific criteria for the analysis of whether or not a difference in treatment is objectively justified. It has been said that this absence of criteria and the resulting uncertainty for the carriers constitutes a disadvantage of Art. 4 I Regulation 4056/86[92]. Yet, it may also be argued that such a lack of rigidity is an advantage of Art. 4 I Regulation 4056/86, since it permits flexible decisions on a case-by-case basis. Art. 4 I Regulation 4056/86 thereby ensures that all possible distortions to competition are caught by that provision[93]. Examples for justified conduct under Art. 4 Regulation 4956/86 are the levying of a currency adjustment factor[94] and the conclusion of service contracts between single shippers and conferences[95].

The consequence of an unjustified difference in freight rates or conditions of carriage according to Art. 4 I Regulation 4056/86 is that the conference agreement in question is automatically void *ab initio* and *erga omnes* by virtue of Art. 4 II Regulation 4056/86 juncto Art. 81 II (ex 85 II) EC. However, if the clause that is contradictory to Art. 4 I Regulation 4056/86 can be separated from the rest of the agreement, then only the part of the agreement that does not correspond to Art. 4 I Regulation 4056/86 is void and the remaining part of the agreement remains valid[96].

---

88 Jacobs, (1991), p. 129.
89 Green, ETL (1988), p. 612 ff, p. 623.
90 Clough and Randolph, (1991), p. 220; Green, ETL (1988), p. 612 ff, p. 624; Werner, WuW (1987), p. 796, p. 801.
91 Green, ETL (1988), p. 612 ff, p. 624.
92 Power, (1992), p. 308; for examples where doubts about the legality of price differentials may arise see: Green, ETL (1988), p. 612 ff, p. 624.
93 Munari, RabelsZ (1990), p. 627 ff, p. 642.
94 Kühne, (1996), p. 155 f; Werner, WUW (1987), p. 796 ff, p. 801.
95 Immenga/Mestmäcker, Vol. 2, (1997), Basedow, p. 2052, rec. 34; Munari, RabelsZ (1990), p. 627 ff, p. 642.
96 G/T/E, Vol. 2/1, (1999), Schröter, Art. 87 2nd part, rec. 37; Munari, RabelsZ (1990), p. 627 ff, p. 643.

cc) Art. 5 Regulation 4056/86

Art. 5 Regulation 4056/86 contains a set of detailed obligations that have to be obeyed in connection with the block exemption for liner conferences. The purpose of the obligations set out in Art. 5 Regulation 4056/86 is to ensure that the interests of transport users are taken into account and that the restrictions to competition connected with the liner conference system are kept at a minimum[97]. These obligations arise in respect to the following five topics: consultations between transport users and conferences, loyalty arrangements, services not covered by freight charges, availability of tariffs to transport users and finally, notification to the Commission of awards at arbitration and recommendations made by conciliators.

Art. 5 I Regulation 4056/86 requires mandatory consultations between shippers and conferences about "*rates, conditions and quality of scheduled maritime transport services*", whenever one of the parties makes a request to that effect. The conferences are only obliged to enter into consultations and to participate in a constructive manner; Art. 5 I Regulation 4056/86 does not impose the duty upon them to end the consultations with a result of any kind[98]. Consequently, the effectiveness of Art. 5 I Regulation 4056/86 as a means to balance the interests between carriers and shippers is limited[99]. Conferences only violate Art. 5 Regulation 4056/86 if they refuse to enter into consultations or if the consultations take place only after the conference has already adopted a final decision on the subject of the consultations.

Art. 5 II Regulation 4056/86 establishes compulsory rules concerning the important issue of loyalty rebate arrangements[100] between carriers and shippers. The carriers are under no obligation to offer rebates to the shippers, but if they decide to do so, then it is necessary that the rebates are subject to consultations between the conference and the shippers association. A conference that wishes to operate a rebate system may instate a system of immediate rebates or a system under which the shippers may choose between immediate and deferred rebates. Art. 5 II Regulation 4056/86, which exhaustively regulates the issue of loyalty rebates, does not mention rebates that are granted depending on the volume of cargo that a shipper transports with a conference. As a consequence, such a system of rebates does not conform to Art. 5 II Regulation 4056/86 and is, therefore, not permissible for conferences that want to profit from the liner

---

[97] G/T/E, Vol. 2/1, (1999), Schröter, Art. 87 2nd part, rec. 38; Rabe/Schütte, RIW (1988), p. 701 ff, p. 702; Werner, WuW (1987), p. 796 ff, p. 801.

[98] Green, ETL (1988), p. 612 ff, p. 625; Jacobs, (1991), p. 134; Kühne, (1996), p. 157; Werner, WuW (1987), p. 796 ff, p. 801.

[99] Jacobs, (1991), p. 134; Kühne, (1996), p. 157; Werner, WuW (1987), p. 796 ff, p. 801.

[100] For a discussion of the different types of rebates see above, p. 47 f.

conference block exemption[101]. Such a system of rebates may, however, be permissible on the basis of an individual exemption according to Art. 12 Regulation 4056/86. Conferences that wish to operate a rebate system in accordance with Art. 5 II Regulation 4056/86 must agree with the shippers on a list of cargo and/or any portion of cargo, which is excluded from the loyalty arrangement and issue a list to that effect. A loyalty arrangement may cover 100 per cent of all transported goods, but such an arrangement may not be imposed unilaterally. A second list must define the circumstances under which the shippers are automatically released from their obligation of loyalty towards the conferences.

A matter for discussion is the question of whether or not Art. 5 II Regulation 4056/86 grants conferences the right to punish carriers in situations where they abandon their loyalty obligation without proper reason. Art. 5 II Regulation 4056/86 does not explicitly permit the conferences to engage in such a practice. Nevertheless, it has been suggested that conferences may sanction disloyal carriers[102]. The main argument to this effect is that Recital 10 of the Preamble to Regulation 4056/86 mentions "*the right of a conference to impose penalties on users who seek by improper means to evade the obligation of loyalty*". In the absence of any explicit recognition of the right of conferences to sanction disloyal carriers in Art. 5 II Regulation 4056/86, such a right can only exist if the Preamble to Regulation 4056/86 is in itself the source of such a right. In this respect, it has been argued that Art. 230 IV (ex 173 IV) EC juncto Art. 253 (ex 190) EC permits the individual to take action against official acts if they do not contain sufficient or correct reasons for their adoption because such a deficit constitutes an infringement of rights of the individual. In a second step, it has then been suggested that if the reasoning for an official act may infringe rights of the individual, it must also be possible that these reasons confer rights upon the individual[103].

This position must be dismissed on several accounts. First, it should be noted that individuals can only take action against Regulations on the basis of Art. 230 IV (ex 173 IV) EC if they can demonstrate that he or she is affected directly and individually. This criterion has been interpreted strictly by the ECJ[104], and it is unlikely that a conference member can satisfy this requirement. In the absence of the possibility of an infringement of individual rights through insufficient reasons it is also not possible to conclude that such reasons may constitute

[101] Jacobs, (1991), p. 136;
[102] Jacobs, (1991), p. 136 ff.
[103] Jacobs, (1991), p. 137 f.
[104] For a discussion of the case law of the ECJ on this issue see: Craig/de Burca, (1999), p. 461 ff.

a source of rights for the individual[105]. A second point of criticism concerns the conclusion that if a lack of sufficient reasoning of an official act damages the legal position of an individual and therefore constitutes an infringement of individual rights, it then is possible that sufficient grounds for an official act constitute an independent source of rights for the individual. The lack of sufficient and/or correct reasons infringes only the *procedural* rights of the individual. As a consequence, it is not possible to conclude that the individual can rely solely on the reasons of an official act, such as the Preamble in the case of a Regulation, as the basis for any *material* rights. For these reasons, the Preamble to Regulation 4056/86 does not constitute an independent source for any material rights of conference members.

The Preamble in a Regulation rather has the function of an interpretory aid for the relevant provisions of that Regulation. Art. 5 II Regulation 4056/86 does not contain any expressions that could be interpreted in such a way as to grant liner conferences the right to sanction disloyal carriers. For these reasons, such a practise violates Art. 5 II Regulation 4056/86 and does not constitute a permissible activity for conferences that wish to profit from the liner conference block exemption.

The non-compliance with the requirements of Art. 5 Regulation 4056/86 does not necessarily lead to the withdrawl of the block exemption as under the regime of Art. 4 Regulation 4056/86. The least restrictive course of action that the Commission might consider by virtue of Art. 7 I Regulation 4056/86 is to address a Recommendation to the persons concerned. In the case that the addressee does not react to the Recommendation, the Commission then may adopt a Decision in which it prohibits or requires the addressee to carry out certain acts. Even more restrictive is the withdrawal of the block exemption in combination with the permission to continue the conference agreement on the basis of an individual exemption, albeit under individually tailored obligations and conditions[106]. Finally, the *ultima ratio* available to the Commission by virtue of Art. 7 I Regulation 4056/86 is the complete withdrawal of the block exemption.

---

[105] *Jacobs* relied on a judgement of the ECJ, which concerned an allegedinfringement of individual rights through insufficient reasons in a Decision of the Commission. He did not take into account that such a Decision is addressed to the individual, whereas a Regulation is a legislative act whose addressees are only defined in a general manner. Due to this difference, it is not possible to argue that insufficient reasons in the Preamble to a Regulation may infringe the rights of an individual.

[106] G/T/E, Vol. 2/1, (1999), Schröter, Art. 87 2nd part, rec. 45.

dd) Specific problems connected to Art. 3 Regulation 4056/86

The following part contains an analysis of three major problems that exist in the interpretation of the block exemption for liner conferences, namely multimodal transport, capacity management programmes and individual service contracts. Special attention will be given to relevant judgements of the CFI, as well as Decisions of the Commission.

aaa) Multimodal transport

The container revolution has strengthened the link between liner shipping and land transport, a circumstance, which has been explained in the introductory chapter of this study[107]. Only containerisation made multimodal transport possible on a large scale[108]. Liner shipping companies began to offer such services and they also started to fix prices for the land leg of such operations, within the conference system. Such behaviour typically contravenes Art. 81 I (ex 85 I) EC. It has been suggested, however, that the fixing of prices for the inland leg of a multimodal transport operation falls under the block exemption of Art. 3 Regulation 4056/86. Yet, the status of multimodal transport under Art. 3 Regulation 4056/86 is ambiguous[109]. The CFI[110] and the Commission[111] both share the view that liner conferences may not fix the price for the land leg of a multimodal transport operation by virtue of Art. 3 Regulation 4056/86. This position has been opposed by many carriers and has also been subject to criticism in legal writing.

(1) Arguments related to the wording of Regulation 4056/86

One first group of arguments centres around the wording of the different provisions of Regulation 4056/86. The CFI and the Commission both stress that Art. 1 II Regulation 4056/86, which defines the scope of Regulation 4056/86, only speaks of "*maritime transport*"[112]. Maritime transport typically refers to transport by sea[113]. This position is confirmed by the fact that Art. 1 II Regulation 4056/86 further states that Regulation 4056/86 is applicable to transport "*from or to one or more Community ports*". Finally, Recital 6 of the Preamble to

---

107 See above , p. 25.

108 Braakman, ETL (1996), p. 265 ff, p. 272.

109 Confavreux, RMC (1996), p. 369 ff, p. 373.

110 Case T-86/95, *Compagnie générale maritime and Others v Commission*, (2002), ECR II, p. 1011 ff, rec. 230 ff.

111 See: "*FEFC*", OJ, (1994), L-378/17; the Commission repeated its opinion in the following two decisions: "*TAA*" , OJ, (1994), L-376/1 and "*TACA*", OJ, (1999), L-95/1.

112 Case T-86/95, *Compagnie générale maritime and Others v Commission*, (2002), ECR II, p. 1011, rec. 232 ff; "*FEFC*", OJ, (1994), L-378/17, rec. 75; "*TAA*", OJ, (1994), L-376/1, rec. 373.

113 Case T-86/95, *Compagnie générale maritime and Others v Commission*, (2002), ECR II, p. 1011 ff, rec. 234.

Regulation 4056/86 mentions transport "*from or to Community ports*". Such an unequivocal choice of words would have required an explicit extension of the scope of Regulation 4056/86 to multimodal transport. The absence of a statement to that effect leads to the conclusion that the scope of Regulation 4056/86 does not cover price fixing agreements concerning land transport, which in turn removes such an activity from the list of practices exemptable under Art. 3 Regulation 4056/86, since the scope of this exemption cannot be wider than that of Regulation 4056/86[114].

Another means by which the supporters of an exemption for collusive pricing practices for multimodal transport seek to incorporate such an exemption into the scope of Regulation 4056/86 is to argue that multimodal transport operations constitute maritime transport because they constitute a single integrated product, subject to Regulation 4056/86 in their entirety[115]. This claim has to be rejected. Inland transport and ocean transport are different insofar, as they can be purchased from and provided by different economic operators. For ocean carriers, land transport rather has the character of an ancillary service that complements their maritime transport activities[116]. The CFI was even more restrictive on this issue. It stated *obiter dictum* that even if it were assumed that multimodal transport is a single composite product, it would not fall within the scope of Regulation 4056/86. Instead, the requirement to interpret exemptions such as Art. 3 Regulation 4056/86 in a narrow manner would also necessitate withdrawing the ocean leg of a multimodal transport operation from the scope of Regulation 4056/86[117].

Those who argue in favour of an exemption of price fixing for multimodal transport operations from Art. 81 I (ex 85 I) EC have put forward that Arts. 5 III and IV Regulation 4056/86 indicate that joint price fixing for the land leg is covered by Art. 3 Regulation 4056/86[118]. Art. 5 III Regulation 4056/86 permits shippers to choose their own land transport operator in situations where the inland leg is not included in the freight rate. If, however, the inland leg is in-

---

[114] Case T-86/95, *Compagnie générale maritime and Others v Commission,* (2002), ECR II, p. 1011 ff, rec. 231;"*FEFC*", OJ, (1994), L-378/17 rec. 75 f; "*TAA*", OJ, (1994), L-376/1, rec. 376; Kreis, ETL (1992), p. 155 ff, p. 166.

[115] Case T-86/95, *Compagnie générale maritime and Others v Commission,* (2002), ECR II, p. 1011ff, rec. 160.

[116] Case T-86/95, *Compagnie générale maritime and Others v Commission,* (2002), ECR II, p. 1011 ff, rec. 262.

[117] Case T-86/95, *Compagnie générale maritime and Others v Commission,* , (2002), ECR II, p. 1011 ff, rec. 262.

[118] Case T-86/95, *Compagnie générale maritime and Others v Commission,* , (2002), ECR II, p. 1011, rec. 182 ff; "*FEFC*", OJ, (1994), L-378/17, rec. 86; "*TAA*", OJ, (1994), L-376/1, rec. 149.

cluded in a common freight rate, then the carriers must be the ones who are allowed to select the operator for the land leg. Carriers can only exercise this right in a sensible manner, if the conference has the right to also extend the common freight rate to the land leg of a multimodal transport operation. As a consequence, land leg price fixing must constitute a permissible activity for liner conferences based on Art. 3 Regulation 4056/86[119]. As far as Art. 5 IV Regulation 4056/86 is concerned, the supporters of an exemption for price fixing on the inland leg of a multimodal transport operation do point to the fact that carriers are thereby under an obligation to make tariff details available to their customers, concerning "*the exact extent of the services covered by the freight charge in proportion to the sea transport and the land transport*". They conclude that both these provisions constitute an acknowledgement of the fact that joint price fixing for the land leg of a multimodal transport operation is permissible under Art. 3 Regulation 4056/86.

This reasoning must be rejected on several grounds. The CFI first pointed to the function of Art. 5 Regulation 4056/86 as a provision which merely has the purpose to set out the obligations that are attached to the block exemption in Art. 3 Regulation 4056/86. This function makes it impossible to rely on Arts. 5 III and IV Regulation 4056/86 in an attempt to widen the scope of Art. 3 Regulation 4056/86[120]. The CFI then went on and stated that Art. 5 III only seeks to ensure that carriers do not use their market power in the markets for maritime transport as a means to force their own choice of land transport contractors upon the shippers. Similarly, Art. 5 IV Regulation 4056/86 only states that the individual carriers are *inter alia* required to bring forward detailed tariff information in situations, in which there is a single price for a transport service composed of a sea as well as a land part[121]. The Commission also refused to accept any reasoning in favour of allowing joint price fixing for multimodal transport based on Art. 5 III and IV Regulation 4056/86. It stated that both provisions do not relate to a common conference tariff, but to the conditions offered by the individual carrier. They contain obligations that the individual carrier has to fulfil if it wants to benefit from the group exemption in Art. 3 Regulation 4056/86[122]. For these reasons, it is not possible to rely on Art. 5 III and IV Regulation 4056/86 as a means to argue that the scope of Art. 3 Regulation 4056/86 must

---

119 Clough/Randolph, (1991), p. 214; Kröger, ETL (1993), p. 423 ff, p. 429; Pernice, (1993), FS Deringer, p. 135 ff, p. 155; Rabe/Schütte, RIW (1988), p. 701 ff, p. 703.

120 Case T-86/95, *Compagnie générale maritime and Others v Commission*, (2002), ECR II, p. 1011 ff, rec. 267.

121 Case T-86/95, *Compagnie générale maritime and Others v Commission*, (2002), ECR II, p. 1011 ff, rec. 267.

122 "*FEFC*", OJ, (1994), L-378/17, rec. 87; "*TAA*", OJ, (1994), L-376/1, rec. 376.

be interpreted in such a way, as to exempt inland price fixing from Art. 81 I (ex 85 I) EC.

The CFI[123] and the Commission[124] also based their view on the wording of Recital 11 of the Preamble to Regulation 4056/86, which states that "*in the case of inland transport organised by the shippers*[125]*, the latter continue to be subject to Regulation (EEC) 1017/68*". Accordingly, this choice of words clearly supports the position that inland transport is not covered by Art. 3 Regulation 4056/86. The carriers interpret this provision in a different manner. They are of the poinion that Recital 11 of the Preamble to Regulation 4056/86 clarifies that conferences, which purchase inland transport services from providers of inland transport services, are not subject to Regulation 4056/86 and, in their function as a buyer, do not fall under the group exemption of Art. 3 Regulation 4056/86[126]. Such an interpretation does not make sense. Recital 11 of the Preamble to Regulation 4056/86 relates to Art. 5 IV Regulation 4056/86, which covers the availability of tariffs to conference customers, as explained in the two preceding paragraphs. Transport users must not be able to inform themselves about conference rates because carriers might act as a cartel when they themselves purchase land transport services[127]. Furthermore, there is no evidence in Regulation 4056/86 that conferences, which buy land transport services, are supposed to be exempted from Art. 81 I (ex 85 I) EC, by virtue of Art. 3 Regulation 4056/86. Art. 3 Regulation 4056/86, which allows the "*fixing of rates and conditions of carriage*", is unequivocal insofar, as the price charged to shipper is meant and not the price that carriers have to pay to inland haulage contractors[128]. For these reasons, the wording of Recital 11 of the Preamble to Regulation 4056/86 does not support the view that conferences are allowed to engage in inland price fixing based on Art. 3 Regulation 4056/86.

(2) Arguments related to the purpose of Art. 3 Regulation 4056/86
Another group of arguments that has been advanced to justify the fixing of prices for multimodal transport within a conference focuses on the purpose of Art. 3 Regulation 4056/86. A prominent argument in this respect is that conferences cannot exert their stabilising role properly, if they are not allowed to fix

---

[123] Case T-86/95, *Compagnie générale maritime and Others v Commission,* (2002), ECR II, p. 1011 ff, rec. 242 ff.

[124] "*FEFC*", OJ, (1994), L- 378/17, rec. 78; "*TAA*", OJ, (1994), L-376/1, rec. 375.

[125] From the German version it becomes clear that the word shipper here means "carrier", it does not mean "transport user".

[126] "FEFC", OJ, (1994), L-378/17, rec. 79.

[127] Case T-86/95, *Compagnie générale maritime and Others v Commission,* (2002), ECR II, p. 1011 ff, rec. 244; "*FEFC*", OJ, (1994), L-378/17, rec. 80.

[128] Case T-86/95, *Compagnie générale maritime and Others v Commission,* (2002), ECR II, p. 1011 ff, rec. 244; "*FEFC*", OJ, (1994), L-378/17, rec. 82.

the price for the inland leg as well[129]. The underlying rationale is that it would otherwise be possible for individual carriers to undercut the commonly established maritime freight rate by offering cheap land transport[130]. However, if the capacity of liner conferences to fix prices is extended to include land transport as well, then such an extension would also have to result in an increased common benefit in return. Price fixing by conferences cannot stabilise prices in other transport sectors[131], such as road or rail transport. As no additional benefit arises from allowing conferences to fix inland prices, such a practise is not permissible.

In this context it is also important to note that the extension of the block exemption for liner conferences to land transport provided within the frame of a multimodal transport operation could lead to a distortion of competition in relation to other modes of transport, where Art. 2 lit. a Regulation 1017/68 prohibits joint price fixing [132]. For example, the carriers could increase the price for the maritime leg and lower the price for the land leg accordingly. Genuine land transport operators could not compete with such a low price for land transport and would lose customers. Finally, it must be stated that block exemptions are not granted for the purpose of enforcing discipline among the members of a cartel[133]. Their possible lack of discipline cannot be used as an argument to increase cartel power.

It has also been argued in favour of an exemption for the fixing of prices for the inland leg of a multimodal transport operation. Conferences, because of their market power as buyers of inland transport services, have the capacity to negotiate especially low rates for the inland leg, which is beneficial for the shippers. Even if such an assumption holds true, this does not mean that such a price reduction is necessarily passed on to the shipper[134], which invalidates the above-made reasoning. These recent arguments show that no conclusive evidence exists to support the thesis that the purpose of the liner conference block exemption, which is to stabilise the maritime transport sector[135], necessitates an extension of this block exemption to price fixing for the inland leg of a multimodal transport operation.

---

[129] Braakman, ETL (1996), p. 265 ff, p. 273; Temple Lang, ETL (1993), p. 405 ff, p. 421.

[130] Temple Lang, ETL (1993), p. 405 ff, p. 407; Pernice, (1993), FS Deringer, p. 135 ff, p. 155.

[131] Temple Lang, ETL (1993), p. 405 ff, p. 421.

[132] Case T-86/95, *Compagnie générale maritime and Others v Commission*, (2002), ECR II, p. 1011 ff, rec. 264; Temple Lang, ETL (1993), p. 405 ff, p. 421.

[133] Temple Lang, ETL (1993), p. 405 ff, p. 421.

[134] Temple Lang, ETL (1993), p. 405 ff, p. 421.

[135] See: Recital 9 of the Preamble to Regulation 4056/86.

(3) Arguments related to the legislative history of Regulation 4056/86
A final aspect in the discussion of the treatment of multimodal transport under Regulation 4056/86 is its legislative history. During the legislative process, the European Parliament and the ECOSOC both suggested an amendment of the legislative proposal, with the aim to explicitly include multimodal transport into the scope of Art. 3 Regulation 4056/86[136]. The Council, however, rejected this proposal and did not explicitly mention multimodal transport in Regulation 4056/86. Supporters of an exemption for land leg price fixing of a multimodal transport operation leg argue that several Member States have reacted positively to American plans to exempt multimodal transport from U. S. antitrust legislation during the deliberations preceding the passage of the U. S. Shipping Act of 1984. They conclude that the position of these Members States remained unaltered in consideration of the adoption of Regulation 4056/86[137]. Furthermore they were of the opinion that the Council saw no need to make explicit mention of multimodal transport because it viewed this type of transport as implicitly being part of the scope of Regulation 4056/86[138]. However, it should be borne in mind that the U. S. Shipping Act of 1984 explicitly removed multimodal transport from the application of the normal antitrust principles in U. S. law. This circumstance, as well as the fact that the European Parliament and the ECOSOC made a proposal to that effect, leads to the conclusion that the Council deliberately decided not to exempt price fixing for the land leg of a multimodal transport operation from Art. 81 I (ex 85 I) EC[139].

There has been support for the view that liner conferences are allowed to engage into inland price fixing, by relying on a statement in the Council minutes on the adoption of Regulation 4056/86, in which it has been stated that: "*in practice, non application of Art. 85 (1) will be the rule as regards the organisation and execution of successive or supplementary multimodal sea/land transport operations and the fixing or application of inclusive rates for such transport operations*"[140]. However, this statement has only been made in connection to Arts. 2 Regulation 4056/86 and Art. 3 Regulation 1017/68 and not in connection to Art. 3 Regulation 4056/86. The aforementioned provisions cover technical agreements which are distinct from liner conference agreements[141].

---

[136] Case T-86/95, *Compagnie générale maritime and Others v Commission*, (2002), ECR II, p. 1011 ff, rec. 284.
[137] Case T-86/95, *Compagnie générale maritime and Others v Commission*, (2002), ECR II, p. 1011 ff, rec. 199 f.
[138] Case T-86/95, *Compagnie générale maritime and Others v Commission*, (2002), ECR II, p. 1011 ff, rec. 205.
[139] "*FEFC*", OJ, (1994), L-378/17, rec. 83 f; "*TAA*", OJ, (1994), L-376/1, rec. 377 f.
[140] Cited from: Kreis, ETL (1992), p. 155 ff, p. 167.
[141] See above, p. 98 ff.

Therefore, it cannot affect the scope of Art. 3 Regulation 4056/86[142]. As far as the block exemption in Art. 3 Regulation 4056/86 is concerned, it is rather the first part of the statement that is of importance, which declares "*that multimodal sea/land transport operations are subject to the rules of competition adopted for land transport and to those laid down for sea transport*". For these reasons, the legislative history of Regulation 4056/86 does not support the finding that agreements on prices for multimodal transport are exempted from Art. 81 I (ex 85 I) EC by virtue of Art. 3 Regulation 4056/86.

(4) Conclusion
This analysis has demonstrated that those arguing in favour of allowing liner conferences to fix prices for land transport as part of a multimodal transport service cannot support their view convincingly. Consequently, the CFI and the Commission have correctly taken the position that such activities are not permissible based on Art. 3 Regulation 4056/86. The approach of both institutions is an inital example of their general tendency to interpret the block exemption in Art. 3 Regulation 4056/86 in a narrow way, in order to ensure its compliance with Art. 81 III (ex 85 III) EC. Further evidence of their strictness on this issue is the fact that an application for an individual exemption of price fixing for multimodal transport from Art. 81 I (ex 85 I) EC has so far never been successful[143].

bbb) Capacity management programmes
A second issue that has caused a considerable debate between carriers and the Commission is the question to what extend Art. 3 Regulation 4056/86 permits the joint adoption of so-called capacity management programmes. The programmes in question normally do not lead to an irrevocable elimination of physical carrying capacity[144], since they only deny the carriers use of a certain percentage of the available transport capacity on each vessel[145]. They typically do not call for a reduction of vessels or sailings. The dispute arises over the question as to whether or not liner conferences may instate such programmes under the protection of the block exemption contained in Art. 3 Regulation 4056/86.

---

[142] "*FEFC*", OJ, (1994), L-378/17, rec. 90; Kreis, ETL (1992), p. 155 ff, p. 168.

[143] The CFI rejected a claim to that effect in: Case T-86/95, *Compagnie générale maritime and Others v Commission*, (2002), ECR II, p. 1011 ff, rec. 401 f. The Commission has rejected applications for individual exemption for inland price fixing in the following Decisions: "*TAA*", OJ, (1994), L-376/1, rec. 462-491; "*FEFC*", OJ, (1994), L-378/17, rec. 92-141; "*TACA*", OJ, (1999), L-95/1, rec. 409-424.

[144] Erdmenger, (1995), FS Raisch, p. 387 ff, p. 403.

[145] "*EATA*", OJ, (1999), L-193/23, rec. 11; "*TAA*", OJ, (1994), L-376/1, rec. 19.

According to the position of the Commission, capacity management programmes do only conform to Art. 3 Regulation 4056/86 if they seek to ensure the regularity, reliability and frequency of liner transport to all ports served by a conference. A reduction of transport capacity is also permissible if it has the purpose to balance seasonal or economical changes, which affect the demand for liner shipping[146]. Capacity management programmes with the primary target to raise rates are not allowed in the eyes of the Commission. As a consequence, the Commission does not approve of capacity adjustment schemes as described in the preceding paragraph. In its view, only such capacity adjustment programmes are exemptable by virtue of Art. 3 Regulation 4056/86, which either reduce the physical shipping capacity or the frequency of services[147]. This view has been opposed by carriers, who are of the opinion that all kinds of capacity management programmes conform to the requirements of Art. 3 Regulation 4056/86.

The starting point for an analysis of this problem is Art. 3 lit. d Regulation 4056/86, which permits conferences "*the regulation of the carrying capacity offered by each member*". The wording of this provision, by not indicating that Art. 3 lit. d Regulation 4056/86 in any way restricts the application of the block exemption for liner conferences to capacity management programmes[148], supports the position of the carriers.

The Commission presents two major arguments in support of its view that Art. 3 lit. d Regulation 4056/86 does not cover all types of capacity management programmes. First, it has been put forward that the activities enumerated in Art. 3 lit. a to c Regulation 4056/86 are only ancillary activities to the main conference activity, which is price fixing[149]. These activities do not in themselves constitute a significant restriction to competition[150]. The adoption of capacity management programmes contrary to the requirements of the Commission and in addition to joint price fixing activities, however, would in itself constitute a fundamental restriction to competition. Such an interpretation of Art. 3 lit. d Regulation 4056/86 is not possible as the different permissible conference objectives, enumerated in Art. 3 lit a to d Regulation 4056/86, would no longer be of equal value. Art. 3 lit. a to c Regulation 4056/86 would allow activities that are not very harmful to competition, whereas Art. 3 lit. d Regulation 4056/86 would contain one of the most serious kinds of restrictions to competition[151].

[146] "*EATA*", OJ, (1999), L-193/23, rec. 178; "*TAA*", OJ, (1994), L-376/1, rec. 365.
[147] "*EATA*", OJ, (1999), L-193/23, rec. 179; "*TAA*", OJ, (1994), L-376/1, rec. 366.
[148] Erdmenger, (1995), FS Raisch, p. 387 ff, p. 400, Jacobs, (1991), p. 115.
[149] "*TAA*", OJ, (1994), L-376/1, rec. 369.
[150] Temple Lang, ETL (1993), p. 405 ff, p. 416.
[151] Temple Lang, ETL (1993), p. 405 ff, p. 416.

From an economic point of view, a restriction of output, such as for example the implementation of a capacity management programme, has the same consequences for the market outcome as an increase in prices. In both situations, the price level rises while the amount of goods or services sold decreases at the same time. There is no indication that Art. 3 lit. d Regulation 4056/86 has a special position in relationship to the other alternatives, contained in Art. 3 Regulation 4056/86. It is, therefore, not permissible to interpret Art. 3 lit. d Regulation 4056/86 in such a way as to contain a completely different provision than Art. 3 lit. a to c Regulation 4056/86[152].

The second major argument of the Commission is that permitting capacity management programmes without any restrictions is not coherent with the aim of the group exemption for liner conferences. One of the main functions of Regulation 4056/86 is to realign EC law with the UNCTAD-code[153], which is evidenced *inter alia* by the fact that both bodies of law define the term *liner conference* in the same way[154]. Art. 19 I UNCTAD provides that: "*Conferences should take necessary and appropriate measures to ensure that their member lines provide regular, adequate and efficient service of the required frequency on the routes they serve and shall arrange such services so as to avoid as far as possible bunching and gapping of sailings. Conferences should also take into consideration any special measures necessary in arranging services to handle seasonal variations in cargo volume*".

Art. 19 UNCTAD is headed "*Adequacy of service*". The Commission concludes from this heading, as well as from the wording of Art. 19 UNCTAD that the main goal of this provision is to ensure a qualitative high standard of liner shipping. Since Regulation 4056/86 seeks to harmonise EC competition law and the UNCTAD-code, it also has the purpose to ensure such a qualitative high standard of liner shipping. For this reason, it is impossible, according to the Commission, to interpret Art. 3 lit. d Regulation 4056/86 in such a way as to exempt capacity management programmes of liner conferences, which primarily aim for an increase of shipping rates[155] from the prohibition contained in Art. 81 I (ex 85 I) EC. Such an interpretation would not be consistent with the purpose of the liner conference block exemption.

It has been argued against the position of the Commission that the teleological limitation of the scope suggested by the Commission does not provide a criterion, by which the different capacity management programmes can be distin-

---

[152] "*TAA*", OJ, (1994), L-376/1, rec. 370.
[153] Recital 3 and 4 of the Preamble to Regulation 4056/86.
[154] See above, p. 59.
[155] "*TAA*", OJ, (1994), L-376/1, rec. 362.

guished properly. Every reduction of shipping capacity affects the price of shipping services and this consequence is typically also intended by those who reduce the capacity, even if they only want to react to seasonal or economical changes in the freight volume[156]. Therefore, all capacity management programmes seek to raise the freight rates through a limitation of transport capacity. Additionally, it has been put forward that it is incomprehensible, according to the Commission's view[157], that an agreement to reduce capacity utilisation by a certain percentage would be illegal, but an agreement to reduce sailings on a certain route, or to reduce the number of ships that operate a certain service, would be lawful[158]. It is emphasised that the Commission's position is inconsequential insofar, as it allows a more severe form of capacity reduction and prohibits capacity reductions of lesser severity.

The underlying rationale for a distinction between capacity management programmes that reduce the number of sailings or vessels and such programmes that simply leave a number of slots empty on every voyage, is that the former alternative, which was considered to constitute a more severe restriction to competition, reduces the fixed operating costs in comparison to the latter alternative. Ships that do not sail reduce the fixed operating costs per unit in comparison to ships sailing partly empty. Such a reduction in capacity, therefore, could prove beneficial to the shippers[159], which in turn allows for a different treatment. An additional reason that supports the Commission's approach towards capacity management programmes is the argument that Art. 3 Regulation 4056/86 has to be interpreted in accordance with Art. 81 III (ex 85 III) EC. The combination of price fixing and output limitation is possibly the most effective way to restrict competition[160]. To allow liner conferences to extensively engage in such a practice by virtue of Art. 3 lit. d Regulation 4056/86 would, with great probability, conflict with Art. 81 III (ex 85 III) EC, leading to the invalidity of the former provision[161].

This analysis of capacity management programmes in the light of Art. 3 Regulation 4056/86 has demonstrated that the approach of the Commission to permit liner conferences only in restricted circumstances to operate capacity management programmes constitutes the proper approach towards such activities. The Commission thereby provided another example of its tendency to interpret Art. 3 Regulation 4056/86 in a restrictive way. So far the CFI has not ruled on the

---

[156] Immenga/Mestmäcker Vol. 2, (1997), Basedow, p. 2053, rec. 35.
[157] "*TAA*", OJ, (1994), L-376/1, rec. 366.
[158] Immenga/Mestmäcker, Vol. 2, (1997), Basedow, p. 2053, rec. 35.
[159] Faull/Nikpay, (1999), p. 897; Wood, (1999), p. 8.
[160] Faull, ETL (1995), p. 3 ff, p. 5; Wood, (1999), p. 9.
[161] Temple Lang, ETL (1993), p. 405 ff, p. 416.

legality of capacity management programmes, but the fact that the CFI also follows a restrictive interpretation of Art. 3 Regulation 4056/86[162] is an indication that it will uphold the Commission's position on this matter.

ccc) Restrictions on the use of individual service contracts

The third major issue of debate in the interpretation of Art. 3 Regulation 4056/86 concerns the practice of some liner conferences to restrict the capacity of their members to enter into service contracts with their customers on an individual basis. In a service contract the shipper promises to commit a fixed amount of cargo over a set period of time to a certain carrier. In consideration, the carrier agrees on a certain rate and on a specifically defined level of service. The negotiated price in such contracts may be lower than the conference tariff, which is beneficial for the shipper. This derogation from the official conference tariff is the reason why conferences often wish to restrict the individual carriers power to conclude such contracts, since otherwise the effectiveness of a common conference tariff may be endangered from a conference point of view. The availability of individual service contracts has other positive effects, apart from a possible reduction of the prices for shipping services. Such contracts can be tailored to suit the shippers' needs for special transport services, and they can be concluded for a longer period of time, thereby creating financial stability for both parties, the shipper as well as the carrier[163].

The importance of the availability of individual service contracts for the maritime transport industry can be seen from the consequences of the passage of the Ocean Shipping Reform Act of 1998 (OSRA) in the United States, which entered into force on the 1st of May 1999. A principle feature of this legislation is that it allows for the unrestricted use of individual service contracts and provides for the possibility to keep key information on these contracts confidential[164]. First evaluations of this new statutory regime indicate that carriers and shippers enter into such contracts in large numbers and that the number of conferences operating in the trades to and from the United States is in decline[165].

The Commission addressed the legality of restrictions imposed by conferences on service contracts in the *TACA* Decision[166]. Individual service contracts as such are not subject to Art. 81 I (ex 85 I) EC, as they do not contain any collu-

---

[162] The CFI stated its restrictive approach towards Art. 3 Regulation 4056/86 in: Case T-86/95, *Compagnie générale maritime and Others v Commission*, (2002), ECR II, p. 1011 ff, rec. 251 f.

[163] "*TACA*", OJ, (1999), L-95/1, rec. 472 f.

[164] FMC, OSRA Report, (2001), p. 8.

[165] FMC, OSRA Report, (2001), p. 2 f.

[166] "*TACA*", OJ, (1999), L-95/1.

sive element. A conflict with Art. 81 I (ex 85 I) EC may arise, however, if a conference agreement contains provisions that regulate if and under what conditions the conference members may enter into such service contracts[167]. The Commission found in its decision that: "*the group exemption for liner conferences contained in Regulation (EEC) No 4056/86 does not authorise: (.....) a prohibition on individual service contracts or restrictions, whether binding or non binding, on the contents of such contracts*"[168].

The part in the Commission's legal analysis, which is concerned with service contracts focused on the relationship between Art. 3 Regulation 4056/86 and joint service contracts, but as the above-cited statement indicates, the Commission must have thought that the application of Art. 3 Regulation 4056/86 to such parts of a conference agreement that regulate individual service contracts is not *a priori* excluded. Some of the arguments that have been used in connection with joint service contracts can also be made fruitful in relationship to those clauses of a conference agreement that cover individual service contracts. The CFI addressed the legality of restrictions to the right of individual carriers to depart from the official conference tariffs in its *TAA* ruling[169]. In its judgement the CFI analysed such restrictions in the light of a possibility for individual exemption. Since the requirements set by Art. 81 III (ex 85 III) EC are the same for both types of exemptions, the position of the CFI in that case provides some guidance for its interpretation of Art. 3 Regulation 4056/86, on the issue of individual service contracts.

The regulation of service contracts is not an activity that is especially mentioned in Art. 3 Regulation 4056/86. The question that arises is, whether or not such an activity is implicitly exempted from Art. 81 I (ex 85 I) EC by virtue of Art. 3 Regulation 4056/86[170]. Such an exemption seems doubtful for a variety of reasons. First, it must be noted that there is traditionally a difference between contractual transport arrangements and transport carried out under a common tariff[171]. Already a British law from 1830 followed this differentiation[172] as

---

[167] "*TACA*", OJ, (1999), L-95/1, rec. 447.

[168] "*TACA*", OJ, (1999), L-95/1, rec. 449.

[169] Case T-395/95, *Atlantic Container Line AB and Others v Commission*, (2002), ECR II, p. 875 ff.

[170] This has been argued by the TACA members in relationship to joint service contracts, see: "*TACA*", OJ, (1999), L-95/1, rec. 451.

[171] "*TACA*", OJ, (1999), L-95/1, rec. 107.

[172] 11° Geo. IV & Gul. IV, which contains the following provision: "*Provided always, and be it further enacted, that nothing in this Act contained shall extend or be construed to annul or in anywise affect any special Contract between such Mail Contractor, Stage Coach roprietor, or Common carrier, and any other Parties, for the Conveyance of Goods and merchandises.*", cited from: Wood, 1999, p. 10.

well as the majority report of the already mentioned[173] Royal Commission on Shipping Rings[174]. The conference system is based on a rate structure governed by a common tariff[175]. Therefore, the regulation of transport arrangements on the basis of an individual contract and not on the basis of the common conference tariff does not constitute a typical conference activity, which can be exempted from Art. 81 I (ex 85 I) EC under Art. 3 Regulation 4056/86. The fact that the regulation of service contracts is not a typical activity of liner conferences as defined in Art. 1 II lit. b Regulation 4056/86 and the UNCTAD-code[176] is furthermore underlined by the fact that such contracts were only introduced after United States legislation banned loyalty contracts[177] in 1984[178]. The definition of the term *liner conference* in the UNCTAD-code that was also employed in Regulation 4056/86 precedes this date. Consequently, it cannot have taken the emergence of individual service contracts into account, which is a further indication of the fact that Art.3 Regulation 4056/86 does not permit the restriction of the capacity of individual carriers to enter into contractual obligations of this kind.

It can further be argued that individual service contracts constitute a form of non-conference competition. Although such contracts are carried out by carriers that are also conference members, they are not carried out within the tariffary framework of the conference. One of the fundamental principles of Art. 81 III (ex 85 III) EC is that restrictions to competition are only permissible if there remains a sufficient degree of competition[179]. The ECJ is of the same opinion by stating that: "*the requirements contained in Articles 3 and 85 of the EEC Treaty that competition shall not be distorted implies the existence on the market of workable competition*"[180]. The supply of transport services on the basis of individual service contracts outside the conference tariff system could be

---

173 See above, p. 23 ff.

174 This report contained the following paragraph: "*Contracts. – We have spoken of the rebate system as superseding the system under which shipowners made separate bargains in the form of contracts with their clients. And so far as general merchandise is concerned this is practically true. To a certain limited extent, however, the contract system still survives, but in the great majority of cases the contracts are collective contracts made by the Con ference as a whole and not contracts made by individual members of the Conference.*", cited from: Wood, (1999), p. 10.

175 Wood, (1999), p. 10.

176 UNCTAD-code, Part 1, Chapter 1, Definition 1.

177 A loyalty contract is an agreement by which a shipper commits all, or a fixed percentage, of his freight to a certain carrier or conference. The shipper benefits from lower rates in consideration. A loyalty contract is typically characterised by a loyalty obligation of the shipper, which is not part of service contracts.

178 "*TACA*", OJ, (1999), L-95/1, rec. 111; Wood, (1999), p. 10-13.

179 See: Kreis, ETL (1988), p. 562 ff, p. 566; Kreis, ETL (1992), p. 155 ff, p. 160.

180 Case 26/76, *Metro v Commission (No. 1)*, (1977) ECR, p. 1875 ff, p. 1905, rec. 20.

seen as a way to ensure the necessary degree of residual competition in the maritime transport sector. It is necessary to interpret Art. 3 Regulation 4056/86 in such as way that it does not allow conferences to restrict individual service contracting, in order to ensure its conformity with Arts. 3 and 81 (ex 85) EC. The CFI recognised the virtue of this reasoning in its *TAA* ruling. It stated therein that restrictions to the right of individual carriers to enter into contracts for the transport of goods outside the common tariff, constitutes an elimination of internal competition[181]. Although the CFI acknowledged that an elimination of internal competition does not in itself lead to the conclusion that an agreement or a type of agreement is contradictory to Art. 81 III (ex 85 III) EC, the CFI asserted that the existence of internal competition is an important aspect in this respect[182].

Finally, that, which has been said earlier[183] in connection to intermodal transport can be repeated: it is not the function of Art. 3 Regulation 4056/86 to prevent indiscipline among the members of a conference[184]. If carriers decide to enter into individual service contracts at prices below the conference rate, it cannot be the purpose of Art. 3 Regulation 4056/86 to hinder them to do so. This analysis has demonstrated that the CFI and the Commission adopted a restrictive approach towards the restriction of the capacity of individual carriers to transport goods on the basis of individual contracts outside the common conference tariff. They thereby demonstrated yet again that the exceptional nature of the liner conference block exemption in Art. 3 Regulation 4056/86 requires a strict interpretation in order to ensure its compliance with Art. 81 (ex 85) EC.

e) Art. 6 Regulation 4056/86 - the exemption for agreements with shippers

Art. 6 Regulation 4056/86 contains two block exemptions for agreements that involve shippers; it thereby seeks to ensure that the interests of the shippers are duly taken into account[185]. Both block exemptions are restricted to agreements that concern "*the rates, conditions and quality of liner services*"[186], a choice of words, which is so wide that it does not substantially limit the scope of issues that may be subject of an exemptable agreement.

---

181 Case T-395/95, *Atlantic Container Line AB and Others v Commission*, (2002), ECR II, p. 875 ff, rec. 321.

182 Case T-395/95, *Atlantic Container Line AB and Others v Commission*, (2002), ECR II, p. 875 ff, rec. 302.

183 See above, p. 116.

184 Temple Lang, ETL (1993), p. 405 ff, p. 421.

185 Pernice, FS Deringer, (1993), p. 149 ff, p. 156; Rycken, ETL (1987), p. 483 ff, p. 492; Werner, WuW (1987), p. 796 ff, p. 804.

186 Jacobs, (1991), p. 140.

The first exemption granted by Art. 6 Regulation 4056/86 covers vertical agreements between conferences and shippers. Two types of vertical agreements are suitable for exemption, according to Art. 6 Regulation 4056/86. First, agreements that result from consultations between carriers and shippers are exempted based on Arts. 6 juncto 5 I Regulation 4056/86. This exemption became necessary in order to provide for a possibility by which the consultations, which constitute an ancillary obligation, attached to the block exemption for liner conferences in Art. 3 Regulation 4056/86, may lead to any tangible results[187]. It has already been explained above that the obligation to enter into consultations does not constitute a very effective measure to safeguard the interests of the shippers[188]. The same is true for any vertical agreement that incorporates the result of such negotiations. A second type of vertical agreements, which is exempted by virtue of Art. 6 Regulation 4056/86 in connection with Art. 5 II Regulation 4056/86 concerns loyalty rebates. Art. 5 II Regulation 4056/86 lays down criteria under which conferences are allowed to grant loyalty rebates. Such a permission can only function, if carriers and shippers are allowed to enter into agreements on the issue of loyalty rebates[189].

The second block exemption applies to horizontal agreements between shippers. Art. 6 Regulation 4056/86 thereby follows a principle that already featured in the findings of the Royal Commission on Shipping Rings, which is that collective bargaining power on the side of the shippers is an adequate tool to balance the powers of liner conferences[190]. According to one view, the mentioning of horizontal agreements between shippers in Art. 6 Regulation 4056/86 does not constitute a block exemption[191]. The wording of Art. 6 Regulation 4056/86 does not support such a position, because it equally and expressly *exempts* both vertical, as well as horizontal agreements. It is true, however, that the exemption for horizontal agreements is merely accessorial to the exemption for vertical agreements in Art. 6 Regulation 4056/86[192]. Shippers are only allowed to enter into agreements among themselves in relation to the types of vertical agreements exempted by virtue of Art. 6 Regulation 4056/86. Through this exemption it is possible for associations of shippers to represent the interests of shippers collectively in negotiations with the conferences[193]. The fact that the shippers may represent their interests in a collective way does not significantly

---

[187] Kühne, (1996), p. 167.
[188] See above, p. 109.
[189] Kühne, (1996), p. 166.
[190] See above, p. 24.
[191] Rabe/Schütte, RIW (1988), p. 701 ff, p. 703.
[192] Immenga/Mestmäcker, Vol. 2, (1997), Basedow, p. 2056, rec. 42.
[193] Werner, WuW (1987), p. 796 ff, p, 805.

improve the position of the shippers, since the conference carriers are under no legal obligation to take the position of the shippers into account.

2) Regulations 870/95 and 823/2000

The second block exemption that has been granted in the field of maritime transport is the exemption for consortia agreements contained in Regulation 823/2000 and its predecessor Regulation 870/95.

a) Introduction

The exemption of consortia from Art. 81 I (ex 85 I) EC has proven much less problematic than that of liner conferences. There has been no Decision or other measure of the Commission during the five years in which Regulation 870/95 has been valid to the effect that a consortium agreement could not be exempted, either based on Art. 3 Regulation 870/95 or in reliance on Art. 81 III (ex 85 III) EC[194]. One of the main reasons for this lack of controversy is the fact that the consortia block exemption does not permit collusive price fixing[195]. As a consequence, there is no need to realign a group exemption, which contains one of the most powerful restrictions to competition thinkable, with the fundamental principles of EC competition law embodied in Art. 81 (ex 85) EC.

Consortia and liner conferences are very different types of agreements. Liner conferences have the purpose of making liner shipping more profitable for the carriers by influencing the price for liner shipping services. They try to raise the profits of carriers through an increase of their total revenue. This goal is pursued directly through agreements on a common freight rate and indirectly through agreements on capacity reduction and/or market partitioning. Consortia on the other side are agreements that mainly affect the expenses incurred by carriers. They seek to increase the profits of liner shipping companies through a reduction of the costs of liner shipping. The primary concern of consortia is the rationalisation of shipping services and the exploitation of economies of scale[196]. Due to this fundamental difference between the two types of agreements, consortia cause less difficulties than liner conferences in relation to Art. 81 III (ex 85 III) EC.

b) The scope of Regulation 823/2000

Arts. 1 and 2 Regulation 823/2000 define the scope of Regulation 823/2000 and consequently of the block exemption for consortia contained therein. As far as

---

[194] Williams, (2000), p. 44 f; for a list of Commission action in this matter see: Commission working document on Regulation 870/95, annex 2.

[195] See: Art. 2 I Regulation 823/2000 and Recital 9 of the Preamble to Regulation 823/2000.

[196] Confavreux, RMC (1996), p. 369 ff, p. 377 f; Immenga/Mestmäcker, Vol. 2, (1997), Basedow, p. 2080, rec. 1.

the territorial scope is concerned, Art. 1 Regulation 823/2000 states that only "*international liner transport services from or to one or more Community ports*" are covered by Regulation 823/2000. The same is true for Regulation 4056/86 by virtue of Art.1 II Regulation 4056/86. For the interpretation of the territorial scope of Regulation 823/2000 it is, therefore, possible to make reference to the analysis of the territorial scope of Regulation 4056/86[197].

In relation to the personal scope of Regulation 823/2000, Art. 1 Regulation 823/2000 stipulates that this Regulation is only applicable to consortia offering liner shipping services. This wording clearly indicates that tramp shipping services are not subject to Regulation 823/2000[198]. Art. 2 II Regulation 823/2000 defines the term liner shipping in an unequivocal manner. It is already more problematic to precisely define the expression *consortium*. Art. 2 I Regulation 823/2000 provides that a consortium within the meaning of this Regulation is: "*an agreement between two or more vessel-operating carriers which provide international liner shipping services exclusively for the carriage of cargo, chiefly by container, in relation to one or more trades, and the object of which is to bring about cooperation in the joint operation of a maritime transport service, and which improves the service that would be offered individually by each of its members in the absence of the consortium, in order to rationalise their operations by means of technical, operational and/or commercial arrangements, with the exception of price fixing*".

This definition has intentionally been kept very broad, as the Commission was of the opinion that such a broad exemption is necessary in order for the consortia block exemption to function in practise[199]. The difficulty of defining the term consortium positively, which is also encountered by the definition in Art. 2 I Regulation 823/2000, arises from the fact that the variety of existing consortia agreements is very large. It has been explained in the introductory chapter of this study that consortia agreements range from limited forms of co-operation in just one trade lane to global alliances that constitute highly sophisticated forms of co-operation[200]. Only a broad definition like the one contained in Art. 2 I Regulation 823/2000 covers the multitude of existing consortia[201]. Art. 2 I Regulation 823/2000 has further clarified the scope of Regulation 823/2000 in relation to its predecessor, since it replaced the expression "*relating to a particular trade*" with the term "*relating to one or more trades*". The only narrowing element that is clearly contained in Art. 2 I Regulation 823/2000 is that

[197] See above, p. 95 ff.

[198] Immenga/Mestmäcker, Vol. 2, (1997), Basedow, p. 2082, rec. 5; Kühne, (1996), p. 191.

[199] Commission working document on Regulation 870/95, (1999), rec. 77.

[200] See above, p. 26 f.

[201] Ginderachter/Durande, ETL (1996), p. 241 ff, p. 247.

agreements that allow price fixing cannot constitute consortia within the meaning of this provision.

Although it is difficult to define the term consortium in a positive way, some clarity can be gained by establishing what a consortium is not. Consortia are different from liner conferences in two ways. First, they can be differentiated from liner conferences insofar, as they do not set uniform or common freight rates[202]. Second, they are a form of co-operation of liner shipping companies that has the purpose of reducing the costs of liner shipping, rather than of increasing the price level in liner shipping like conferences[203]. Consortia cannot be considered to be technical agreements in the sense of Art. 2 Regulation 4056/86 either, as these agreements aim exclusively at the technical improvement of liner shipping services [204]. Consortia typically have the purpose of reducing the costs of liner shipping through rationalisation and thereby pursuing a commercial motive, which does not conform to Art. 2 Regulation 4056/86[205]. Finally, consortia do not constitute mergers either[206] because they normally contain a clause that regulates the possible termination of the agreement[207], and therefore, they do not create permanently fused new entities, which are legally separate from the undertakings that created them[208].

A further aspect of the scope of Regulation 823/2000 is that Regulation 823/2000 neither applies to agreements between different consortia nor to agreements between consortia and single individual carriers[209]. The exclusion of so-called tolerated outsider agreements from the scope of Regulation 823/2000 corresponds to the approach of Regulation 4056/86 on this issue. It is also unlikely that an application for individual exemption on this issue will be successful for the same reasons that such an exemption is unlikely in the case of liner conferences[210]. Finally, Arts. 5 and 6 Regulation 823/2000 as well as Recital 8 of the Preamble to Regulation 823/2000 indicate that the block exemption for consortia covers consortia that operate within a liner conference as well as consortia that exist outside a conference.

---

[202] Ruttley, ETL (1993), p. 487 ff, p. 489.
[203] See above, p. 27.
[204] Immenga/Mestmäcker, Vol. 2 , (1997), Basedow, p. 2046, rec. 21; Munari, RabelsZ (1990), p. 627 ff, p. 641.
[205] See above, p. 99 ff.
[206] Commission working document on Regulation 870/95, (1999), rec. 15.
[207] Kreis, ETL (1992), p. 155 ff, p. 164.
[208] Kreis, ETL (1992), p. 155 ff, p. 164; Ruttley, ETL (1993), p. 487 ff, p. 489.
[209] See: Recital 21 to the Preamble of Regulation 823/2000.
[210] See above, p. 104.

c) The relationship between Regulation 4056/86 and Regulation 823/2000

Regulation 4056/86 contains detailed rules for the application of EC competition law to the field of maritime transport, with the exception of tramp shipping. Its scope covers all kinds of restrictions to competition that are within the scope of Arts. 81 and 82 (ex 85 and 86) EC. As a consequence, consortia agreements also fall within the scope of Regulation 4056/86[211]. The provisions of Regulation 823/2000, therefore, constitute *leges speciales* to those of Regulation 4056/86[212]. Support for this position can be found in Art. 1 I Regulation 479/92, which provides that the Commission may pass a Regulation containing a block exemption for consortia "*without prejudice to the application of Regulation (EEC) No. 4056/86*". In addition, Art. 7 I Regulation 823/2000 refers to Regulation 2834/98, which lays down procedural details concerning the application of Regulation 4056/86[213]. This reference indicates that Regulation 4056/86 and its ancillary Regulation 2834/98 regulate the application of Arts. 81 and 82 (ex 85 and 86) EC in relation to consortia agreements, if Regulation 823/2000 does not provide any detailed rules[214]. The interplay between the two Regulations is especially important in the context of procedural provisions. Regulation 823/2000, as its predecessor Regulation 870/95, only contains rudimentary procedural rules. The more general rules embodied in Regulation 4056/86 become applicable as soon as Regulation 823/2000 does not contain the necessary procedural provisions[215]. For example, Art. 12 Regulation 4056/86 also regulates the application for an individual exemption according to Art. 81 III (ex 85 III) EC in relation to consortia agreements[216]. As far as material law is concerned it has been demonstrated above that consortia agreements are not exemptable under Art. 3 Regulation 4056/86.[217], but it may nevertheless be necessary to analyse an agreement in the light of both Regulations in order to establish which block exemption is applicable.

Difficulties may arise between the two block exemptions in relationship to agreements that contain rules on joint price fixing activities. Art. 2 I Regulation 823/2000 and Recital 8 of the Preamble to Regulation 823/2000 state that this Regulation is applicable to consortia that operate within a liner conference as well as to consortia that exist outside the framework of a conference, as long as they do not engage in joint price fixing. An agreement within a conference that

[211] Immenga/Mestmäcker, Vol. 2, (1997), Basedow, p. 2083, rec. 9, the scope of Regulation 4056/86 is not to be confused with the scope of the block exemption contained in Art. 3 Regulation 4056/86, the latter of which does not include consortia, see p. 105 f.

[212] Immenga/Mestmäcker, Vol. 2, (1997), Basedow, p. 2083, rec. 9.

[213] Similarly, Art. 7 VII Regulation 823/2000 refers to Arts. 10 - 26 Regulation 4056/86.

[214] Immenga/Mestmäcker, Vol. 2, (1997), Basedow, p. 2083, rec. 9.

[215] Immenga/Mestmäcker, Vol. 2, (1997), Basedow, p. 2083, rec. 9.

[216] Ginderachter/Durande, ETL (1996), p. 241 ff, p. 261.

[217] See above, p. 105 f.

contains rules on price fixing cannot be exempted under Art. 3 Regulation 823/2000. Such an agreement does not constitute a consortium within the definition of Art. 2 I Regulation 823/2000. Since Art. 3 Regulation 823/2000 only exempts activities of agreements that constitute consortia according to the definition of Art. 2 I Regulation 823/2000, the whole agreement, including those parts that do not relate to price fixing, falls outside the scope of Regulation 823/2000[218]. An exemption under Art. 3 Regulation 4056/86 is also doubtful, because this provision does not cover all forms of co-operation, which are typical for consortia[219]. Furthermore consortia typically do not offer a uniform or common freight tariff, as required by Art. 3 Regulation 4056/86[220], even if there is some sort of agreement on prices-related affairs. As a result, it is only possible in such situations to apply for an individual exemption based on Art. 81 III (ex 85 III) EC[221] according to Art. 12 Regulation 4056/86.

Agreements that do not operate within a conference and do not constitute a conference themselves cannot benefit from the consortia block exemption for the above-explained reasons, as long as they engage in price fixing. As they do not constitute a conference, they may not benefit from the exemption contained in Art. 3 Regulation 4056/86, either. The only possibility to avoid conflict with Art. 81 (ex 85) EC is again to apply for an individual exemption based on Art. 81 III (ex 85 III) EC. Another problem related to the interplay between the two Regulations is the question of whether it is possible to exempt a consortium from Art. 81 I (ex 85 I) EC by virtue of Art. 3 Regulation 823/2000 that requires its members to participate in a certain conference. The exemption of such an agreement under Art. 3 Regulation 823/2000 would circumvent the prohibition of price fixing contained in Art. 2 I Regulation 823/2000[222]. As a consequence, it is not possible to exempt agreements that contain an obligation to join a certain conference on the basis of Art. 3 Regulation 823/2000[223].

d) Overview of the main provisions of the consortia block exemption

Art. 3 Regulation 823/2000 contains the actual block exemption for consortia. It states that only activities carried out within the framework of a consortium, as defined by Art. 2 I Regulation 823/2000, may be exempted from Art. 81 I (ex 85 I) EC. Art. 3 II lists activities to which Art. 81 I (ex 85 I) EC is not applicable. The wording of Art. 3 II Regulation 823/2000 is misleading insofar, as it is not

---

[218] Immenga/Mestmäcker, Vol. 2, (1997), Basedow, p. 2084, rec. 11.
[219] Immenga/Mestmäcker, Vol. 2, (1997), Basedow, p. 2084, rec. 11.
[220] Ginderachter/Durande, ETL (1996), p. 241, p. 251.
[221] Ginderachter/Durande, ETL (1996), p. 241, p. 251; Immenga/Mestmäcker, Vol. 2, (1997), Basedow, p. 2084, rec. 11.
[222] Commission working document on Regulation 870/95, (1999), rec. 117.
[223] Commission working document on Regulation 870/95, (1999), rec. 116.

the activity in itself that can lead to a conflict with Art. 81 I (ex 85 I) EC, but only the collusive engagement in these activities[224]. The list of collusive activities that can be exempted from the application of Art. 81 I (ex 85 I) EC by virtue of Art. 3 II Regulation 823/2000 is exhaustive[225].

Arts. 5 to 9 Regulation 823/2000 lay down a system of conditions and obligations that are attached to the block exemption in Art. 3 Regulation 823/2000. The differentiation between conditions and obligations is merely declaratory[226]. Any consortia agreements that do not fully comply with either type of requirement are void according to Art. 81 II (ex 85 II) EC. If the clause that is contradictory to any of the requirements in Arts. 5 to 9 Regulation 823/2000 can be separated from the rest of the agreement, then the rest of the agreement remains valid and does not become automatically void[227]. In the case that a consortium does not correspond to the requirements established by Arts. 5 to 9 Regulation 823/2000, it is also possible to apply for an individual exemption according to Art. 12 Regulation 4056/86 or Art. 12 Regulation 1017/68 if the agreement also relates to land activities[228].

Art. 5 Regulation 823/2000 contains several alternative conditions that seek to ensure that there still is a sufficient degree of competition in the markets in which the consortium operates[229]. Consortia may only operate within a conference if there is effective competition on prices or in relation to the quality of service. Irrespective of the question of whether or not a consortium exists inside or outside a conference, the condition of Art. 5 Regulation 823/2000 isalso fulfilled if actual or potential competition exists from shipping lines that operate outside the consortium.

Arts. 6 and 7 Regulation 823/2000 also have the purpose of ensuring that the markets in which the consortia operate remain competitive[230]. These two provisions establish a system of maximum market shares that consortia may not exceed, if they want to benefit from the block exemption in Art. 3 Regulation 823/2000[231]. Any consortium (within a conference) with a market share below

---

[224] Immenga/Mestmäcker, Vol. 2, (1997), Basedow, p. 2085, rec. 14.

[225] Ginderachter/Durande, ETL (1996), p. 241 ff, p. 252.

[226] Kühne, (1996), p. 195; under Regulation 4056/86 conditions can be distinguished from obligations according to the different legal consequences in case of a violation of either type of requirement; see above, p. 107 ff.

[227] Ginderachter/Durande, ETL (1996), p. 241 ff, p. 255.

[228] Ginderachter/Durande, ETL (1996), p. 241 ff, p. 259.

[229] Immenga/Mestmäcker, Vol. 2, (1997), Basedow, p. 2088, rec. 21.

[230] Ginderachter/Durande, ETL (1996), p. 241 ff, p. 255.

[231] Arts. 6 and 7 Regulation 823/2000 contain the most important change in comparison to Regulation 870/95, in that the trade share thresholds were replaced by market share thres-

30 per cent on all markets within which it operates or 35 per cent (outside a conference) automatically qualifies for exemption according to Art. 6 Regulation 823/2000 if it fulfils the other requirements attached to the block exemption. If the market share of a consortium exceeds these numbers, but remains below 50 per cent on all markets within which it operates, then the agreement must be notified to the Commission. The consortium automatically benefits from the block exemption if the Commission has not opposed the agreement within six months from the date of notification. A consortium that has a market share of more than 50 per cent in any market within which it operates, cannot benefit from Regulation 823/2000, but can only apply for individual exemption[232] according to Art. 12 Regulation 4056/86[233].

Art. 8 Regulation 823/2000 attaches four cumulative conditions to the consortia block exemption. These conditions concern the availability of individual service contracts, the right to withdraw from the consortium and the right to engage in independent marketing if the consortium operates a joint marketing structure. Art. 8 I Regulation 823/2000 requires consortia to allow their members to enter into service contracts on an individual basis. Art. 8 I Regulation 823/2000 thereby avoids any discussions on this issue, like under Regulation 4056/86[234]. Finally, Art. 8 IV Regulation 823/2000 contains a non-discrimination clause. As this clause corresponds to the clause contained in Art. 4 I Regulation 4056/86, reference can be made to the remarks made in respect to Art. 4 Regulation 4056/86[235]. Art. 9 Regulation 823/2000 lays down four cumulative obligations concerning such issues as consultations with shippers or their representative organisations, the availability of service details to the shippers, notification of any results of arbitration measures to the Commission and the availability of proof to the Commission that a consortium conforms to the requirements of Arts. 5 to 9 Regulation 823/2000.

e) Consortia and land activities

It has been explained above that a consortium within the meaning of Art. 2 I Regulation 823/2000 may not engage in price fixing[236]. This prohibition also extends to price fixing for inland activities such as in connection with the provi-

---

olds. The main difference between these two criteria is that only the latter takes substitute ports into account. Regulation 870/95 employed the trade share criterion, because initially thecarriers were of the opinion that it would be difficult to establish the exact market shares. Experience has demonstrated however that the carriers were able to provide numbers on their market shares; per: Williams, (2000), p. 46.

232 Williams, (2000), p. 46.

233 Ginderachter/Durande, ETL (1996), p. 241 ff, p. 259.

234 See above, p. 122 ff.

235 See above, p. 107 ff.

236 See above, p. 127 f.

sion of multimodal transport services. The question remains whether other inland activities constitute permissible activities for consortia according to Art. 3 Regulation 823/2000. Art. 1 I Regulation 479/92 limits the scope of consortia activities that may be exempted from Art. 81 I (ex 85 I) EC through a Commission Regulation to activities "*that have as an object to promote or establish co-operation in the joint operation of maritime transport services between liner shipping companies*". As a consequence, the block exemption in Art. 3 Regulation 823/2000, which is based on the enabling Regulation 479/92, only covers maritime activities; the common provision of land services, such as for example the provision of land transport as part of a multimodal transport operation, is not covered by Art. 3 Regulation 823/2000[237], even if the carriers refrain from joint price fixing.

This clear limitation of the scope of Art. 3 Regulation 823/2000 is supported by the fact that the initial Commission proposal for the enabling Regulation[238] suggested an extension of the authorisation for a consortia group exemption, also to such agreements that offer multimodal transport services[239]. However, the European Parliament in its comment on this proposal[240] demanded that multimodal transport should be excluded from the scope of such a Regulation. The European Parliament was of the opinion that the problem of multimodal transport should be addressed in a general way, not limited to maritime transport[241]. The Commission amended its proposal accordingly. This change of the initial proposal, which was accepted by the Council, suggests that the legislator intentionally wanted to exclude inland activities from the scope of Regulation 479/92. As Regulation 823/2000 is based on Regulation 479/92, provisions of Regulation 823/2000 cannot be extended to such activities either. Therefore, Art. 3 Regulation 823/2000 does not cover inland activities.

The only inland activities that may be carried out by a consortium under the block exemption of Art. 3 Regulation 823/2000 are those that are explicitly mentioned in Art. 3 II lit. a ii Regulation 823/2000 (pooling of port installations) and Art. 3 II lit. c Regulation 823/2000 (joint operation of port terminals and related services). It has been suggested that already the joint installation of port facilities is not covered by these provisions[242]. Such an interpretation does not conform to the intention of Regulation 823/2000, which is to foster the ra-

237 Ginderachter/Durande, ETL (1996), p. 241 ff, p. 250; Immenga/Mestmäcker, Vol. 2, Basedow, p. 2084,rec. 12; Ruttley, ETL (1993), p. 487 ff, p. 493.
238 OJ (1990), C-167/9.
239 Ginderachter/Durande, ETL (1996), p. 241 ff, p. 250.
240 OJ (1991), C-305/35.
241 Ginderachter/Durande, ETL (1996), p. 241 ff, p. 250.
242 Immenga/Mestmäcker, Vol. 2, (1997), Basedow, p. 2086, rec. 19.

tionalisation of maritime transport services. Rationalisation may not only occur through the use of port facilities, but also during their construction. For this reason, Art. 3 Regulation 823/2000 should be interpreted accordingly. Any other land transport activities are subject to Regulation 1017/68. Inland activities that do not constitute transport services fall under Regulation 17/62. In order to avoid a conflict with Art. 81 I (ex 85 I) EC it is necessary to apply for an individual exemption in such situations.

f) Consortia and capacity management programmes

Under Art. 3 Regulation 4056/86 it was highly disputed as to what extend liner conferences were permitted to operate capacity management programmes. The position is much clearer under Regulation 823/2000. Arts. 3 II lit. b juncto 4 Regulation 823/2000 allow temporary capacity adjustments. These programmes may not be simply an agreement with the effect that a certain percentage of the available container slots stays empty; instead such agreements must lead to a reduction in the number of sailings or the size of the vessels commissioned to the service on a certain route[243]. The Commission ensured through this limitation that the same rules apply to capacity reduction arrangements that are permissible for liner conferences in accordance with the *TAA* Decision and to capacity reduction arrangements of consortia suitable for exemption under Art. 3 II lit. b juncto 4 Regulation 823/2000. The Commission thereby avoided that conference carriers circumvent the *TAA* Decision through a transfer of the clauses on capacity management that were not considered to be exemptable under Art. 3 Regulation 4056/86 to a consortium agreement that exists within a conference[244].

3) Conclusion

The analysis of the block exemption for liner conferences has demonstrated that it is necessary to interpret Art. 3 Regulation 4056/86 and related provisions in a narrow manner. The CFI and the Commission follow this principle as can be seen from their rulings and Decisions on inland price fixing, capacity management programmes and the availability of individual service contracts, where they both firmly rejected any attempts on the part of the conference carriers to interpret Art. 3 Regulation 4056/86 in their favour.

It has been noted above that the general principles of EC competition law embodied in Arts. 81 and 82 (ex 85 and 86) EC are fully applicable in the maritime transport sector[245]. The principal idea behind Art. 81 (ex 85) EC is that competitive markets are the best way to ensure efficiency, increased innovation,

[243] Ginderachter/Durande, ETL (1996), p. 241 ff, p. 254.

[244] Commission working document on Regulation 870/95, (1999) rec. 57.

[245] See above, p. 54 ff.

lower prices and, as a consequence, optimal resource allocation[246]. The applicability of Art. 81 (ex 85) EC in the field of maritime transport has been acknowledged by Recitals 1 and 13 of the Preamble to Regulation 4056/86, the latter of which states that *"there can be no exemption if the conditions set out in Article 85 (3) are not satisfied"*. Regulation 4056/86 contains several provisions that have the purpose of avoiding such a violation of Art. 81 III (ex (85 III) EC. Yet, it has been demonstrated that the effectiveness of these provisions is limited. They do not decisively limit the power of conferences to fix the price for maritime transport operations. The CFI and the Commission, which have both shown their will to interpret Art. 3 Regulation 4056/86 in a restrictive manner, have also not challenged the general assumption that price fixing in liner shipping is beneficial for the liner shipping markets, contrary to traditional economic beliefs. The often-found statement that liner shipping requires such a special treatment due to the peculiar characteristics of this industry has been evaluated and dismissed in the preceding chapter on liner shipping economics. Nevertheless, Regulation 4056/86 relys exactly on this assumption by stating that stability and efficiency in the markets for liner shipping may not be achieved *"without the cooperation that shipping companies promote within conferences in relation to rates"*[247]. For these reasons, it is justified to ask whether Regulation 4056/86 conforms to Art. 81 III (ex 85 III) EC or whether a group exemption for price fixing cartels cannot be reconciled with this provision.

The preceding analysis of the consortia block exemption contained in Regulation 823/2000 has demonstrated that it is far less controversial than the block exemption for conference agreements. Regulation 823/2000 does not exempt any joint activities in connection with the fixing of prices. The problematic areas of inland transport, capacity management and the availability of individual service contracts are regulated in a precise manner. It may be argued that the existence of such precise rules[248] in Regulation 823/2000 results from the fact that the Commission had already experienced severe problems in relation to liner conferences on these issues[249]. The Commission also demonstrated its positive attitude towards a block exemption for consortia through the fact that it was prepared to extend the block exemption for another five years without substantial amendments[250]. These circumstances indicate that Regulation 823/2000

---

246 Bellamy/Child, (1993), p. 35, rec. 1-075.

247 See: Recital 8 of the Preamble to Regulation 5067/86.

248 Compare for example Art. 3 lit. d Regulation 4056/86 and Art. 3 II lit. b Regulation 823/2000.

249 Proceedings in the FEFC affair began in 1989 and in the TAA affair in 1992.

250 Commission working document on Regulation 870/95, (1999), rec. 145.

has far less potential for conflict with Art. 81 III (ex 85 III) EC than Regulation 4056/86.

Chapter six - The liner conference block exemption and relevant provisions of the EC Treaty

The preceding chapter has paved the way for the last and crucial question concerning the relationship between conferences and consortia and European competition law. The question that remains is whether or not the block exemptions for liner conferences and consortia are compatible with the EC Treaty and especially with Art. 81 (ex 85) EC. The analysis will begin with an evaluation of the scope of Art. 81 (ex 85) EC in relation to liner shipping, followed by an evaluation of Art. 3 Regulation 4056/86 in the light of Art. 81 (ex 85) EC and other relevant Treaty provisions and finally focus on the compatibility of Art. 3 Regulation 823/2000 with the EC Treaty.

Art. 81 I (ex 85 I) EC contains a definition of such practices, which constitute a restriction to competition and which, as a consequence, are incompatible with the Common Market. Measures that fall under Art. 81 I (ex 85 I) EC are regularly automatically void, according to Art. 81 II (ex 85 II) EC. There is, however, one important exception to this rule, which is in turn embodied in Art. 81 III (ex 85 III) EC. This provision lays down criteria under which the behaviour in question may be exempted from the prohibition of Art. 81 I (ex 85 I) EC because of its overall economic utility, even though it constitutes a restriction to competition in the sense of Art. 81 I (ex 85 I) EC. The evaluation of the block exemption for price fixing activities in liner shipping follows this pattern. After an examination of the scope of Art. 81 (ex 85) EC the analysis of price fixing arrangements of liner conferences will first focus on the question of whether or not such a conduct constitutes a restriction of competition according to Art. 81 I (ex 85 I) EC. In case this question is answered in the affirmative, it is then necessary, as a second step, to find out if price fixing activities of liner carriers fulfil the criteria for exemption laid down in Art. 81 III (ex 85 III) EC.

1. Applicability of Art. 81 (ex 85) EC to liner shipping

It has been described in chapter three how the ECJ through a string of rulings established that the Treaty provisions on competition are applicable to the sector of maritime transport[1]. However, Art. 81 (ex 85) EC can only be applied to agreements in liner shipping if the geographical as well as the personal scope of that provision permits its application to such activities.

a) The geographical scope of Art. 81 (ex 85) EC

The geographical scope of Art. 81 (ex 85) EC requires limitation in two directions. On the one hand, the scope of Art. 81 (ex 85) EC must be defined in

---

[1] See above, p. 54 ff.

situations where that provision is applied to circumstances that have a link to natural or legal persons outside the EC, and, on the other hand, it is necessary to determine the scope of Art. 81 (ex 85) EC in relationship to equivalent provisions of the Member States.

aa) The extraterritorial application of Art. 81 (ex 85) EC

Agreements among liner shipping operators are predestined to raise the question of the extraterritorial application of Art. 81 (ex 85) EC, since the partners of such agreements are normally not only undertakings from the EC, but also from abroad[2]. Art. 299 I (ex 227 I) EC lays down the geographical scope of the EC Treaty in general. It is defined therein that the application of the EC Treaty is confined to the area of the Member States. As a consequence, any application of EC Treaty provisions that affects third countries, their citizens or commercial entities that are established abroad, warrants a special justification.

Some legal writers turned to the expression "*which may affect trade between Member States*" in their search for an answer to the question of the extraterritorial application of Art. 81 (ex 85) EC. They were of the opinion that this clause expressly regulates the international applicability of Art. 81 (ex 85) EC[3]. Today, most legal writers agree that this expression does not regulate the international applicability of Art. 81 (ex 85) EC, but that its purpose is to define the relationship between Art. 81 (ex 85) EC and parallel provisions in the legal orders of the Member States[4]. The wording of Art. 81 (ex 85) EC, as well as the fact that the Treaty does not contain provisions that govern the extraterritorial application of its rules in other places, support the latter interpretation of Art. 81 (ex 85) EC[5]. Due to the absence of any Treaty provisions that expressly regulate the extraterritorial application of Art. 81 (ex 85) EC, the answer to this problem may instead be found in an analysis of the material scope of that provision[6]. In this respect, the above cited clause from Art. 81 I (ex 85 I) EC does play an important role.

Since the extraterritorial application of Community competition law necessarily touches upon the legal orders of third countries, fundamental principles of public international law that have the purpose of balancing the differing interests of the affected states also influence the application of EC competition law in such

---

[2] Kühne, (1996), p. 87.

[3] Jacobs, (1991), p. 48; Meessen, EuR (1973), p. 18 ff, p. 22.

[4] Immenga/Mestmäcker, Vol. 1, (1997), Rehbinder, p. 70, rec. 50; Kühne, (1996), p. 88; Meessen, EuR (1973), p. 18 ff, p. 22.

[5] Jacobs, (1991), p. 49.

[6] Immenga/Mestmäcker, Vol. 1, (1997), Rehbinder, p. 70, rec. 50; Jacobs, (1991), p. 49; Kühne, (1996), p. 88.

incidents. In this respect, it is important to note that the Member States have equipped the EC with legal personality in the sphere of public international law by virtue of Art. 281 (ex 210) EC[7]. As a consequence, the EC is obliged to obey any relevant fundamental principles of public international law. The paramount principle of public international law in this respect is the principle of sovereign equality. According to this principle, all states have the same formal legal position, irrespective of such factors as territorial size, population, wealth or military might[8]. In order to protect the formal equality of all states, no state has the right to interfere with domestic affairs of other states[9]. The EC has to respect this principle of public international law in its application of Art. 81 (ex 85) EC[10].

aaa) The principle of territoriality and the doctrine of effects

The principle of sovereign equality does not restrict the application of domestic laws solely to the territory of the state in question, in the case of the EC to the territory of her Member States[11]. This position was already acknowledged in the *Lotus* decision[12] of the Permanent Court of International Justice in 1927, in which the court was of the opinion that states have a wide discretion when it comes to the application of their domestic laws to persons, property and acts outside their own territory, but that public international law in some situations limits this power. As far as the extraterritorial application of competition law is concerned, there are two main positions on how such an application must be restricted.

The traditional principle that governs the applicability of domestic competition law to situations that involve third country nationals or undertakings established abroad, is the principle of territoriality. According to this principle, it is required that the situation in question is genuinely linked to the territory of the state that wishes to regulate the affair. An application of Art. 81 (ex 85) EC in consistency with this principle demands that the restrictive behaviour does at least partially take place on EC territory[13]. Another position, called the doctrine of effects, was developed in the U. S.. This principle shifts the emphasis away from the restrictive behaviour to the consequences of such a conduct. As a result, states may apply their domestic competition rules to all such situations, in which the consequences of anti-competitive behaviour are felt within their ter-

[7] Ipsen, (1999), p. 77, rec. 19.
[8] Ipsen, (1999), p. 329, rec. 7 f.
[9] G/T/E, Vol. 5, (1997), Meng, p. 1224, rec. 34.
[10] Jacobs, (1991), p. 52.
[11] Ipsen, (1999), p. 285, rec. 94.
[12] PCIJ Ser. A, No. 10, (1927), p. 18 f.
[13] Meessen, EuR (1973), p. 18 ff, p. 20.

ritory[14], even if the conduct originates in another state. In order to counterbalance the interests of both states, the application of domestic competition law is only permissible in such situations, wherein the consequences of the anti-competitive conduct are substantial, direct and forseeable[15].

bbb) The position of the ECJ and the Commission

Until the present day, the position of the ECJ on the question of the extraterritorial application of EC law has remained somewhat ambiguous[16]. The Court first touched upon the subject of extraterritoriality in the *Béguelin* case[17], which was concerned with an exclusive distribution agreement between a producer of disposable cigarette lighters established in Japan and a French, as well as a Belgian distributor. The Court stated in its judgement that it is irrelevant if one of the partners to the agreement is established in a non-EC country, as long as the effects of the agreement occur within the EC[18]. This ruling seems to indicate that the ECJ accepted the doctrine of effects, even if the problem was only addressed *obiter dictum* in this case[19]. In a consecutive ruling, the so-called *Dyestuffs* case[20], the ECJ however demonstrated that it was not ready to accept this principle and that it relied on the concept of territoriality instead. That case concerned a secret price cartel of producers of dye; which was composed not only of companies from the different Member States, but also of companies from Switzerland and the United Kingdom[21]. The ECJ did not emphasise the fact that the consequences of the price agreement took effect within the Community, instead it considered Art. 81 (ex 85) EC to be applicable, because the agreement had been carried out on Community territory. In this respect, the Court focused on the fact that the EC-based subsidiary of the plaintiff increased the prices for sale within the Common Market in accordance with the cartel agreement concluded by the parenting company in the UK. The latter was responsible for actions of its subsidiary in the Community, since it was the UK-based parent company, which controlled the market behaviour of its subsidiary, established within the Community[22]. Due to this constellation, the non-EC company in the UK was held responsible for acts that took place within the Community.

---

[14] Ipsen, (1999), p. 288, rec. 100; Jones/Sufrin, (2001), p. 1041.

[15] G/T/E, Vol. 5, (1997), Meng, p. 1228, rec. 49; Ipsen, (1999), p. 288, rec. 100.

[16] Immenga/Mestmäcker, Vol. 1, (1997), Rehbinder, p. 71, rec. 56.

[17] Case 22/71, *Béguelin Import Co. v S.A.G.L. Import Export*, (1971), ECR, p. 949 ff.

[18] Case 22/71, *Béguelin Import Co. v S.A.G.L. Import Export,* (1971), ECR, p. 949 ff, p. 959 f, rec. 10/12.

[19] The ECJ did not have to decide on the extraterritorial application of EC competition law in the *Béguelin* case, since the Japanese producer was not party to the proceedings.

[20] Case 48/69, *Imperial Chemical Industries Ltd. v Commission,* (1972), ECR, p. 619 ff.

[21] At that time the United Kingdom was not yet a member of the then EEC.

[22] Case 48/69, *Imperial Chemical Industries Ltd. v Commission*, (1972), ECR, p. 619 ff, p. 665, rec. 125 ff.

The last major judgement in which the ECJ considered the question of the extraterritorial application of Art. 81 (ex 85) EC was the *Wood Pulp* case[23]. This time, the case concerned agreements among non-European producers of wood pulp, and again the Court was not ready to fully accept the doctrine of effects[24]. The ECJ acknowledged that it was too narrow an interpretation of Art. 81 (ex 85) EC to demand that an agreement be formed on EC territory. Instead, the Court saw a link to Community territory by emphasising that the cartel in question was implemented on the territory of the Member States and, as a consequence, found Art. 81 (ex 85) EC to be applicable based on the principle of territoriality[25]. The Court was prepared to adopt a wide definition of the term *implementation* of an agreement by stating that it was sufficient for the implementation of an agreement on EC territory to engage in a transaction with a consumer in the EC, according to the rules of an agreement that was formed outside the EC[26]. In departure from its earlier ruling in *Dyestuffs*, the Court did not consider the existence of subsidiaries, agencies or branches within the EC necessary[27].

It has been stated that the Court's ruling in *Wood Pulp* must be considered as an acceptance of the principle of effects[28]. Although it is true that the Court also referred to the impact of the price cartel on the Common Market[29], it is not sound to infer from this fact that the Court implicitly accepted the doctrine of effects. AG *Darmon*, as well as the Commission, explicitly referred to the principle of effects. The absence of any statement to that effect in the Court's own judgement must be understood as a refusal to accept this principle[30]. Nevertheless, the position of the Court is not radically different from that of those who rely on the principle of effects[31].

From the beginning, the Commission based its decisions on the applicability of Art. 81 (ex 85) EC to agreements or practices including non-EC undertakings, more on the effect of the conduct in question, than on the formation or imple-

---

[23] Joint cases 98, 104, 114, 116, 117 and 125 - 129/85, *A. Ahlström Osakeyhtiö and others v Commission*, 1988), ECR, p. 5193 ff.

[24] Immenga/Mestmäcker, Vol. 1, (1997), Rehbinder, p. 72, rec. 57.

[25] Joint cases, 98, 104, 114, 116, 117 and 125 - 129/85, *A. Ahlström Osakeyhtiö and others v Commission*, (1988), ECR, p. 5193 ff, p. 5243, rec. 16 - 18.

[26] Lange/Sandage, CMLR (1989), p. 137 ff, p. 155.

[27] Joint cases, 98, 104, 114, 116, 117 and 125 - 129/85, *A. Ahlström Osakeyhtiö and others v Commission*, (1988), ECR, p. 5193 ff, p. 5243, rec. 17.

[28] Jacobs, (1991), p. 50.

[29] Joint cases, 98, 104, 114, 116, 117 and 125 - 129/85, *A. Ahlström Osakeyhtiö and others v Commission*, (1988), ECR, p. 5193 ff, p. 5242 f, rec. 12 ff.

[30] Lange/Sandage, CMLR (1989), p. 137 ff, p. 157.

[31] Immenga/Mestmäcker, Vol. 1, (1997), Rehbinder, p. 72, rec. 58.

mentation of such agreements[32]. In the *Grosfillex* Decision[33], the agreement in question was concluded between a French and a Swiss undertaking. The Commission did not especially mention the problem of extraterritoriality, but it focused only on the consequences of that agreement for the Common Market, which may be viewed as a first indication that this criterion is of paramount importance for the Commission. In the subsequent *Bendix* Decision[34], which was concerned with an agreement between an American and a Belgian undertaking, the Commission was more outspoken. It was explicitly stated therein that even though one of the partners to the agreement was established outside the Community, this did not constitute an obstacle to the application of Art. 81 (ex 85) EC because it is sufficient, in this respect, that the agreement take effect within the confines of the Common Market.

In the *Dystuffs* Decision[35], the opinion of the Commission differed from that of the ECJ. For the Commission, the behaviour of the non-EC parenting company was in itself the reason for an infringement of Art. 81 (ex 85) EC[36], and, therefore, the Commission did not have to take recourse to the construction of accountability as did the ECJ. The clearest confirmation of the effects principle by the Commission is contained in the *Wood Pulp* Decision[37]. Therein, it emphasised again the importance of the effects of the agreement in question and then went on to state that these effects were not only substantial, but also intended[38] and the primary and direct result of the agreement in question[39]. This limitation of the applicability of Art. 81 (ex 85) EC has the purpose of ensuring that the interests of other states are duly respected, as demanded by public international law. The fact that the Commission also referred to the implementation of the agreement in the form of direct exports from the non-EC undertakings into the Community, as well as to the circumstance that some of those undertakings had subsidiaries, agencies or other establishments within the Com-

---

[32] Jacobs, (1991), p. 50.

[33] "*Grosfillex-Fillistorf*", OJ, (1964), 58/915.

[34] "*Bendix*", OJ, (1964), 92/1426.

[35] "*Dyestuffs*", OJ, (1969), L-195/11.

[36] "*Dyestuffs*", OJ, (1969), L-195/11, p.13.

[37] "*Wood Pulp*", OJ, (1985), L-85/1.

[38] On this point, the American and the European position differ. Whereas the Commission demands that the consequences must have been *intentional*, U. S. legislation only requires them to be *forseeable*. Another difference between the EC and the U. S. position is that the U. S. also consider their laws to be applicable in situations where a restriction to competition is only *probable*. The EC, on the other hand, only applies Art. 81 (ex 85) EC to *actual* restrictions of competition; per: G/T/E, Vol. 5, (1997), Meng, p. 1227, Rec. 45; Lange/Sandage, CMLR (1989), p. 137 ff, p. 162.

[39] "Wood Pulp", OJ, (1985), L-85/1, rec. 79.

munity, is merely an ancillary way of reasoning[40], in order to conform to the jurisdiction of the ECJ.

ccc) Evaluation

The position of the Commission is preferable to that of the ECJ. One criticism of the approach of the Court is that the concept of creating a territorial link through the implementation of a foreign agreement within the EC forms at best a quasi-territorial basis[41] for jurisdiction. It is difficult to understand how the mere import of goods or services into the area of the Common Market is sufficient to create a *genuine* territorial link to the EC and its jurisdiction. One possible explanation for the reluctance of the Court to accept the principle of effects may be the fact that this rule has not gained universal acceptance so far. The ECJ might also have hesitated to expressly confirm this principle since the UK vehemently argues against the principle of effects in the context of extraterritorial application of competition rules[42].

One of the main disadvantages of the position of the ECJ is that the principle of territoriality cannot form a coherent basis for the extraterritorial application of European competition law in a globalised economy[43]. Art. 81 (ex 85) EC focuses more on the economical consequences of restrictive practises and less on the question of where the agreement in question was formed or carried out. As a result, the principle of territoriality does not match the purpose and the wording or Art. 81 (ex 85) EC. The effects doctrine, on the other hand, does correspond to the purpose and the wording of this provision[44]. A good example that displays the inability of the concept of territoriality to function as a proper basis for the extraterritorial application of competition law is the change in the Court's own jurisdiction from the *Dyestuffs* to the *Wood Pulp* ruling. Whereas the ECJ in the former judgement considered it necessary for the establishment of a genuine territorial link to the EC that the undertaking in question be represented in the Community by a subsidiary, agent, or similar entity, it could not maintain this position in the latter ruling.

In this respect, it is also important to note that the application of the principle of territoriality, as developed by the ECJ, may lead to arbitrary results. For example, if several non-EC producers agree on a selling price for their product and

---

[40] Immenga/Mestmäcker, Vol. 1, (1997), Rehbinder p. 73, rec. 59.

[41] Grabitz/Hilf, Vol. 1, (1999), Koch, pre Art. 85, p. 7, rec. 14; Lange/Sandage, CMLR (1989), p. 137 ff, p. 157.

[42] Lange/Sandage, CMLR (1989), p. 137 ff; p. 153 f.

[43] Per AG *Darmon* in: Joint cases, 98, 104, 114, 116, 117 and 125-129/85, *A. Ahlström Osakeyhtiö and others v Commission*, (1988), ECR, p. 5193 ff, p. 5224.

[44] Immenga/Mestmäcker, Vol. 1, (1997) Rehbinder, p. 73, rec. 60; Knebel, EuZW (1991), p. 265 ff, p. 266.

later on only some of them import these goods to the area of the Common Market, then only those members of the cartel would come under the jurisdiction of Art. 81 (ex 85) EC, in spite of the fact that all producers were partners of the restrictive agreement[45]. Another example would be, if several producers agree that some of them withdraw from the European Market in order to reduce the pressure of competition. In case of such behaviour, it would not be possible to subject those producers to the European jurisdiction, despite the adverse consequences of such conduct for the Common Market[46]. For these reasons, the principle of effects forms the only reasonable basis for the extraterritorial application of EC competition law[47].

The acceptance of the doctrine of effects as the valid basis for extraterritorial application of EC competition law in respect to liner shipping leads to the result that Art. 81 (ex 85) EC is applicable to all conference and consortia agreements, inbound and outbound, which call at ports within the Common Market. EC competition law is, however, not applicable to agreements that cover routes between third countries. such agreements may have a negative impact on the Common Market (e.g. through a re-direction of trade away from a Community port), but the impact would only be of an indirect nature and, as such, would not warrant a subjection to European jurisdiction[48].

bb) Art. 81 (ex 85) EC and correspondent domestic provisions of the Member States

As a second aspect of the geographical scope of Art 81 (ex 85) EC, it is necessary to define its relationship to equivalent provisions of the legal orders of the Member States. For this purpose, the clause "*which may affect trade between Member States*" constitutes the crucial element of Art. 81 (ex 85) EC. First, the analysis of this expression will focus on its interpretation by the ECJ, the CFI and the Commission. In a second step, it is then necessary to establish how Art. 81 (ex 85) EC regulates any possible conflict with equivalent provisions of the Member States.

aaa) Liner conferences and their effect on trade between the Member States

The Court interpreted the above quoted expression in a very broad way. According to the ECJ, any agreement has an effect on trade between the Member States if it is reasonably forseeable "*that the agreement in question may have an*

[45] Immenga/Mestmäcker, Vol. 1, (1997), Rehbinder, p. 72, rec. 57.
[46] Grabitz/Hilf, Vol. 1, (1999), Koch, pre Art. 85, p. 7, rec. 14; Immenga/Mestmäcker, Vol. 1, (1997), Rehbinder, p. 72, rec. 57.
[47] Grabitz/Hilf, Vol. 1, (1999), Koch, pre Art. 85, p. 7, rec. 14; Kühne, (1996), p. 89.
[48] Grabitz/Hilf, Vol. 1, (1999), Koch, pre Art. 85, p. 6a, rec. 11; Jacobs, (1991), p. 54.

influence, direct or indirect, actual or potential, on the pattern of trade between Member States"[49]. In practice, this requirement is met if the agreement leads to a change in trade flows[50] or if the competitive structure within the Common Market experiences an appreciable alteration[51]. Due to this wide interpretation, a large number of agreements falls within the scope of Art. 81 (ex 85) EC[52].

Trade in the sense of Art. 81 I (ex 85 I) EC does not only include trade in goods, but also the provision of services[53], such as scheduled maritime transport. Conference agreements that cover routes between two or more Community ports or such agreements that regulate shipping from ports within the Common Market to ports situated abroad, are capable of influencing trade patterns between the Member States and thus they fall within the scope of Art. 81 (ex 85) EC[54]. The CFI and the Commission have identified several ways in which agreements in liner shipping may influence trade patterns between the Member States. Through centralised cargo allocation, they have the power to decide on the ports through which the goods enter the Common Market. Conferences and consortia may thereby alter the amount of goods that is shipped through one port or another, which in turn has an effect on competition between the different ports in the different Member States[55]. Apart from having an influence on competition between ports, the choice of ports may also affect the flow of goods in-between Member States. Most goods require further transport from the port to their final destination inland. If conference agreements have an effect on the cargo volumes of different ports, they consecutively also influence the pattern of the successive land transport operation[56]. Since the final destination of the transported goods is not necessarily situated in the same Member State, as the port through which the goods entered the Community, this effect may also take place in the sphere between the Member States. Another way in which conference agreements in particular may exert influence over trade patterns between the Member States is through the reduction of competition on prices. Carriers that operate efficiently cannot convert this advantage into a larger market share, since they are not allowed to pass their cost advantage on to

---

[49] Case 56/65, *Société Technique Minière v Maschinenbau Ulm GmbH,* (1966), ECR, p. 282 ff, p. 303.
[50] Bellamy/Child, (1993), p. 110, rec. 2-129.
[51] Bellamy/Child, (1993), p. 113, rec. 2-131.
[52] Bellamy/Child, (1993), p. 108 f, rec. 2-128; Craig/de Burca, (1998), p. 915.
[53] G/T/E, Vol. 2/1 (1999), Schröter, Art. 85, p. 230, rec. 164.
[54] Kühne, (1996), p. 93 f.
[55] Case T-86/95, *Compagnie générale maritime and others v Commission*, (2002), ECR II, p. 1011 ff, rec. 147; "*FETTSCA*", OJ, (2000), L-268/1, rec. 140 f.
[56] "*FETTSCA*", OJ, (2000), L-268/1 rec. 142; Case T-395/94, *Atlantic Container Line and others v Commission*, (2002), ECR II, p. 875 ff, rec. 81.

their customers[57]. For these reasons, conference and consortia agreements constitute agreements that have an effect on trade between the Member States in the sense of Art. 81 (ex 85) EC.

bbb) The concept of "*effect on trade between Member States*" as a rule of jurisdiction

Another consequence of the expansive interpretation of the scope of Art. 81 (ex 85) EC by the ECJ, is the fact that in many situations Art. 81 (ex 85) EC and comparable domestic provisions of the Member States may both be applicable. Since domestic and European competition law is by no means required to be identical, situations are likely to arise where the application of these provisions imposes a duty upon the addressees to comply with contradictory measures. It is, therefore, necessary to reconcile the application of Art. 81 (ex 85) EC with that of equivalent domestic provisions of the Member States. The clause "*which may affect trade between Member States*" has the purpose of defining the relationship between Art. 81 (ex 85) EC on the Community level and the relevant national provisions[58]

(1) The *double hurdle* test

The traditional position on the resolution of a jurisdictional conflict between national provisions of the Member States and Art. 81 (ex 85) EC was that both laws have a different purpose and that they, therefore, coexist on an equal footing next to each other[59]. It is the object of national provisions to protect an environment of free competition within the single Member States. On the Other hand, Art. 81 (ex 85) EC intends to ensure fair competition in relation to trade between the Member States. Due to this difference in purpose, a conflict between the two provisions is deemed not possible[60], and they can both be applied to the same agreement. An agreement is permissible if it masters both hurdles, the one established through Art. 81 (ex 85) EC, as well as the one imposed by Member State law. If the agreement fails to pass either of these two hurdles, it then is illegal and must be abandoned. This rule has been called the factual precedent of the stricter rule[61], since it is always the stricter law that dictates whether or not an agreement is legal. As a consequence, it may be possible that an agreement is successfully prohibited through an action of a national author-

[57] "*FETTSCA*", OJ, (2000), L-268/1, rec. 140; "*FEFC*", OJ, (1999), L-95/1, rec. 48.

[58] Cases 56 and 58/64, *Consten SARL & Grundig-Verkaufs GmbH v Commission*, (1966), ECR, p. 299 ff, p. 389; Bellamy/Child, (1993), p. 107, rec. 2-126; Jones/Sufrin, (2001), p. 121.

[59] Bunte, WuW (1989), p. 7 ff, p. 12.

[60] Grabitz/Hilf, Vol. 1, (1999), Koch, pre Art. 85, p. 11, rec. 31; Lieberkenecht, FS Pfeiffer, (1988), p. 589 ff, p. 591.

[61] Bunte, WuW (1989), p. 7 ff, p. 12.

ity, based on national law, even though it does not contradict Art. 81 (ex 85) EC[62].

(2) The position of the ECJ

The landmark ruling of the ECJ on this issue is the *Walt Wilhelm* judgement[63], which was concerned with a cartel of aniline producers from several Member States. In its judgement, the Court concurred with the above presented position insofar, as it stated that national rules, as well as Art. 81 (ex 85) EC may be applicable to the same agreement[64]. The Court then continued and stated that the application of domestic laws is only permissible under the condition that the uniform application of EC law throughout the Community is not endangered. If, however, an action of a national authority on the basis of relevant domestic laws is contradictory to a measure of the Commission based on Art. 81 (ex 85) EC, then the latter takes precedent over the former[65].

The ECJ established through this ruling that the principle of supremacy of EC law is also valid in the sphere of competition law[66]. The basis for this principle is the famous *Costa v. ENEL*[67] judgement of the ECJ. In the absence of any Treaty provisions on this issue, the Court therein adopted a teleological approach and founded the principle of supremacy on the fact that EC law is not simply public international law, but a new source of law, independent from the legal orders of the Member States. According to the ECJ, this special character of EC law warrants a doctrine of supremacy, otherwise the uniform application of EC law throughout the whole Community may be jeopardised. The supremacy of EC law is not absolute, but relative. Therefore, a national provision that is contradictory to Community law does not become automatically void, but is simply not applicable in a situation of conflict and therein the Community provision thus prevails[68].

(3) Evaluation

The opinion of the Court is preferable on several accounts. One argument is that the Court's position recognises that many agreements influence not only the economic situation within the individual Member States, but that they also affect economic relations in-between the Member States. The assumption that these two spheres are completely separate artificially divides one single factual

---

[62] Bunte, WuW (1989), p. 7 ff, p. 12; Gleiss/Hirsch, (1978), p. 40, rec. 58.
[63] Case 14/68, *Walt Wilhelm and others v Bundeskartellamt*, (1969), ECR, p. 1 ff.
[64] Case 14/68, *Walt Wilhelm and others v Bundeskartellamt,* (1969), ECR. p. 1 ff, p. 13, rec. 3.
[65] Case 14/68, *Walt Wilhelm and others v Bundeskartellamt,* (1969), ECR, p. 1 ff, p. 14, rec. 7.
[66] Bunte, WuW (1989), p. 7 ff, p. 12.
[67] Case 6/64, *Costa (Flaminio) v ENEL*, (1964), ECR, p. 585 ff.
[68] Streinz, (1999), p. 65, rec. 200; Zuleeg, EuR (1990), p. 123 ff, p.126 f.

situation into a Community and a domestic part, whereby in reality, no such division exists[69]. A second advantage of the position of the ECJ is that it ensures the uniform application of EC competition law throughout the Community. It has been described above how the application of the double hurdle test may lead to differences in the application of Art. 81 (ex 85) EC from Member State to Member State, depending on the domestic laws of the Member States[70]. The rules on competition play a central role for the establishment and the functioning of the Common Market and as a consequence, it is equally important that they are applied in the same way throughout the whole Community. Finally, it is possible to draw some support for the position of the Court from the Treaty itself. Art. 83 II lit. e (ex 87 II lit. e) EC empowers the Council to enact measures that are appropriate *to "determine the relationship between national laws and the provisions"* on competition, contained in the EC Treaty. This expression permits the conclusion that the Treaty itself envisions possible conflicts between domestic and European competition law. Hence, the double hurdle test, which negates the possibility of such conflicts, does not find the support of the Treaty.

(4) Resolution of jurisdictional conflicts in maritime transport according to the principle of supremacy

In the field of maritime transport, jurisdictional conflicts may primarily arise between Art. 81 (ex 85) EC, on the one hand, and domestic competition laws of the Member States, on the other hand, in consideration of the fact that Regulation 4056/86 exempts certain collusive practices of carriers from the prohibition contained in Art. 81 I (ex 85 I) EC. The ECJ stated in the *Walt Wilhelm* ruling that Art. 81 (ex 85) EC permits "*the Community authorities to carry out certain positive, though indirect, actions with a view to promoting a harmonious development of economic activities within the whole Community*"[71]. While it is clear that this expression is a reference to exemptions based on Art. 81 III (ex 85 III) EC[72], the exact meaning of this phrase is under dispute. According to one position, all exemptions based on Art. 81 III (ex 85 III) EC automatically take precedence over any conflicting national rules[73]. Others argue against such an automatism. It is their opinion that exemptions based on Art. 81 III (ex 85 III) EC only dominate over national laws of the Member States if the explicit purpose of the former is to promote a harmonious development of economic activ-

[69] Grabitz/Hilf, Vol. 1, (1999), Koch, pre Art. 81, p. 11, rec. 32.
[70] See above, p. 148.
[71] Case 14/68, *Walt Wilhelm and others v Bundeskartellamt*,(1969), ECR, p. 1 ff, p. 14, rec. 5.
[72] Gleiss/Hirsch, (1978), p. 41, rec. 61.
[73] Bunte, WuW (1989), p. 7 ff, p. 16 f; Gleiss/Hirsch, (1978), p. 42, rec. 62; Immenga/Mestmäcker, Vol. 1, (1997), Rehbinder, p. 103, rec. 18; Lieberknecht, FS Pfeiffer, (1988), p. 589 ff, p. 595 ff.

ity within the Community. This needs to be established individually in every single case[74].

The latter opinion is flawed insofar, as it does not take into account that the criteria for exemption laid down in Art. 81 III (ex 85 III) EC have the purpose of ensuring that restrictions to competition may only be legal if they somehow have a positive effect on the economy. Therefore, they ensure that any measures permissible under Art. 81 III (ex 85 III) EC promote, at the same time, a harmonious development of the economy within the Common Market. As a consequence, any exemption that complies with the conditions enumerated in Art. 81 III (ex 85 III) EC is automatically a positive measure in the sense of the *Walt Wilhelm* ruling[75].

The finding that exemptions under Art. 81 III (ex 85 III) EC always dominate over conflicting national rules is not only true for individual exemptions, but also for block exemptions. Already their function as a tool to replace a large number of individual exemptions through one legislative act indicates that both types of exemptions must be treated in the same manner[76]. Another argument to this effect is that Art. 81 III (ex 85 III) EC does not differentiate between block exemptions and individual exemptions; both have to fulfil the same criteria, as laid down in that provision[77]. For these reasons, the block exemptions contained in Regulations 4056/86 and 823/2000 take precedent over all conflicting measures adopted by national authorities, on the basis of domestic laws of the Member States.

b) The personal scope of Art. 81 (ex 85) EC

Addressees of Art. 81 (ex 85) EC are undertakings and associations of undertakings. Nowhere does the Treaty provide a definition of the term *undertaking* and it has been left up to the European Courts to fill in that gap through their jurisdiction. According to the ECJ, any entity that is engaged in an economic activity, regardless of its legal status and the way in which it is financed, constitutes an undertaking in the sense of Art. 81 (ex 85) EC[78]. The CFI ruled on this matter that undertakings are entities that are made up of a collection of physical and human resources which also pursue a defined commercial purpose with some permanence[79]. Carriers that operate liner shipping services do qualify as

[74] Bunte, WuW (1989), p. 7 ff, p. 15;

[75] Bunte, WuW (1989), p. 7 ff, p. 17; Lieberknecht, FS Pfeiffer, (1988), p. 589 ff, p. 596.

[76] Immenga/Mestmäcker, Vol. 1, (1997), Rehbinder, p. 105, rec. 24;Lieberkenecht, FS Pfeiffer, (1988), p. 589 ff, p. 597.

[77] Bunte, WuW (1989), p. 7 ff, p. 17; Lieberknecht, FS Pfeiffer, (1988), p. 589 ff, p. 597.

[78] Case C-41/90, *Höfer & Elser v Macroton GmbH*, (1991), ECR-I, p. 1979 ff, p. 1993.

[79] Case T-11/89, *Shell International Chemical Co. Ltd. v Commission*, (1992), ECR-II, p. 757 ff, p. 885, rec. 312.

undertakings in this sense. Therefore, the block exemptions in Art. 3 Regulation 4056/86 (conferences) and Art. 3 Regulation 823/2000 (consortia) are properly addressed to the carriers as undertakings.

The more interesting question is whether the personal scope of Art. 81 (ex 85) EC also includes conferences and consortia themselves as addressees and whether it would consequently be possible to address a measure based on that provision directly to a conference or consortium. Liner conferences would be directly subjected to Art. 81 (ex 85) EC if their actions constitute decisions by an association of undertakings. According to one position, conferences are not an association of undertakings. The basis for this opinion is the view that the expression *associations of undertakings* does not have a distinctive meaning next to the term *undertakings* in Art. 81 (ex 85) EC[80]. The assumption that there is no intended difference between these two expressions is difficult to maintain, since this would imply that there are redundant parts in such a condensed text as the EC Treaty. A better line of argument is to emphasise that conferences, and similarly consortia, are not sufficiently independent from their member carriers to be seen as associations of undertakings. As far as conferences are concerned, the conference secretary may only decide independently on matters of routine administration. All important decisions are taken by the owners committee, which is solely composed, as the name suggests, of representatives of the member carriers[81]. Therefore, the management of the conference is under the control of its members. The Commission decided in a similar situation concerning associations of steel producers that the fact that they were under the control of the senior management of their members precluded their subjection to Art. 81 (ex 85) EC[82]. For this reason, it is correct to say that conferences do not fall within the personal scope of Art. 81 (ex 85) EC and that it is not possible to address measures based on this provision directly against them.

2. Liner conferences and Art. 81 (ex 85) EC

Once it has been established that Art. 81 (ex 85) EC is applicable to conference and consortia agreements, even if they are not the direct addresses of this provision, the analysis will now focus on the compatibility of the block exemption for conference agreements in Art. 3 Regulation 4056/86 with Art. 81 (ex 85) EC.

a) Restriction to competition

Art. 81 I (ex 85 I) EC prohibits all agreements between undertakings that "*have as their object or effect the prevention, restriction or distortion of competition*

---

[80] Kühne, (1996), p. 84 f.

[81] See above, p. 44.

[82] "*Welded Steel Mesh*", OJ, (1989), L-260/1, rec. 207.

within the common market". The Council expressed its fear of such a negative impact of liner conferences on competition within the Community in the Preamble to Regulation 4056/86. This Regulation not only exempts price fixing activities of liner conferences in Art. 3, but also specified types of co-operation of a more technical nature by virtue of Art. 2. The Council stated in Recital 9 of the Preamble to Regulation 4056/86 that the reason for the latter exemption is the fact that these technical agreements normally do not constitute a restriction to competition[83]. The absence of such a statement in relation to the exemption for price fixing activities is a first indication that the Council was of the opinion that such conduct has a negative impact on competition within the Common Market. This impression is confirmed by the fact that the Council defines the object of Regulation 4056/86 in relation to price fixing activities among carriers as the prevention of unnecessary restrictions to competition[84]. The Council thereby expresses its belief that price fixing constitutes a restriction to competition in the sense of Art. 81 I (ex 85 I) EC. It is the purpose of the following analysis to establish whether or not such an assumption of the Council holds true.

aa) Price fixing of liner conferences and the mechanisms of Art. 81 (ex 85) EC

Disagreement exists over the question of how to proceed with the analysis of the block exemption for price fixing arrangements in liner shipping. It has been argued that those who oppose a block exemption for price fixing in the maritime industry must justify their view, as they demand a change from the current regulatory system and therefore carry the burden of proof[85]. In terms of EC competition law this would mean that it is necessary to establish that joint price fixing of liner conferences actually constitutes a restriction of competition according to Art. 81 I (ex 85 I) EC[86].

Others emphasise that those who seek an exemption from the normal application of competition law must show that such an exemption is possible on grounds of public interest[87]. In the sphere of EC competition law this position

[83] It may be argued that it is not possible to exempt certain types of conduct from the prohibition of Art. 81 I (ex 85 I) EC, if they do not contravene that provision; the rationale for Art. 2 Regulation 4056/86 is, however, to relievethe Commission from the workload connected to the adoption of a large number of individual decisions concerning such agreements, which justifies the incorporation of Art. 2 into Regulation 4056/86.

[84] Recital 12 of the Preamble to Regulation 4056/86.

[85] Brian Mankins, submission to the Australian Productivity Commission, (1999), p. 6; WSC submission to the OECD, (2001), p. iii.

[86] This position is doubtful insofar, as there is a general rule of interpretation that renders it necessary to justify any derogations from a basic principle and not vice versa.

[87] ESC submission to the OECD, (2001), p. 3-4.

would mean that it is necessary to show that a regime that allows joint price fixing agreements of liner conferences, fulfils the criteria for exemption laid down in Art. 81 III (ex 85 III) EC. The question remains as to whether joint price fixing constitutes *per se* a restriction to competition in the sense of Art. 81 I (ex 85 I) EC that may be exempted according to Art. 81 III (ex 85 III) EC, or whether it instead is necessary to prove that joint price fixing of liner conferences has such a detrimental impact on the Common Market that it constitutes a restriction to competition in accordance to Art. 81 I (ex 85 I) EC? This question may become relevant in connection with the re-evaluation of Regulation 4056/86, which is carried out by the Commission[88]. Only if the latter position holds true, is the Commission required to actually establish the fact that price fixing in liner shipping has a negative impact on the economy within the Common Market.

bb) The *Rule of Reason* and *per se* restrictions to competition

The concept of a *rule of reason* in competition law originates from United States antitrust law. It means that antitrust provisions do not prohibit all agreements that restrain competition, but only those that restrict competition unreasonably. In order to decide whether or not a restriction to competition is reasonable, it is necessary to identify the pro- and anti-competitive effects of an agreement and to weigh them against each other, for the purpose of establishing whether or not the agreement has an overall positive or negative impact on competition within the Common Market[89]. A transfer of this approach to EC competition law would necessitate the interpretation of the prohibition contained in Art. 81 I (ex 85 I) EC in such a way that not all agreements restricting competition be prohibited, but only those that cannot be justified on an objective basis[90]. In the ECJ's jurisprudence, there is a line of cases in which the Court expresses its favour for such an approach[91]. The Court did not go so far as to expressly adopt the rule of reason doctrine, since it did not use this expression in any of these rulings. On the other hand, the ECJ stated that it is necessary for the purposes of Art. 81 I (ex 85 I) EC to judge an agreement in its actual economic context[92]. The Court was prepared to rule that those parts of an agreement that have some negative impact on competition within the Common Market nevertheless do not constitute a restriction to competition in the sense of

---

[88] For a good description of that review process see: Stragier, (2002), p. 9 ff.

[89] Craig/de Burca, (1998), p. 904.

[90] Bellamy/Child, (1993), p. 79, rec. 2-080.

[91] Case 56/65, *SociétéTechnique Minière v Maschinenbau Ulm GmbH*, (1966), ECR, p. 282 ff; Case 42/84, *Remia BV and others v Commission*, (1985), ECR, p. 2545 ff; Case 161/84, *Pronuptia*, (1986), ECR, p. 353 ff.

[92] Case 56/65, *Société Technique Minière v Maschinenbau Ulm GmbH*, (1966), ECR, p. 282 ff, p. 303; Case 161/84, *Pronuptia*, (1986), ECR, p. 353 ff, p 384, rec. 27.

Art. 81 I (ex 85 I) EC, because the positive impact of these clauses was predominant[93].

These rulings indicate that the ECJ tends to balance the advantages and the disadvantages of an agreement in relation to competition, and if the former prevail, then the agreement does not restrict competition in the sense of Art. 81 I (ex 85 I) EC[94]. In case this approach could be applied to price fixing arrangements of liner conferences, a situation might arise where arguments have to be brought forward to justify that such conference activities actually constitute a restriction of competition. This would conform to the first opinion presented above.

However, the rule of reason approach cannot be applied to price fixing arrangements of maritime carriers. First, there are doubts as to whether a rule of reason approach is correct at all under Art. 81 I (ex 85 I) EC. The EC Treaty provides Art. 81 III (ex 85 III) EC as a means of recognising that some practises, which restrict competition, are beneficial and, therefore, should not be prohibited by EC competition law[95]. United States antitrust legislation does not contain an equivalent provision[96]. Consequently, there is much greater need for including a rule of reason in the definition of what constitutes a restraint of trade under United States law than in the definition of what is a restriction of competition under EC law. In the latter body of law such a doctrine is not necessary, as Art. 81 III (ex 85 III) EC already provides for a possibility of recognising positive aspects of agreements that restrict competition[97], by allowing their exemption from the prohibition contained in Art. 81 I (ex 85 I) EC.

Second, the CFI has recognised that some practises *per se* constitute a restriction of competition, regardless of any positive impact they may have on competition[98]. In such situations, there is no room for the application of the rule of

---

[93] For example, in the *Maschinenbau Ulm* ruling the Court stressed that an exclusive distribution agreement does not constitute a restriction to competition since such an agreement allows an undertaking to penetrate a new market. Another example of the Court's way of thinking is its ruling in *Remia*. The ECJ had to establish *inter alia* whether or not a non-competition clause in connection with the sale of a business constituted a restriction to competition. Even though the Court was of the opinion that the agreed 10-year span of such a clause was too long, it stated in a more general way that such clauses not necessarily constitute a restriction of competition, since they may be necessary in order to make the sale of the business possible at all.

[94] Bellamy/Child, (1993), p. 68 f, rec. 2-063.

[95] Craig/de Burca, (1998), p. 905; Immenga/Mestmäcker, Vol 1, (1997), Emmerich, p. 190, rec. 259.

[96] Jones/Sufrin, (2001), p. 143.

[97] Immenga/Mestmäcker, Vol. 1, (1997), Emmerich, p. 190. rec. 259.

[98] Case T-141/89, *Montepide SpA v Commission*, (1992), ECR II, p. 1155 ff, p. 1246, rec. 265; CaseT-148/89, *Tréfilunion v Commission*, (1995), ECR II, p. 1063 ff, p. 1108, rec. 109.

reason doctrine[99]. The price is the main instrument of competition. Agreements to fix prices are expressly prohibited by Art. 81 I lit. a (ex 85 I lit. a) EC. Such agreements would effectively exclude competition from the crucial part of any market. As a result, any agreement to fix prices would constitute, by its very nature, a restriction to competition within the meaning of Art. 81 I (ex 85 I) EC[100]. For these reasons, it is not possible to argue that price fixing arrangements, even if they do not raise prices above the market equilibrium, do not constitute a restriction to competition. Agreements to fix prices entered into by carriers, organised in a liner conference, constitute by their very nature a restriction of competition in the sense of Art. 81 I (ex 85 I) EC.

b) Regulation 4056/86 and Art. 81 III (ex 85 III) EC

The Final step of the evaluation of Regulation 4056/86 under Art. 81 (ex 85) EC is its analysis in the light of Art. 81 III (ex 85 III) EC. This provision contains four cumulative criteria that exempt agreements, which conform to these conditions, from the scope of the prohibition contained in Art. 81 I (ex 85 I) EC[101]. The general purpose of Art. 81 III (ex 85 III) EC is to exempt agreements from the prohibition in Art. 81 I (ex 85 I) EC, because they are beneficial to the public interest, even though they constitute a restriction to competition. Although Art. 81 III (ex 85 III) EC only makes explicit reference to goods, it is equally applicable to services[102]. In the Preamble to Regulation 4056/86 there are some general statements to the effect that a block exemption for liner conferences fulfils the criteria of Art. 81 III (ex 85 III) EC[103]. Yet, these statements do not indicate that there has been a thorough analysis of Art. 3 Regulation 4056/86 in light of the conditions, laid down in Art. 81 III (ex 85 III) EC[104]. As far as the position of the Commission is concerned, it has been stated repeatedly in the recent past that there is no need to change or even abolish the block exemption for price fixing activities of liner conferences[105]. Up until now, the standpoint of the Commission has been that Art. 3 Regulation 4056/86 must only be interpreted narrowly, in order to ensure its compliance with the EC Treaty[106]. However, the fact that the Commission has started a review process of Regulation 4056/86 may be a first indication for a change of position on the issue of price fixing in liner shipping within the Commission.

---

99 Immenga/Mestmäcker , Vol. 1, (1997), Emmerich, p. 190. rec. 259.

100 Joint Cases T-68/89, T-77/89, T-78/89, *Socieata Italiano Vetro v Commission*, (1992), ECR II, p. 1403 ff, p. 1539, rec. 350.

101 Grabitz/Hilf, Vol. 1, (1999), Koch, Art. 85, p. 38, rec. 155.

102 Bellamy/Child, (1993), p. 154, rec. 3-026.

103 Recital 8 of the Preamble to Regulation 4056/86.

104 Dolfen, (1991), p. 280.

105 Fitzgerald, (1999), p. 5; Pons, (2000), p. 15; Wood, (1999), p. 18.

106 Temple Lang, ETL (1993), p. 405 ff, p. 406.

aa) The positive conditions of Art. 81 III (ex 85 III) EC

The first requirement under Art. 81 III (ex 85 III) EC is that the agreement or the type of agreement must improve the production or distribution of goods or further technical or economic progress. The resulting benefit must at least partially be passed on to the consumers. Although the Treaty follows the basic principle that a competitive market is generally the best way to ensure an efficient allocation of resources[107], it is possible to depart from this fundamental assumption, if it can be shown that the restrictive agreement also results in objective benefits for the economy. In a balancing process this benefit must outweigh any negative consequences that accrue from such an agreement[108].

aaa) Volatility of rates

One alleged advantage of liner conferences is their stabilising effect on rates. Stable rates are beneficial for the customers of carriers insofar, as they have more certainty over the development of transport costs in the future. Already the Royal Commission on Shipping Rings and the Alexander Committee emphasised the positive impact that conferences have on rate stability[109]. However, the reality of the shipping industry does not support such a finding. The OECD asked interested parties to comment on the topic of regulatory reform in the maritime industry in the preparation of its recent study on this issue. Associations of shippers from the United States, Canada and Europe were among those who submitted statements to the OECD. They all conducted a survey among their members, which *inter alia* covered the topic of rate volatility. All three submissions stated that under the present system, which grants anti-trust immunity to price fixing agreements under the different legal orders, rates are more volatile than stable[110]. This finding was supported by the relevant numbers contained in each survey. It may be argued that such a result was foreseeable, as it suits the interests of the groups that conducted those surveys. Yet, even data provided by groups representing the liner shipping industry, which were arguing in favour of allowing joint price fixing, show that rates do not develop in a stable way[111]. As a result, the finding is true that liner conferences do not effectively stabilise rates.

---

[107] Grabitz/Hilf, Vol. 1, (1999), Koch, Art. 85, p. 41, rec. 162; Immenga/Mestmäcker, Vol. 1, (1997) Sauter, Art. 85, p. 346, rec. 6.

[108] Bellamy/Child, (1993), p. 155, rec. 3-027; G/T/E, Vol. 2/1, (1999), Schröter, Art. 85, p. 309, rec. 298; Immenga/Mestmäcker, Vol. 1, (1997), Sauter, Art. 85, p. 345, rec. 5.

[109] See above, p. 23 and p. 168.

[110] CSC submission to the OECD, (2001), p. 5 f; ESC submission to the OECD, (2001), p. 8; NITL submission to the OECD, (2001), p. 7.

[111] TSA submission to the OECD, (2001), exhibit 2 and 3; WSC submission to the OECD, (2001), p. 13 f; these groups have submitted data on rates to prove that the overall rate level dropped.

bbb) Higher standard of service

A second argument that has been advanced in favour of exempting price fixing activities of liner conferences from the prohibition in Art. 81 I (ex 85 I) EC is that such a behaviour is justified because conferences in return provide a higher level of service[112]. However, since the advent of container shipping, the maritime transport industry has witnessed the emergence of new independent operators that provide liner services of a quality that is comparable to that of conference carriers[113]. Through co-operation with land transport companies, they are also able to offer intermodal transport services. Consequently, the argument that conference services are of a distinctively higher quality in comparison to non-conference services has lost much of its virtue as a means to justify the existence of liner conferences.

ccc) The position of the Commission

The finding that price fixing agreements, such as liner conferences, do not conform to the requirements of Art. 81 III (ex 85 III) EC is backed up by several decisions of the Commission on this issue[114]. It is the position of the Commission that the assessment of the overall economic utility of an agreement must take into account the basic principles and objectives of the EC Treaty. If it is the foremost purpose of an agreement to reduce competition between the suppliers in a market, then such an agreement does not conform to the basic objectives of the Treaty[115], especially not to Art. 3 lit. g EC, which seeks to ensure a functioning system of competition within the Common Market. Price fixing agreements are designed to primarily protect the interests of the suppliers and as a consequence, they conflict with the basic principles of the Treaty[116]. Through this approach the Commission has established that price fixing is not an activity that corresponds to the conditions of Art. 81 III (ex 85 III) EC; a finding that is also applicable to price fixing in the liner shipping industry.

bb) Indispensability

Art. 81 III (ex 85 III) EC, furthermore, requires that the agreements in question, respectively the type of agreements in the case of block exemptions, be indispensable for the attainment of their objectives. Through this provision, the gen-

---

112 WSC submission to the OECD, (2001), p. 3.

113 Fink/Mattoo/Neagu, (2001), p. 9.

114 *"Papiers peints de Belgique"*, OJ, (1974), L-237/3; *"Preserved Mushrooms"*, OJ, (1975), L-29/26; *"Cast iron and steel rolls"*, OJ, (1983), L-317/1; *"Zink producer group"*, OJ, (1984), L-220/27.

115 *"Zink producer group"*, OJ, (1984), L-220/27, rec. 87.

116 *"Cast iron and steel rolls"*, OJ, (1983), L-317/1, rec. 61.

eral principle of proportionality[117] finds entry into the assessment of agreements under Art. 81 III (ex 85 III) EC[118]. An agreement is indispensable in the sense of that provision if it is not possible to realise the benefits that are supposed to arise out the agreement in the same period of time, to the same extent or with the same degree of probability through less restrictive means[119]. The Council stated in the Preamble to Regulation 4056/86 that liner conferences, which have the power to fix prices, are beneficial for the shipping industry, because they stabilise the markets for liner shipping and because they promote the provision of efficient, reliable and adequate shipping services[120].

It is doubtful, however, that collusive pricing practises of carriers are the only way to ensure a stable shipping industry. One argument featuring in this discussion is that only the existence of joint price fixing agreements ensures investments that lead to technological progress and thus enhanced efficiency of liner shipping[121]. On the other hand, many practises that have the purpose of increasing efficiency exist outside the framework of conference agreements[122]. The typical agreement that aims at a reduction of costs and an enhancement of service quality is the consortium, which does not include rules on price fixing.

The underlying rationale for the different kinds of agreements among carriers is that the liner shipping industry is burdened with several peculiar characteristics, such as the uneven distribution of cargo by season, different cargo volumes on outbound and inbound legs of a journey and high fixed costs[123]. These are structural difficulties of the industry. Therefore, the consortium, which is a form of structural co-operation, is the best answer to solve or at least reduce the impact of such structural problems. For example, the problem of uneven distribution of cargo on the inbound and outbound leg of a journey can, at least in parts, be overcome by offering round-the-world services. The consortium is the forum to co-ordinate the complicated logistics of such an activity. The problems arising out of seasonal changes in the cargo volume can be battled by shipping more refrigerated products. The investment in warehouses and containers with refrigeration capacities could again be shared among the members of an alliance, such as the consortium. These examples show that agreements that do not include price fixing are also adequate to ensure a functioning liner

117 This principle is one of the fundamental principles of EC law, which the ECJ developed through its case-law, in the absence of any explicit recognition of this principle through the EC Treaty.
118 Goyder, (1998), p. 142.
119 Faull/Nikpay, (1999), p. 113; Grabitz/Hilf, Vol. 1, (1999), Koch, Art. 85, p. 45, rec. 181.
120 Recital 10 of the Preamble to Regulation 4056/86.
121 Butz, CPI (1993), Issue 3, p. 69, p. 71.
122 Reitzes, CPI (1993), Issue 3, p. 81, p. 82.
123 See above, p. 16 .

shipping industry. As a result, price fixing is not indispensable in the sense of Art. 81 III (ex 85 III) EC.

This finding is also supported by experiences from other transport sectors. In the areas of road haulage and rail transport, agreements, similar to consortia in their activities, have emerged increasing efficiency without having the power to fix prices[124]. A final argument that underlines the fact that price fixing is not a *condicio sine qua non* for the operation of a functioning shipping service can be drawn from the experiences with the U. S. Ocean Shipping Reform Act (1998)[125]. Since the coming into force of OSRA in the United States on the 1st of May 1999, transport to and from the United States is conducted in large parts under individual service contracts outside the conference tariff system[126]. The number of conferences operating in trades to and from the United States dropped from 35 to 19[127] between 1998 and June 2001. Yet, in 1999 and 2000, the average profitability of liner shipping companies increased[128]. This indicates that a reduced power of conferences to fix prices does not lead to a breakdown of the liner shipping markets due to *cut-throat* competition. Therefore, liner conferences are not essential for ensuring stability in the markets for maritime transport services.

Based on these reasons the conclusion is correct that collusive pricing practices are not absolutely necessary to ensure a stable and efficient maritime transport industry. This goal can also be reached through co-operation in the form of consortia agreements. Since these agreements do not allow for joint price fixing, they constitute a less restrictive way to stabilise the liner shipping industry in comparison with conference agreements.

cc) The elimination of competition

Art. 81 III (ex 85 III) EC finally stipulates that only those agreements are suitable for exemption that do not eliminate "*competition in respect of a substantial part of the products in question*". Again, this requirement is equally applicable to the provision of services[129]. The purpose of this condition is to give effect to Art. 3 lit. g EC, which has as its objective to protect competition within the Common Market from distortions[130]. In order to assess the intensity of competition in the face of an agreement that constitutes a restriction thereof, two as-

---

[124] Reitzes, CPI (1993), Issue 3, p. 81, p. 82.

[125] Chapter seven provides an analysis of the U. S. position on price fixing activities in liner shipping.

[126] FMC, OSRA Report, (2001), p. 17 f..

[127] FMC, OSRA Report, (2001), p. 3.

[128] Submission of the WSC to the OECD, (2001), p. 13.

[129] Faull/Nikpay, (1999), p. 114.

[130] Immenga/Mestmäcker, Vol. 1, (1997), Sauter, Art. 85, p. 355, rec. 28.

pects have to be taken into account. The first aspect is the degree of competition among those market participants that are party to the agreement, and the second aspect is the intensity of competition from outsiders[131].

aaa) The remaining competition among the members of a liner conference

One indicator for the position that Regulation 4056/86 does not ensure a sufficient degree of residual competitiveness in the markets for liner shipping is the fact that the price is the main device by which business rivals compete with each other[132]. To eliminate competition in this field leaves only very restricted possibilities for competition on other levels. This is especially true for liner shipping. The introduction of containerised shipping made the handling of the different cargoes easier for the carriers, since they now could fill their ships with standardised boxes irrespective of their actual content. As a consequence, the quality of shipping services became much more uniform, which in turn reduced the possibilities for competition with regard to the service quality. With respect to competition between the members of a liner conference, it is also important to note that Regulation 4056/86 not only allows joint price fixing of carriers, but that these carriers may also engage in revenue and/or cargo pooling by virtue of Art. 3 lit. e Regulation 4056/86. It has been explained in chapter two how the combination of such practices eliminates virtually all competition between the members of a conference[133]. These circumstances indicate that Regulation 4056/86 does not ensure a sufficient degree of residual competition among the members of a liner conference.

bbb) The remaining competition with outsiders

An evaluation of competition between the members of a conference and independent carriers is the second element of the assessment, whether or not the exemption for price fixing activities in liner shipping leaves a sufficient amount of competition intact. The market shares[134] of liner conferences and independent carriers are a decisive factor in such an analysis. There is no fixed percentage from which on the market share of the participants of an agreement precludes that agreement from being suitable for exemption. The Commission decided in *Fedetab*[135] that a market share of 80 per cent precluded the exemption of the agreement in question and the Court confirmed this position in its subsequent

---

131 Faull/Nikpay, (1999), p. 114; Grabitz/Hilf, Vol. 1, (1999), Koch, Art. 85, p. 45, rec. 184; G/T/E, Vol. 2/1, (1999), Schröter, Art. 85, p. 332 f, rec. 317 f; Immenga/ Mestmäcker, Vol. 1 (1997), Sauter, Art. 85, p. 355 f, rec. 28.

132 Bellamy/Child, (1993), p. 173, rec. 4-002.

133 See above, p. 50 ff.

134 G/T/E, Vol. 2/1, (1999), Schröter, Art. 85, p. 333, rec. 318; Immenga/Mestmäcker, Vol. 1, (1997) Sauter, Art. 85, p. 353, rec. 28.

135 "*Fedetab*", OJ (1978), L-224/29, rec. 133.

ruling[136]. Others have stated that a market share of 60 per cent in an oligopolistic market is sufficient to eliminate competition contrary to Art. 81 III (ex 85 III) EC[137]. These figures relate to Decisions for individual exemption. For block exemptions, the respective numbers need to be somewhat smaller[138], since a safety margin is necessary, in order to ensure that the individual agreements covered by such a general exemption actually do not eliminate competition unduly. The Commission seems to be of the same opinion, since it laid down in Art. 7 Regulation 823/2000 that the maximum market share for a consortium, which wishes to benefit from the exemption in Art. 3 Regulation 823/2000, may not exceed 50 per cent.[139].

According to Regulation 4056/86 there is no limit upon the market share that a conference may have, in order to benefit from the exemption in Art. 3 Regulation 4056/86. As a result, liner conferences that control nearly the entire market on their route are also eligible for exemption under the current regime. In this respect, it is not important that world-wide conference coverage has declined in recent years and that it typically ranges at present around 60 per cent in the major trade lanes[140]. This factor is irrelevant, as there may well be markets in which conferences have a larger market share and also because of the fact that the evaluation of Regulation 4056/86 must take into account what is permissible under that Regulation *in extremis*. An illustrative example of the effects of a very high market share of an agreement among carriers are the dealings of the TSA in the Asia - U. S. trade in 1998. This cartel of carriers combined around 90 per cent of the available transport capacity. The effect of this cartel was an elimination of nearly all competition in the affected trade. Shippers could not chose between alternative operators, but they faced a single entity on the supply side of the market[141]. In the absence of any quantitative restrictions on the market shares of a conference, such an agreement as the TSA would also be permissible under Regulation 4056/86. As a result, Regulation 4056/86 does not ensure the existence of sufficient competition between the conference and outsiders.

Regulation 4056/86 neither ensures an acceptable degree of competition within a liner conference, nor between a conference and independent carriers. Due to

---

[136] Joint cases 209 - 215 and 218/78, Heinz van Landewyck Sàrl and others v Commission, (1980), ECR, p. 3125 ff, p. 3279 f, rec. 186 ff.

[137] Grabitz/Hilf, Vol. 2, (1999), Koch, Art. 85, p. 46, rec. 185.

[138] G/T/E, Vol. 2/1, (1999), Schröter, Art. 85, p. 333, rec. 318.

[139] Art. 7 I Regulation 823/2000.

[140] Meyrick, (1999), p. 16; OECD, (2001), p. 20.

[141] Won, (1999), p. 17 f.

this shortcoming, Regulation 4056/86 does not fulfil the last requirement of Art. 81 III (ex 85 III) EC.

3. Arguments connected to the legal basis provisions of Regulation 4056/86 and to Art. 73 (ex 77) EC

Regulation 4056/86 is based *inter alia* on Art. 83 (ex 87) EC. This provision aims at giving""*effect to the principles set out in Articles 81 and 82*" (ex 85 and 86) EC. Typically a block exemption contains some restrictions of competition but it leaves the principle of free competition intact in principle. The liner conference block exemption differs from the other block exemptions, insofar, as it does not only affect ancillary aspects of competition in the relevant market (i. e. the market for liner shipping services), but it restricts competition in this market at its very centre through allowing joint price fixing. To permit such a fundamental restriction of competition contradicts the basic principle of EC competition law, which is to ensure a process of effective competition in order to achieve an efficient allocation of resources. The efficient allocation of resources is best achieved in competitive markets[142]. Consequently, Art. 3 Regulation 4056/86 constitutes a contradiction to Art. 83 (ex 87) EC[143].

Secondly, Regulation 4056/86 is based on Art. 80 II (ex 84 II) EC. It has been noted above that, in the interpretation of the ECJ, this provision does not restrict the application of competition law to the field of maritime transport[144]. Therefore, a measure may be based on Art. 80 II (ex 84 II) EC if it complements general EC competition law in the field of maritime transport, based on the specialties of this sector. Secondary legislation that constitutes a fundamental restriction to, or the exclusion of, the application of basic principles of EC competition law to the maritime transport industry, cannot be based on Art. 80 II (ex 84 II) EC[145]. An exemption for price fixing activities of liner conferences however would constitute such a fundamental restriction to the application of EC competition law in the field of maritime transport and, therefore, conflicts with Art. 80 II (ex 84 II) EC.

A third argument can be derived from Art. 73 (ex 77) EC. This provision contains special derogatory rules for the granting of state aids in the transport sector. There is no similar provision, which would allow derogations from the basic principles laid down in Arts. 81 and 82 (ex 85 and 86) EC. From the absence of such a provision in the case of price fixing arrangements in the transport sector, it must be concluded that such a derogation was not envisioned by the

[142] Jones/Sufrin, (2001), p. 4.
[143] Immenga/Mestmäcker Vol. 2, (1997), Basedow, p. 2049, rec. 26.
[144] See above, p. 54 ff.
[145] Immenga/Mestmäcker Vol. 2, (1997), Basedow, p. 2050, rec. 27.

EC Treaty. As a result, Art. 3 Regulation 4056/86, which contains such a derogation cannot be considered to conform to the Treaty[146].

4. Conclusion

The evaluation of Regulation 4056/86, and particularly Art.3 thereof, in light of Art. 81 (ex 85) EC and other relevant Treaty provisions raises serious doubts as to whether the block exemption for liner conferences conforms to the EC Treaty. Since joint price fixing constitutes a restriction to competition in the sense of Art. 81 I (ex 85 I) EC, it is necessary to justify an exemption for such an activity according to the four cumulative criteria provided in Art. 81 III (ex 85 III) EC. This provision is designed to ensure that only those restrictions of competition are legal which balance this negative aspect with some other advantage for the economy as a whole. The preceding analysis has demonstrated that joint price fixing of liner conferences does not have any such positive effects, and, as a consequence, Art. 3 Regulation 4056/86 contradicts Art. 81 (ex 85) EC. In addition, Art. 3 Regulation 4056/86 does not conform to Art. 83 (ex 87) and 80 II (ex 84 II) EC either.

5. The block exemption for consortia and Art. 81 (ex 85) EC

In chapter five it has been demonstrated that the block exemption for consortia did not trigger a similar amount of legal controversy as the liner conference block exemption. Correspondingly, the question as to whether or nor Art. 3 Regulation 823/2000 conforms to the EC Treaty, and especially to Art. 81 (ex 85) EC, can be answered without much debate. Consortia do limit competition[147] and, therefore, constitute agreements that restrict competition in the sense of Art. 81 I (ex 85 I) EC. Thus a justification of the consortia block exemption in light of the requirements of Art. 81 III (ex 85 III) EC is necessary.

At this point the evaluation of consortia differs from that of liner conferences since the consortia block exemption conforms to Art. 81 III (ex 85 III) EC. Under the regime of Regulation 823/2000, agreements on price fixing are prohibited by virtue of Art. 2 No. 1 Regulation 823/2000. Therefore, the gravest impediment of the liner conference block exemption, as far as coherence with Art. 81 (ex 85) EC is concerned, does not exist under Regulation 823/2000. The block exemption for consortia is sufficiently beneficial for the public interest as defined in Art. 81 III (ex 85 III) EC. Consortia rationalise liner shipping[148] through activities related to the joint provision of shipping services such as, for example, vessel sharing. The consequence is a more efficient shipping industry. The shippers profit from such a rationalisation in the form of a better quality of

---

[146] Immenga/Mestmäcker, Vol. 2, (1997), Basedow, p. 2050, rec. 27.

[147] Kreis, ETL (1992), p. 155 ff, p. 165.

[148] Immenga/Mestmäcker, Vol. 2, (1997), Basedow, p. 2080, rec. 1.

shipping services. Finally, shippers may benefit from reduced costs[149]. This does not contradict the observation made above that a reduction in costs does not necessarily lead to lower prices[150]. That statement was made in connection to Regulation 4056/86, which allows collusive action on prices. Under Regulation 823/2000, such behaviour is not permissible, and consequently, the forces of competition will ensure that a reduction in costs be passed on to the shippers.

Based on this reasoning, the conclusion is justified in stating that the consortia block exemption conforms to Art. 81 III (ex 85 III) EC. This finding is backed by the fact that the Commission was prepared to extend this block exemption for another five years without substantial amendments[151] and, more importantly, by the fact that shippers also judge the consortia block exemption positively[152]. This is the best proof that a block exemption for consortia is sufficiently beneficial, not only for the carriers, but also for the shippers.

[149] Kreis, ETL (1992), p. 155 ff, p. 165.

[150] See above, p. 116.

[151] Commission working document on Regulation 870/95, (1999), rec. 145.

[152] ESC submission to the OECD, (2001), p. 5.

Chapter seven - U. S. antitrust laws and agreements in liner shipping

The purpose of this chapter is to describe the development of U. S. antitrust law in relation to liner conferences and similar agreements as well as to evaluate current tendencies in U. S. policy on this issue. American antitrust law is important for the European Community, not only because the U. S. are one of the main trading partners of the Community, but also because the U. S. have a much longer history of regulating liner shipping than Europe.

1. Liner conferences after the passage of the Sherman Act in 1890

The central piece of U. S. legislation in the field of antitrust law is the Sherman Act, which was enacted in 1890 at about the same time, when shipping conferences started to operate in U. S. trades[1]. Section 1 of that act declares "*every contract, combination in the form of trust or otherwise conspiracy, in restraint of trade or commerce (......) to be illegal*". The prohibition of collusive actions that constitute a restraint of trade is the fundamental principle of U.S. antitrust law until this day. Early rulings of the American courts could not develop a consistent position on the question of whether or not shipping conferences constitute a violation of section 1 of the Sherman Act[2]. In 1911 the practices of the Atlantic Conference came under scrutiny of the Circuit Court of New York (S. D.). The carriers bound together in the conference agreed on such matters as the division of traffic among themselves, the pooling of receipts and the right of the carriers to command their fellow conference members to adjust their rates, if carriers with a combined share of traffic of at least 75 per cent considered such a move necessary. In its ruling, the court held that such a conduct was contradictory to section 1 of the Sherman Act[3]. Two years later the U. S. Supreme Court ruled that the practice of several steamship and railway companies to fix rates for the transport of passengers and freight on the White Pass & Yukon route did constitute a violation of the requirements of the Sherman Act[4]. A third judgement from the year 1915 by the same court, which prohibited a conference agreement in 1911, now ruled the opposite, and it was held that the conference agreement in question did not in itself constitute an unreasonable restraint of trade according to section 1 of the Sherman Act[5]. These rulings indicate that there existed no common accord within the American judiciary as to whether or not liner conferences violate section 1 of the Sherman Act.

[1] Munster, (2001), p. 3.
[2] Herman, (1983), p. 12; Munster, (2001), p. 3.
[3] *U. S. v. Hamburg-Amerikanische Packet-Fahrt-Actien-Gesellschaft et al*, (1911), Circuit Court, S. D. New York, 200 F 806.
[4] *U.S. v. Pacific and Arctic Railway and Navigation Company et al*, (1913), 228 U.S. 87.
[5] *U. S. v. Prince Line et al*, (1915), District Court, S. D. New York, 220 F 230.

2. The Shipping Act of 1916

The first major step in the regulation of liner conferences under U. S. law was the passage of the Shipping Act of 1916. Although this Act was primarily concerned with the establishment, promotion and development of the U. S. merchant marine[6], it also contained provisions on the antitrust immunity of agreements in the liner shipping industry. Such legislation became necessary since the American courts had until that time not been able to develop a consistent approach on the legality of liner conference agreements. In 1912 the so-called *Alexander Committee*[7] was charged with the task to enquire into the practices of shipping conferences. It delivered its report to Congress in 1914 and it was this report that became the principal basis for the antitrust exemption for liner conferences, embodied in the U. S. Shipping Act of 1916[8]. The *Alexander Committee* stated in its report its general support for the conference system, similarly to the majority report of *the Royal Commission on Shipping Rings*[9] in the UK, but its support of the conference system was not unconditional and the suggestions for the control of liner conferences made therein went further than those of the British commission.

It was stated in the Alexander Report that conferences ensure rate stability as well as the uniform application of rates, that they lead to the provision of a high quality service, that they reduce wasteful competition, as sailing dates are rationalised, and finally that the conference tariffs take the value of the shipped goods into account[10]. However, the *Alexander Committee* also paid attention to the monopolistic effects of liner conferences. It was stressed that under the conference system the carriers sometimes charged excess rates, that they did not experience sufficient pressure to deliver a proper service due to the lack of competition and that the fact that conference tariffs were not made public to the shippers could lead to secret rebates for large shippers[11]. The system of deferred rebates was considered as a measure, which tied shippers too closely to a conference.

The committee suggested that all conference agreements should be brought under the supervision of the Interstate Commerce Commission, which should have the power to strike down agreements which it considered discriminatory, unfair or harmful for national interests of the United States. The committee also rec-

---

[6] Reisener, (1968), p. 12.

[7] Named after the chairman of the House of Representatives Merchant Marine and Fisheries Committee, *Joshua Alexander*.

[8] Munster, (2001), p. 5; Reisener, (1968), p. 12; Zerby, (1984), p. 8.

[9] See above, p. 23.

[10] Munster, (2001), p. 4

[11] Munster, (2001), p. 4; Reisener, (1968), p. 20.

ommended that all rebates on freight rates and other discriminatory measures between shippers should be declared illegal. Deferred rebates and the use of fighting ships were explicitly considered unlawful. It was furthermore suggested that the Interstate Commerce Commission should have the power to initiate proceedings concerning conference behaviour, not only after a complaint has been filed, but also at its own initiative. In order to prevent the violation of these rules, the *Alexander Committee* advised the establishment of a system of penalties.

Following these recommendations Congress tried to preserve the identified benefits of the conference system through its legislation, while eliminating its inherent disadvantages. The most prominent provision of the Shipping Act of 1916 as far as the antitrust immunity of shipping conferences is concerned is section 15, as it lays down the requirements of the antitrust exemption for agreements in liner shipping[12]. The scope of this exemption is not limited to liner conference agreements, but it extends to "*understandings, conferences and other arrangements*"[13]. An agreement in this sense is illegal, if it does not conform to the requirements laid down in section 15 of the Shipping Act of 1916. That provision establishes three conditions which agreements must fulfil in order to be exemptable. First, agreements may not be discriminatory; second, agreements among carriers may not be detrimental to the commerce of the U. S. Finally, carriers may not engage in such activities as are specifically listed in section 14 of the Shipping Act of 1916. This list comprises the use of deferred rebates and fighting ships as well as the engagement in retaliatory measures against shippers that also use the services of non-conference carriers.

The Shipping Act of 1916 further established the U. S. Shipping Board[14] as a new authority which was charged *inter alia* with the control of conference agreements[15]. All agreements among carriers had to be filed with this new ad-

---

[12] Reisener, (1968), p. 37.

[13] In 1973 the U. S. Supreme Court defined this expression as to encompass all such agreements that create continuous obligations between their partners, but not agreements that impose one-time obligations, such as for example the sale of assets; see: *Federal Maritime Commission v. Seatrain Lines Inc.* (1973), U. S. Supreme Court, 411 U. S. 726.

[14] The U. S. Shipping Board was what eventually became the Federal Maritime Commission, which is the U. S. authority that oversees liner shipping today. For a brief account of the different authorities that were charged with the oversight of agreements in liner shipping since 1916; see: Reisener, (1968), p. 87.

[15] The U. S. Shipping Board was also responsible for the promotion of the U. S. merchant marine. It has been stated that this dual responsibility of the U. S. Shipping Board did not work well, since the two objectives could come into conflict with each other; see: Zerby, (1984), p. 8 f. As a consequence, the Federal Maritime Commission, as its successor, is only charged with the control of agreements in the liner shipping industry.

ministrative body, and they were only lawful if the U. S. Shipping Board considered them so according to the standards described in the preceding paragraph. The U. S. Shipping Board had to issue an order within which it voiced its consent, but it could also reject or modify an agreement. In addition, the U. S. Shipping Board had the right to conduct an enquiry upon the complaint by a third person or upon its own initiative. A final aspect of the Shipping Act of 1916 was that it instated a system of penalties in case carriers were found to violate the provisions of this Act. If the U. S. Shipping Board, upon the complaint of another person, found a carrier in violation of the Shipping Act of 1916, it could then issue an order for the full reparation of any financial loss that occurred to the complainant as a consequence of the violation of the Shipping Act of 1916[16]. Through this new administrative regime the Shipping Act of 1916 established a system of mandatory government control over agreements in the liner shipping industry.

The essence of the Shipping Act of 1916 is that shipping conferences find limited acceptance under U. S. law, but only under the condition of active government control[17]. Several reasons have been advanced for the rather generous approach of Congress towards liner conferences, which is insofar surprising, as the general sentiment of the time in the U. S. opposed the permission of monopolistic structures such as liner conferences[18]. First, the shippers that commented on the conference system during the enquiry of the *Alexander Committee* expressed their satisfaction with the system as it was[19]. Another prominent reason for the exemption of liner conferences from section 1 of the Sherman Act was the problem of international comity. At the beginning of the 20th century, the conference system was the organisational backbone for liner shipping all over the world. The U. S. legislator feared disadvantages for the American economy if conferences were not allowed in the American trades[20]. A final reason for the exemption of liner conferences from the antitrust prohibition of section 1 of the Sherman Act may have been that in the latter part of the 19th century, the American economy witnessed instances of ruinous competition in the nation's railway industry. It may well be that Congress wanted to avoid similar conflicts within the field of maritime transport and consequently assented to measures which intended to stabilise the liner shipping industry[21], at the expense of general antitrust policy.

---

16 Section 22 of the Shipping Act of 1916.
17 Munster, (2001), p. 5.
18 Zerby, (1984), p. 9.
19 Zerby, (1984), p. 9.
20 Zerby, (1984), p. 9 f.
21 Zerby, (1984), p. 10.

3. The *Bonner Act Amendments* in 1961

On October 3rd 1961 a law amending the Shipping Act of 1916 came into force, often referred to as the *Bonner Act Amendments*[22]. Its following discussion in light of relevant rulings of the U. S. Supreme Court will focus on the legality of dual rate contracts and the relationship between general antitrust laws and the Shipping Act of 1916 as amended.

a) The legality of dual rate contracts

Section 14 of the Shipping Act of 1916 explicitly prohibited the use of deferred rebates by liner conferences in U. S. trades[23]. However, the Shipping Act of 1916 did not contain any provision concerning rebates based on the dual rate system[24]. Many conferences operating in U.S. trades inferred from this circumstance that dual rate contracts were legal under the U. S. Shipping Act of 1916 and they, therefore, became the principle rebate system employed by conferences serving the U. S.[25]. Yet, there remained some uncertainty as to whether the Shipping Act of 1916 permitted the use of dual rate contracts and the matter finally came before the U. S. Supreme Court in 1958. In that year the U. S. Supreme Court held in *Maritime Board v. Isbrandtsen Co.*[26] that the dual rate system of the Japan-Atlantic and Gulf Freight Conference did not conform to section 14 of the Shipping Act of 1916. The court emphasised in its ruling that section 14 of the Shipping Act of 1916 not only specifically prohibited the use of deferred rebates and fighting ships, but that it also outlawed in more general terms the "*resort to other discriminating or unfair methods*". According to the U. S. Supreme Court, this clause constituted a catchall clause by which Congress sought to ban all practices which were similar in purpose and effect to the use of deferred rebates as well as fighting ships[27]. Based on this line of reasoning, the U. S. Supreme Court ruled that the dual rate system of the Japan-Atlantic and Gulf Freight Conference was in violation of section 14 of the Shipping Act of 1916.

It has been stated that the ruling of the U. S. Supreme Court in *Isbrandtsen* did not declare the dual rate system illegal *per se*, but only dual rate regimes with

---

[22] Named after the Representative *Bonner*, who chaired the House Merchant Marine and Fisheries Special Subcommittee on Steamship Conferences, charged with the enquiry into the current dealings of liner conferences under special consideration of the use of dual rate contracts. A second parallel enquiry was conducted by the Antitrust Subcommittee of the House Judiciary Committee under the chairmanship of Representative Celler.

[23] See above, p. 47.

[24] Munster, (2001), p. 5; Reisener, (1968), p. 69.

[25] Herman, (1983), p. 64 f; Munster, (2001), p. 5.

[26] *Maritime Board v. Isbrandtsen Co.*, (1958), U. S. Supreme Court, 356 U. S. 481.

[27] *Maritime Board v. Isbrandtsen Co.*, (1958), U. S. Supreme Court, 356 U. S. 481, 492.

the intention to impede non-conference competition[28]. Yet, this judgement of the U. S. Supreme Court gave rise to increased doubts and insecurities on the issue of legality of dual rate systems under the Shipping Act of 1916. In order to mitigate these insecurities, Congress passed three interim laws that specifically permitted the use of dual rate contracts in U. S. trades[29] in the period from August 1958 to September 1961. Through these laws Congress bought itself the time it needed to enquire into and decide on the revision of the existing laws on liner shipping. The result of this process was the passage of the *Bonner Act Amendments*.

One major issue of this new legislation was the explicit antitrust exemption of dual rate contracts. To this effect, the Shipping Act of 1916 as amended contained a new section 14 (b). This lengthy provision specifically legalised the use of dual rate contracts by carriers in U. S. trades under a number of detailed conditions. It was specifically provided that the discount that carriers may grant to shippers may not exceed 15 per cent in relation to the common conference tariff. Through this new statutory provision, Congress eliminated any uncertainties, which existed after the *Isbrandtsen* ruling of the U. S. Supreme Court, concerning the legality of dual rate contracts[30].

b) The new public interest standard

A second main element of the *Bonner Act Amendments* was the addition of the public interest standard as the fourth general criterion for the legality of agreements in liner shipping to the already existing three conditions in section 15 of the Shipping Act of 1916. According to this new standard, conference agreements were from then on only legal according to section 15 of the Shipping Act of 1916 as amended if they were not contrary to the public interest. It was the subsequent interpretation of the public interest criterion that lead to an erosion of the antitrust immunity for conference agreements under U. S. law.[31]

The main question was whether the public interest clause was to be construed to relate only to the ability of U. S. shippers to trade fairly and competitively, or whether this expression also connected to broader antitrust principles, thereby incorporating the more general notion of freely competitive markets for liner shipping services into the analysis under section 15 of the Shipping Act of 1916

[28] Herman, (1983), p. 66. However it should be noted that the dual rate system of the Japan-Atlantic and Gulf Freight Conference was typical of its kind, which permits the conclusion that such regimes regularly function to impede non-conference competition.

[29] Herman, (1983), p. 67.

[30] Herman, (1983), p. 69; Munster, (2001), p. 6.

[31] Gilman, (1983), p. 84.

as amended[32]. The U. S. Supreme Court addressed this question in 1968, in its ruling in *Federal Maritime Commission v. Aktienbolaget Svenska Amerika Linien*[33]. Therein the court argued that an illegal restraint of trade is by its very nature contrary to the public interest[34]. As a consequence, the court approved the policy of the Federal Maritime Commission to allow only such agreements that are required by a serious transportation need, or in order to secure important public benefits, or that are necessary in furtherance of a valid regulatory purpose of the Shipping Act of 1916 as amended[35]. A second important aspect of the *Svenska* ruling is its acceptance of the fact that the carriers or conferences are responsible for bringing forth such evidence, as is necessary to demonstrate that their agreements do not run contrary to the public interest[36]. Now the FMC would only declare an agreement as legal if the carriers could demonstrate that the agreement would yield some continuous benefit in comparison to the situation that would exist without the agreement[37].

c) The Shipping Act of 1916 as amended and general antitrust laws

Another important topic that required the attention of the American judiciary in the 1960s was the relationship between the Shipping Act of 1916 as amended and the general antitrust laws such as the Sherman Act. The question was of importance because under the latter laws it was possible to claim three times the injury suffered as damages in civil proceedings, whereas under the Shipping Act of 1916 as amended it was only possible to claim full reparation[38] respectively to fine the carriers a maximum sum of $ 1.000 per day of violation[39]. The U. S. Supreme Court first addressed this issue in 1932, in its ruling in *United States Navigation Co. v. Cunard S. S. Co.*[40]. It had to answer the question of whether or not it was possible for the plaintiff to bring an action for a treble-damage claim directly in the federal courts according to general antitrust laws, or whether the matter came primarily within the exclusive jurisdiction of the then U. S. Shipping Board. Since the U. S. Shipping Board is an administrative

---

[32] Zerby, (1984), p. 11.

[33] *Federal Maritime Commission v. Aktienbolaget Svenska Amerika Linien*, (1968), U. S. Supreme Court, 390 U. S. 238.

[34] *Federal Maritime Commission v. Aktienbolaget Svenska Amerika Linien*, (1968), U. S. Supreme Court, 390 U. S. 238, 244.

[35] *Federal Maritime Commission v. Aktienbolaget Svenska Amerika Linien*, (1968), U. S. Supreme Court, 390 U. S. 238, 243.

[36] *Federal Maritime Commission v. Aktienbolaget Svenska Amerika Linien*, (1968), U. S. Supreme Court, 390 U. S. 238, 245 f.

[37] Gilman, (1983), p. 85.

[38] Section 21 U. S. Shipping Act of 1916 as amended.

[39] Section 15 U. S. Shipping Act of 1916 as amended.

[40] *United States Navigation Co. v. Cunard S. S. Co.*, (1932), U. S. Supreme Court, 284 U. S. 474.

authority with a considerable degree of expert and technical knowledge the court considered it necessary that the matters primarily had to be resolved by recourse to this institution, thereby giving preference to the latter position presented above[41]. Although the court only decided that a matter must first be brought before the U. S. Shipping Board, its ruling may be interpreted in such a way as to indicate that it was not possible to take recourse in the remedies of general antitrust laws if the matter fell within the scope of the Shipping Act of 1916 as amended[42]. The U. S. Supreme Court stated in the *Cunard* judgement that the remedies of the Shipping Act superseded the general antitrust laws[43] and the court also emphasised that the Shipping Act contained sufficient instruments to police agreements in the liner shipping industry[44].

In 1966 the U. S. Supreme Court changed its approach on the issue of the relationship between the Shipping Act of 1916 as amended and the general antitrust laws, in its ruling in *Carnation Co. v. Pacific Westbound Conference et al*[45]. This case was concerned with the right of a shipper to file a treble-damage action on the basis of general antitrust laws, because of a rate increase that had neither been filed with nor approved by the FMC contrary to the requirements of the Shipping Act of 1916 as amended. The court was of the opinion that the present ruling did not overturn the previous *Cunard* ruling[46]. According to the position of the U. S. Supreme Court *Cunard* only defined the right of the FMC to primary jurisdiction concerning activities of debatable legality under the Shipping Act of 1916 as amended. The present case on the other side was concerned with a situation where a violation of the Shipping Act of 1916 as amended was evident, with the consequence that the right of the FMC to primary jurisdiction could not be jeopardised. The view of the U. S. Supreme Court, that the two cases do not overlap is doubtful. The *Cunard* judgement may have been interpreted in a wider manner as to regulate the relationship between the Shipping Act of 1916 as amended and antitrust provisions in general as it has been demonstrated in the preceding paragraph. Secondly, the distinction between situations that constitute a clear breach of the Shipping Act of

41 *United States Navigation Co. v. Cunard S. S. Co.*, (1932), U. S. Supreme Court, 284 U. S. 474, 486; the court repeated its position in: *Far East Conference et al v. United States et al*, (1952), U. S. Supreme Court, 342 U. S. 570.

42 Zerby, (1984), p. 11 f.

43 *United States Navigation Co. v. Cunard S. S. Co.*, (1932), U. S. Supreme Court, 284 U. S. 474, 485.

44 *United States Navigation Co. v. Cunard S. S. Co.*, (1932), U. S. Supreme Court, 284 U. S. 474, 486.

45 *Carnation Co. v. Pacific Westbound Conference et al*, (1966), U. S. Supreme Court, 383 U. S. 213.

46 *Carnation Co. v. Pacific Westbound Conference et al*, (1966), U. S. Supreme Court, 383 U. S. 213, 220.

1916 as amended and situations where such a violation is not evident may not be clear.

In the present case the court was of the opinion that the Shipping Act of 1916 as amended did not remove the liner shipping industry as a whole from the scope of general antitrust laws, but it held instead that agreements which are illegal according to the relevant provisions of the Shipping Act of 1916 as amended may be the subject of a treble-damage claim under the general antitrust provisions. It could be argued on behalf of the respondent shipping conferences that such a position did not take the general conception of the Shipping Act of 1916 as amended into account. In this respect it is important that the Shipping Act of 1916 as amended provided for a system of fines and also gave the injured person the possibility to obtain full reparation for any damages, because of a violation of the Shipping Act of 1916 as amended. Finally, it is also important that the FMC had the right to investigate into possible violations of the Shipping Act of 1916 as amended at its own will. These provisions could indicate that the Shipping Act of 1916 as amended instated a closed legal regime in the sector of liner shipping that precluded the application of the general antitrust laws.

The U. S. Supreme Court dismissed such a line of reasoning by stating that any rights that a damaged party might have under the general antitrust laws were entirely collateral to the rights of such a person under the Shipping Act of 1916 as amended[47]. In its ruling, the court relied on the fact that the antitrust laws embodied a fundamental policy of American law, which did not permit the withdrawal of a whole industry from their field of application without a clear indication that the legislator did wish for such a limitation of the scope of general antitrust provisions[48]. The court could not find any evidence that the Shipping Act of 1916 as amended was supposed to constitute such a general exemption. It stated that the Shipping Act of 1916 as amended only contained an explicit exemption for activities that were legal according to section 15 of the Shipping Act of 1916 as amended[49]. This circumstance implied that activities that did not conform to the requirements of section 15 of the Shipping Act of 1916 as amended were not exempted from the general antitrust provisions and not vice versa. Finally, the U. S. Supreme Court emphasised the general support of antitrust laws through Congress in 1916 in support of its view that ac-

---

47 *Carnation Co. v. Pacific Westbound Conference et al*, (1966), U. S. Supreme Court, 383 U. S. 213, 224.

48 *Carnation Co. v. Pacific Westbound Conference et al*, (1966), U. S. Supreme Court, 383 U. S. 213, 217 f.

49 *Carnation Co. v. Pacific Westbound Conference et al*, (1966), U. S. Supreme Court, 383 U. S. 213, 216 f.

tivities, which were illegal according to the Shipping Act of 1916 as amended, could be subjected to the general antitrust laws[50].

Based on these reasons, the U. S. Supreme Court decided in *Carnation Co. v. Pacific Westbound Conference et al* that conference practices, which were contradictory to the requirements of the Shipping Act of 1916 as amended, fell within the scope of general antitrust provisions.

d) Conclusion

While the U. S. position on agreements in liner shipping did not experience a fundamental change with the passage of the *Bonner Act Amendments* in 1961, it is still true that government control of such agreements became stricter in the wake of the legislative change of 1961[51]. Evidence of this new strictness is the adoption of the public interest standard as the fourth criterion by which the FMC had to evaluate the legality of agreements in liner shipping. The U. S. Supreme Court especially did not look benevolently upon liner conference agreements. Its hostility towards such agreements was displayed in its rulings discussed above which established that the FMC had to take the general antitrust principles into account in its evaluation whether or not an agreement is in the public interest. Furthermore, conferences had to provide proof of their compliance with the public interest criterion. Finally, conference agreements, which did not conform to the requirements of the Shipping Act of 1916 as amended, could be subject to a treble damages claim under general antitrust laws. The combined effect of these changes has lead some commentators to state that liner shipping in U. S. trades had to operate in a harsh and legalistic environment in the 1960s and 1970s[52].

4. The Shipping Act of 1984

The first general overhaul of U. S. legislation on the issue of agreements in liner shipping came about in 1984 with the passage of the Shipping Act of 1984, which entered into force on June 18th 1984[53]. Although it retained the antitrust immunity for ocean carrier agreements and the requirement to file all tariffs and agreements with the FMC[54], it substantially altered the laws on agreements in liner shipping and gave a new direction to the regulation of that industry. The two main aspects of the Shipping Act of 1984 were, on the one hand the intro-

---

[50] The court did so by citing passages from the Alexander Report where the committee expressed its reservations to the conference system. Yet, it should be borne in mind that the Alexander Committee generally supported the conference system.

[51] Zerby, (1984), p. 11 f.

[52] Gilman, (1983), p. 95; Munster, (2001), p. 6.

[53] Campbell/Shin, (1987), p. 151 ff, p. 151; Wilson/Casavant, (1991), p. 427 ff, p. 428.

[54] Munster, (2001), p. 6.

duction of new pro-competitive instruments into the rate structure and, on the other hand the limitation of administrative intervention and supervision of the liner shipping industry.

a) New competitive instruments

Section 5 (b) (8) of the Shipping Act of 1984 provided that the individual conference members had the right to depart from the official conference tariffs on any rate or service item after ten days notice to the conference. This device is known as the right to mandatory independent action, since the conference agreements may not restrict the right of the individual carriers to set the official conference tariff aside in such a manner. The underlying rationale behind the introduction of mandatory independent action was the belief that conferences should not be in a position to cause detriment to the individual carrier[55]. If a carrier considers it necessary to set the conference tariff aside for a certain transaction, then it must be able to do so. Independent rate action quickly became popular after the passage of the Shipping Act of 1984[56] and transportation rates for commodities transported under independent action were typically 10 - 20 per cent lower than the corresponding tariff rates[57].

A second novelty of the Shipping Act of 1984 was the legal acceptance of service contracts as an alternative to the common conference tariff in section 8 (c) of the Shipping Act of 1984. Now the carriers could individually, or together as a conference, agree with a shipper or a shippers' association on rates and the level of service, if the shipper promised in return to commission a certain minimum quantity of cargo over a fixed period of time to the individual carrier or to the conference. This new contractual device replaced dual rate contracts[58] which were outlawed by section 10 (b) (9) of the Shipping Act of 1984. The discussion of service contracts in chapter five of this study has demonstrated the importance of such contracts for a competitive shipping industry[59]. Yet, under the regime of the Shipping Act of 1984, service contracting only marginally increased the competitive pressure on conference carriers. The first reason for such a limited impact was the fact that the right of carriers to enter into individual service contracts was not mandatory as the right to independent action, but conferences could and did restrict the right of carriers to offer individual service contracts to their customers or they could prohibit such a practise

---

[55] Casavant/Wilson, (1991), p. 109 ff, p. 111 f.

[56] In the years immediately following the passage of the Shipping Act of 1984, over 19.000 independent actions were filed with the FMC; see: Wilson/ Casavant, (1991), p. 427 ff, p. 427.

[57] Casavant/Wilson, (1991), p. 109 ff, p. 112.

[58] Munster, (2001), p. 7.

[59] See above, p. 122.

altogether. Secondly, the introduction of service contracts as an alternative to the common tariff was of limited consequence because section 8 (c) of the Shipping Act of 1984 required carriers to publish the essential terms of such a contract through the FMC[60] and to grant the same conditions to all similarly situated shippers. This clause, commonly referred to as the "*me too*" clause, often had the effect to make it undesirable for a carrier to offer lower rates to a single customer on the basis of a service contract, since it did not want to commit itself to the obligation to offer the same low rates to all similarly situated customers.

b) The new role of the FMC under the Shipping Act of 1984

The second major change of the Shipping Act of 1984 was the alteration of the supervisory powers of the FMC. Until the passage of the Shipping Act of 1984, the FMC had to assent to all agreements in liner shipping after it had established their conformity with the valid shipping laws. Since there was no time limit within which the FMC was required to terminate its evaluation of an agreement, it could take years for the FMC to decide on the legality of a single agreement[61]. This process was changed in 1984. Although carriers were still required to file all agreements and tariffs with the FMC, they did not have to await its explicit consent anymore. Instead, according to section 6 (c) of the Shipping Act of 1984, the agreements became automatically valid, either 45 days after they were filed with the FMC or 30 days after the filing of the agreement or tariff had been published in the Federal Register[62]. The FMC could only reject an agreement if it found the agreement in question to contradict the requirements enumerated in section 5 (b) of the Shipping Act of 1984. The requirements enumerated therein concern *inter alia* the admission and readmission of conference members and the right of individual carriers to mandatory independent action. Based on this provision it was no longer possible for the FMC, to reject an agreement because it considered it to be detrimental to the public interest or to the commerce of the United States. Such a decision was now left exclusively to the American judiciary[63]. Section 6 (g) of the Shipping Act of 1984 stated that the FMC had to apply for an injunction at the U. S. District Court for the District of Columbia if it considered an agreement to be substantially anti-competitive. In such proceedings, the FMC carried the burden of proof for the alleged anti-competitive effects of the agreement in question. Thereby, the Shipping Act of 1984 reversed

[60] It was not required to disclose the name of the shippers, but data that have to be made public, include the origin and destination ports, the commodity or commodities involved, the duration of the contract, the line-haul rates, the minimum cargo volume, any service commitments and provisions concerning liquidated damages for non-performance.

[61] Casavant/Wilson, (1991), p. 109 ff, p. 111; Wilson/Casavant, (1991), p. 427 ff, p. 428.

[62] Note that not the agreement or tariff itself has to be published in the Federal Register, but only a notice that an agreement or tariff has been filed with the FMC.

[63] Casavant/Wilson, (1991), p. 109 ff, p. 111.

the judgement of the U. S. Supreme Court in *Svenska*[64] as far as the proceedings for an injunction to prohibit a certain agreement were concerned.

c) Conclusion

It has been stated that the Shipping Act of 1984 constituted a compromise between the interests of both carriers and shippers[65]. Yet, after careful consideration, it seems that it primarily catered to the interests of the carriers and only to a lesser degree to those of the shippers. The former benefit mainly from the application of the "*less governmental*" approach, typical for the Reagan administration[66], to liner shipping as well as from a clarification of the extent of the antitrust immunity[67]. Due to the decreased powers of the FMC and the streamlined administrative procedure, it was now easier to form conference agreements, and they could enter into effect much faster. The new competitive measures introduced with the Shipping Act of 1984 had only a limited impact on the liner shipping industry. As far as the right to mandatory independent action is concerned, it must be kept in mind that this device essentially functioned as a rebate system from the official conference tariff and, as such, did not constitute anything radically new in liner shipping. In addition, the right to mandatory independent action was not seen as a measure for the benefit of the shippers, but it was included into the Shipping Act of 1984 in order to increase the freedom of the individual carriers[68]. However, the introduction of individual as well as group service contracts had the potential to bring new competition into the liner shipping industry. Since conferences could and did control the right of independent carriers to deviate from the conference tariffs by means of an individual service contract, this new feature in the pricing for liner shipping service was only of limited impact[69].

Finally, the wording of section 4 (a) (1) of the Shipping Act of 1984, which permitted the carriers to "*discuss, fix or regulate transportation rates, including through rates*" extended the antitrust exemption in two ways beneficial to the carriers. First, this section clarified the right to fix the price for the inland leg of intermodal transport operations through the conference mechanisms under the Shipping Act of 1984 and second, it exempted agreements that did not establish a common conference tariff, but that only had the purpose of discussing the

---

[64] *Federal Maritime Commission v. Aktienbolaget Svenska Amerika Linien*, (1968), U. S. Supreme Court, 390 U. S. 238.

[65] Casavant/Wilson, (1991), p. 109 ff, p. 110; Munster, (2001), p. 8.

[66] President Reagan stated that the Shipping Act of 1984 "*will minimise Government intervention in the Shipping industry*" and he considered it to be "*a milestone in our struggle to end the overregulation of American shipping*"; see: Munster, (2001), p. 6.

[67] Casavant/Wilson, (1991), p. 109 ff, p. 110.

[68] See above, p. 177.

[69] FMC, OSRA Report, (2001), p. 16.

subject of rates without any definite conclusions on the matter. Congress thereby extended the antitrust exemption to talking agreements. Due to these changes in the legal regime of liner shipping through the Shipping Act of 1984, it is permissible to state that it constituted a departure from the hitherto strict and somewhat hostile control of agreements in liner shipping towards a more conference-friendly position.

5. The Ocean Shipping Reform Act of 1998

The most recent change of U. S. policy on agreements in liner shipping is embodied in the Ocean Shipping Reform Act of 1998 (OSRA), which entered into force on May 1, 1999. After a brief description of its legislative history, the analysis of OSRA will focus on an evaluation of the main regulatory changes to the laws governing liner shipping and the impact thereof on the markets for liner shipping services. The final remarks in this chapter will contain a brief outlook on possible future changes of U. S. legislation on the issue of agreements in liner shipping.

a) The legislative history of the Ocean Shipping Reform Act of 1998

Already the Shipping Act of 1984 foresaw the formation of an "*Advisory Commission on Conferences in Ocean Shipping*" five and a half years after its coming into force[70]. The Advisory Commission was charged with the task to establish "*whether the Nation would be best served by prohibiting conferences, or by closed or open conferences*"[71]. Despite such clear and unequivocal statutory instructions, the report delivered by the Advisory Commission on April 10th 1992 did not contain any own conclusions or recommendations of the Advisory Commission, since its members could not agree on a common position[72]. Instead, the report listed the differing opinions of the concerned parties, including shippers, carriers and conferences[73]. The apathy on the subject of regulatory reform of liner shipping resulting from the indecisive character of the report of the Advisory Commission, was only overcome in 1994. At that time, the shippers and especially the NITL started to press for a complete removal of antitrust immunity in liner shipping, a position that was strongly opposed by the carriers[74]. In the subsequent deliberations involving all groups of the ocean transportation

---

[70] Section 18 (d) (1) of the Shipping Act of 1984.

[71] Section 18 (f) of the Shipping Act of 1984.

[72] It may be that the inability of the Advisory Commission to agree on a common position resulted from the multitude of interests that were represented in this body. The Advisory Commission consisted of one cabinet member, four U. S. Senators, four U. S. Representatives and eight representatives from the private sector; see: section 18 (d) (2) of the Shipping Act of 1984.

[73] Munster, (2001), p. 8.

[74] Shashikumar/Schatz, (2000), p. 5

industry[75], carriers and shippers agreed on a compromise and it was this compromise that formed the nucleus for what was to become OSRA[76], which Congress passed in the summer of 1998 and which was signed by President Clinton on October 14, 1998[77].

b) The main changes introduced by the Ocean Shipping Reform Act of 1998

It has been stated that OSRA dramatically changed the regulatory landscape of liner shipping[78] and it has also been said that it constitutes a logical continuation of the Shipping Act of 1984[79]. The following analysis will demonstrate that the apparent contradiction between continuity and dramatic change in the description of OSRA does not exist in reality and that both statements properly display the impact of the Ocean Shipping Reform Act of 1998 on the liner shipping industry.

In a formal sense, OSRA does not abolish the Shipping Act of 1984, but merely amends it. OSRA follows the fundamental structure of the Shipping Act of 1984 as it retains the antitrust immunity for agreements among liner shipping operators, and it also retains the FMC as the authority to oversee the liner shipping industry[80], albeit with somewhat altered competences[81]. For these reasons, it is justified to say that OSRA continues to regulate liner shipping according to the same basic principles as the Shipping Act of 1984.

Nevertheless, OSRA introduces substantial changes, the most important of which concerns service contracts. These contracts were first introduced by the Shipping Act of 1984, but conferences could and did effectively restrict the right of individual carriers to enter into contractual transport obligations of this type[82]. Such a practice became illegal with the coming into force of OSRA,

---

75 Creel, (2002), p. 1.

76 Munster, (2001), p. 11.

77 For a more detailed description of the legislative history of OSRA see: Munster, (2001), p. 8 ff.

78 FMC, OSRA Report, (2001), p. 8; Reitzes/Sheran, (2002), p. 51 ff, p. 54.

79 Lewis/Vellenga, (2000), p. 3.

80 During the deliberations prior to the passage of OSRA, it had been suggested to abolish the FMC as oversight authority for liner shipping; see: Munster, (2001), p. 11; Shashikumar/Schatz, (2000), p. 5.

81 OSRA maintains the requirement to file service contracts and agreements with the FMC, but cancelled the requirement to file tariffs with the FMC. The latter now have to be made available to shippers electronically, and the FMC only oversees the proper publication of tariffs in an electronic form; see: section 8 (a) of the Shipping Act of 1984 as amended by OSRA.

82 See above, p. 177 ff.

which removed individual service contracts effectively from the control of liner conferences. Sec. 8 (c) (1) of the Shipping Act of 1984 as amended by OSRA expressly grants carriers the right to enter into individual service contracts, and sec. 5 (c) of the Shipping Act of 1984 as amended by OSRA provides that agreements among carriers may neither prohibit nor restrict this right[83], nor force the carriers to disclose any data to the conference that can remain confidential according to this act.

The removal of the regulation of service contracts from the scope of permissible activities for agreements in liner shipping was complemented by new rules on the confidentiality of key data of service contracts. While the carriers still have to file the contracts with the FMC, section 8 (c) (3) of the Shipping Act of 1984 as amended by OSRA now provides that the agreed rate and service commitments may not be made public anymore by the FMC. Finally, the Shipping Act of 1984 as amended by OSRA does not foresee anymore that carriers have to offer the same contractual conditions to all similarly situated shippers. Through these changes, Congress removed individual service contracts effectively from the control of liner conferences. A second change made by OSRA with the purpose of increasing the flexibility of carriers, was the reduction of the period of notice for independent rate action from ten to five days[84].

c) The impact of the Ocean Shipping Reform Act of 1998 on liner shipping in U. S. trades

The principal difference between the Shipping Act of 1984 and OSRA is that the former, in large part, relied upon the common carriage principle and mainly catered to the interests of carriers, whereas the latter also addressed the wish of the shippers to organise the markets for liner shipping in a more market oriented manner[85]. It is this change in paradigms that prompted commentators to state that OSRA constitutes a fundamental change in the regulation of liner shipping under U. S. law.

A first consequence of the passage of OSRA is that most goods transported to and from the U. S. by ship are not transported under a common tariff structure anymore, but rather on the basis of individual service contracts. According to

[83] The only way in which conferences may influence the practices of the individual carriers to enter into service contracts is through the adoption of voluntary guidelines; see: section 5 (c) of the Shipping Act of 1984 as amended by OSRA.

[84] See: section 5 (b) (8) of the Shipping Act of 1984 as amended by OSRA.

[85] Evidence for the new direction of OSRA is the insertion of a new statutory purpose provi sion in section 2 of Shipping Act of 1984 as amended by OSRA, where it is provided that this act seeks "*to promote the growth and development of United States exports through competitive and efficient ocean transportation and by placing a greater reliance on the marketplace*".

the FMC, 98 per cent of all filed service contracts are individual service contracts, and the overall number of filed service contracts has increased by 200 per cent since OSRA took effect, with the consequence that in some trade lanes, nearly all goods are now transported under individual service contracts. Therefore, they now constitute the primary rate setting vehicle in liner shipping transport in trade lanes to and from the U. S.[86]. In structural terms, OSRA represents a shift away from the common carriage principle to contractual shipping arrangements. The common carriage principle denotes a system, whereby everyone has access to transportation services under the same conditions. The carriage of goods under a publicly available common tariff and the *me-too* right of shippers ensured this principle under the regime of the Shipping Act of 1984[87]. Under OSRA, the confidentiality of service contracts and the cancellation of the *me-too* right emphasise the importance of contractual transport arrangements at the expense of the common carriage principle.

Another consequence of OSRA is the decline of the traditional conference agreement. Liner conferences embody the common carriage principle based on a common tariff structure. It has just been explained that both elements only play a reduced role in American Shipping, since the coming into force of OSRA. Cartel effectiveness of conferences is also impeded by the fact that OSRA acts as an incentive for the carriers to differentiate their service offerings. In a heterogeneous liner shipping industry it is increasingly difficult for conferences to exist[88], since they require a uniform shipping service as a prerequisite for a common conference tariff. The fact that OSRA now permits multiple trade lane service contracts[89] also works to the disadvantage of conferences, since they typically cover only one trade route. It is, therefore, not surprising that the number of conferences operating in U. S. trades has fallen by nearly one third after the implementation of OSRA[90] and that membership in the still existing conferences is declining as well[91].

The shift away from a common tariff structure towards individual and confidential service contracts alters the relationship between carriers and shippers. In the past, both groups often eyed each other with some degree of inherent distrust. The fact that transport conditions including prices are now mainly a product of business negotiations between carriers and shippers[92], and not of de-

[86] FMC, OSRA Report, (2001), p. 17.
[87] Reitzes/Sheran, (2002), p. 54; Rodriguez/Craig, (2001), p. 1.
[88] Reitzes/Sheran, (2002), p. 55.
[89] FMC, OSRA Report, (2001), p. 19; where it is stated that 18 per cent of all service contracts cover more than one trade lane.
[90] FMC, OSRA Report, (2001), p. 25.
[91] Lewis/Vellenga, (2000), p. 5.
[92] Lewis/Vellenga, (2000), p. 5.

liberations between carriers only, necessitates that both groups or individuals from those groups, communicate on a frequent basis. For the successful functioning of such business relations, it will be necessary to establish a minimum amount of trust and benevolence between carriers and shippers. The basis for such a change is that both sides feel that they can gain from individual service contracts. Carriers and shippers can profit from the confidentiality of service contracts, since it allows them to avoid sensitive business information from becoming public knowledge. It is, therefore, not surprising that around one third of all service contracts contains a confidentiality clause[93], and two per cent of all contracts even provide for penalties in the case of a breach of confidentiality[94].

Carriers have the chance to attract more customers though individual rate setting and they can develop a distinctive service profile, which allows them to differentiate themselves from other carriers. Shippers can profit from individual service contracts insofar, as they can negotiate service requirements that specifically meet their individual needs[95], and they may also be in a position to negotiate lower rates, especially if they require the shipment of large amounts of cargo[96]. The absence of the *me-too* requirement acts as an incentive for shippers to negotiate with skill, since they now are in a position, in which a successful negotiation practise can give them an advantage over their fellow shippers and competitors[97], that are no longer automatically able to contract with the carrier on the same terms. For these reasons, it is correct to state that OSRA allows and requires the development of business relations between carriers and shippers that are mutually beneficial[98].

d) Conclusion and outlook

The preceding analysis has demonstrated that the U. S. have a much longer tradition in the regulation of agreements in liner shipping than Europe. Whereas the Shipping Act of 1984 followed, in large part, a traditional approach to the regulation of liner shipping, meaning that the industry was left in largely to itself and that carriers could collude on a wide array of matters, OSRA in 1998 constituted a departure from this doctrine. With the passage of OSRA in 1998, the American legislator successfully strengthened pro-competitive elements in

[93] FMC, OSRA Report, (2001), p. 22.
[94] FMC, OSRA Report, (2001), p. 23.
[95] FMC, OSRA Report, (2001), p. 18.
[96] Reitzes/Sheran, (2002),
[97] Munster, (2001), p. 9 claims that, under the old system, such an incentive did not exist, neither for the carriers, nor the shippers.
[98] Munster, (2002), p. 9.

the markets for liner shipping. Yet, this act does not constitute a deregulation of the liner shipping industry, but rather a re-regulation of this sector[99].

Although the American and the European position share the general trend that they display a more cautious attitude towards agreements in liner shipping, the two positions differ in detail. The chief difference is that, according to the EC law position, it is not permissible for carriers to jointly determine the price for the inland leg of an intermodal transport operation[100]. In the U. S., section 4 (a) (1) of the Shipping Act of 1984 explicitly extends the scope of the antitrust exemption for agreements in liner shipping to multimoldal transport operations. OSRA did not alter this provision. A second major difference concerns talking or discussion agreements. The Commission and the CFI clarified in the *TAA* proceedings that such agreements may not benefit from the group exemption in Art. 3 Regulation 4056/86, since they do not constitute a liner conference in the sense of that Regulation[101]. Section 4 (a) (1) of the Shipping Act of 1984 on the other hand also explicitly extends to agreements with the intention to "*discuss*" transportation rates.

The subject of agreements in liner shipping and their treatment under U. S. law continues to cause controversy, a circumstance which is evidenced by the fact that Congress already conducted three post-OSRA hearings on this issue[102]. One issue featuring in the post-OSRA discussions is the concern that OSRA will pave the way for increased rate differentials in the markets for liner shipping, now that the rates are predominantly determined through individual negotiations[103]. Section 10 (5) of the Shipping Act of 1984 as amended by OSRA prohibits unjust discrimination in service contracts with regard to certain ports, but the law does not rule out discriminatory practises against shippers in service contracts in general[104]. Even if a discriminatory practice were considered illegal, it would be difficult to prove such a claim in the face of confidential service contracting[105] and an emerging heterogeneity of shipping services.

---

[99] Rodriguez/Craig, (2001), p. 1.

[100] It should be noted, however, that the individual carrier may offer through rates.

[101] See above, p. 102.

[102] The Committee on the Judiciary of the House of Representatives conducted a hearing on antitrust aspects of the Ocean Shipping Reform Act of 1998 on May 5, 1999, a hearing on the Free Market Antitrust Immunity Reform Act (FAIR) of 1999 on March 22, 2000 and a hearing on the Free Market Antitrust Immunity Reform Act (FAIR) of 2001 on June 5, 2002.

[103] Danas, (1998), p. 2.

[104] Danas, (1998), p. 2; Shashikumar/Schatz, (2000), p. 6.

[105] Lewis/Vellenga, (2000), p. 6; who are mistaken in their assumption that discrimination against shippers generally remains prohibited. Sec. 10 (b) (5) and (9) only mention discrimination with regard to certain ports.

A second point of criticism in connection with OSRA concerns the reduced rate transparency as a consequence of confidential contractual transport arrangements. Especially small shippers argue that the new regulation puts them at a disadvantage in comparison with large shippers, that can negotiate lower rates because of their large freight volume[106]. Small shippers fear that they have to pay more for transport services under the contractual rate making system than under the common carriage principle, where they could profit from generally applicable tariffs and the right to enter into service contracts under the same favourable conditions as their competitors. This concern of the small shippers can partially be overcome if they co-operate in the purchase of transport services[107]. To this effect, OSRA permits shippers' associations and otherwise unrelated groups of shippers to enter into service contracts[108]. Such entities represent a larger freight volume and can therefore negotiate lower freight rates as do large shippers.

Nevertheless, the discussion of transparency of shipping markets highlights the fact that market transparency develops unevenly as a consequence of OSRA. While it is increasingly difficult for shippers to assess whether the rates they negotiate with the carriers correspond to the rates carriers offer to their competitors, carriers can still obtain information on rates from fellow liner shipping operators and discuss rate related issues with them. Even if confidentiality clauses in service contracts bar them from revealing customer specific information to other carriers, they can still discuss general price aspects, such as, for example, the general development freight rates or minimum rates that they offer. It is, therefore, not surprising that small shippers advocate a termination of antitrust immunity for agreements in liner shipping, as a means to counter the uneven information flow in the liner shipping industry[109].

However, such suggestions have caused negative comment from those who are concerned that a complete repeal of antitrust immunity for agreements in liner shipping under U.S. law would be disadvantageous for domestic shipping operators in comparison to foreign carriers[110]. Liner conferences enjoy worldwide antitrust immunity until this day and the unilateral repeal of this immunity through the U. S. could lead to disruptive and unpredictable consequences. In the event of a change of U. S. legislation on this issue, American carriers would have to withdraw from all agreements in liner shipping, and U. S. authorities would need to police all agreements among liner shipping operators that have

---

[106] Danas, (1998), p. 2.
[107] Danas, (1998), p. 2
[108] Sec. 3 (19) and (22) of the Shipping Act of 1984 as amended by OSRA.
[109] Danas, (1999), p. 53; see also: Nannes, (1999), p. 22.
[110] Creel, (1999), p. 11.

an effect on U. S. commerce. One initial disadvantage arising for American carriers from such a step would be that, only they feel the strict enforcement measures of the U. S. authorities, since it is generally more difficult to prove allegations against foreign based carriers and especially since it is even more difficult to enforce any consecutive decisions against them. It is also feared that American carriers might become the target of retaliatory measures of foreign countries, if the U. S. starts to police collusive practises in liner shipping that are considered legal or even fostered by these countries[111].

In order to avoid such detrimental practices for American liner operators, it is considered necessary to co-ordinate any steps towards the repeal of antitrust immunity on an international basis with the major U. S. trading partners, for example through the OECD[112]. One possible solution could be the partial withdrawal of the antitrust immunity only from those collusive practices that concern prices and a retention of antitrust immunity for forms of operational cooperation among liner shipping operators[113]. Such a measure would ensure that consortia agreements, which have proven positive due to their efficiency enhancing effect[114], are not outlawed. The partial withdrawal of antitrust immunity in addition has the virtue that it follows the current trend in liner shipping away from traditional liner conferences and towards forms of operational cooperation. Under such a system, it would, however, become necessary for American carriers to withdraw their participation from any agreements that discuss or even fix prices. Only such a step could remedy the uneven distribution of information on prices in the liner shipping industry which caused the protest of shippers against the current regime after the implementation of OSRA.

[111] Creel, (1999), p. 30.
[112] Creel, (1999), p. 30.
[113] Won, (2000), p. 46.
[114] See above, p. 164 f.

Conclusion

The present study has sought to evaluate how far the current European legal regime, applicable to agreements in liner shipping, requires legislative action of the European legislator. This question is of importance considering the fact that the OECD has issued a report on April 16, 2002, in which it recommended *inter alia* the removal of any existing antitrust exemptions for price fixing and rate discussions in liner shipping in the laws of its member countries[1]. In this context, it is important to note that at the same time the U. S., one of the main trading partners of the European Community, introduced a bill in the House of Representatives entitled "Free Market Antitrust Immunity Reform (FAIR) Act of 2001". Should this bill become law, the U. S. would repeal the antitrust immunity currently granted to agreements among carriers, as described in chapter seven of this study. The Commission reacted to the OECD report with the beginning of its own review of Regulation 4056/86. Regulation 823/2000, which contains the block exemption for consortia agreements is not subject to this inquiry[2]. These circumstances demonstrate that the question of whether it is sufficient to interpret Art. 3 Regulation 4056/86 in a strict manner, as do the CFI and the Commission, or whether it is instead necessary to modify or abandon the liner conference block exemption, is of fundamental importance for the current and future development of European maritime transport law.

The answer to the thus phrased question offered in this study is simple: repeal the block exemption for price fixing agreements in liner shipping.

A first argument to support the cancellation of Art. 3 Regulation 4056/86 is of a factual nature. Today, liner conferences are no longer the dominant form of cooperation in the liner shipping industry, as they were 15 years ago at the time Regulation 4056/86 came into force and even more so at the time the UNCTAD code was drafted in the early 1970s. Conference coverage has dropped from a high of 80 to 90 per cent in the 1970s to an average of 60 per cent in the major trade lanes today[3]. Since the enactment of OSRA in 1999 the number of conferences serving the U. S. has dropped, and the remaining conferences have often lost some of their members[4]. OSRA has also seriously diminished the capacity of conferences to enforce their common tariff against its members through the introduction of mandatory, individual and confidential service contracting. Most cargoes to and from the U. S. are now being transported on the basis of individual contracts and not on the basis of common conference tariffs. The type of

[1] OECD, (2002), p. 78.
[2] Stragier, (2002), p. 9 ff.
[3] See above, p. 43.
[4] See above, p. 183 f.

agreement by which carriers today seek to ameliorate their market position is the consortium. Carriers enter into both types of agreements with the intention to strengthen their position in the market. The principal difference between a liner conference and a consortium is that the former seeks to increase the carriers profits through price control, whereas the latter does not influence the price as the main competitive element, but aims at the rationalisation of shipping services. The decreasing practical importance of conference agreements for the liner shipping industry is a circumstance, which European competition law cannot dismiss. As a consequence, the cancellation of the block exemption for liner conferences is the proper course of action.

A second argument, by which carriers often try to support their demand for a continued exemption of price fixing agreements in liner shipping from the regular mechanisms of competition law, is that the liner shipping industry is special[5]. It is argued that the abolishment of the exemption for price fixing agreements would lead to chaotic and destructive market structures, which would eventually also hurt the shippers requiring reliable transport services. The economic analysis of the markets for liner shipping services in chapter four has not yielded any evidence for such a special character of the liner shipping industry[6]. Instead, liner conferences constitute collusive oligopolies, as standard economic analysis would suggest. Carriers often attempt to negate the oligopolistic character of liner conferences by saying that the profitability of liner shipping operators is low. The absence of supernormal profits, however, does not constitute a contradiction to the finding that liner conferences are an oligopolistic structure, since oligopolies are inherently unstable as a consequence of the diverging interests of the individual cartel members. The finding that liner shipping is not of such a special nature that it requires price fixing agreements, is supported by the development of liner shipping in the American trades after the enactment of OSRA. Although the U. S. markets for liner shipping services now operate according to regular market principles and not on the basis of a commonly agreed tariff structure, the envisioned chaos has so far not hit the U. S. markets for liner shipping.

A further argument in support of a cancellation of the block exemption for price fixing agreements in liner shipping, concerns the development of the European liner fleet. It has been said that Regulation 4056/86 has the purpose to foster and protect the development of a European liner fleet, although such a purpose is not mentioned explicitly in Regulation 4056/86[7]. Despite the passage of Regulation 4056/86, the European liner shipping industry has not recovered from the emer-

[5] See above, p. 89.
[6] See above, p. 91.
[7] Temple Lang, ETL (1993), p. 405 ff, p. 408.

gence of the independent Asian carriers, a development which has been identified in chapter two as one of the major trends in liner shipping since the 1980s. The share of slots of European carriers among the top twenty carriers worldwide has dropped from 34 per cent in 1985 to 25 per cent in 1998[8]. The finding that the exemption of price fixing agreements in liner shipping from the regular mechanisms of competition law does not function as a means to secure the survival of the domestic liner fleet is supported by U. S. experience. In spite of the long tradition of exempting such agreements from sec. 1 of the Sherman Act, none of the 20 largest carriers in the world today are American[9]. As a consequence, it is correct to state that a block exemption for liner conferences cannot be justified by saying that such an exemption is necessary for the survival of European liner shipping[10].

The discussion of U. S. legislation on the issue of liner conferences and like agreements in chapter seven has raised the issue of international comity in the context of a possible abolishment of the antitrust exemption for agreements in liner shipping. It was feared that such a move would be detrimental to domestic carriers, since they would have to withdraw from conference agreements and because foreign countries might direct retaliatory measures against U. S. carriers as a consequence of such a change of U. S. legislation. If such concerns were rational, they would also apply to the cancellation of the liner conference block exemption at the level of European competition law. Yet, there are severe doubts as to whether the cancellation of either exemption would hurt domestic carriers disproportionately in comparison to their foreign counterparts.

First, all carriers, European as well as foreign, would be subjected to a prohibition of conference agreements, as soon as they engage in trade on routes that call at Community ports. As it has been explained in chapter six of this study, Art. 81 (ex 85) EC is applicable in such situations. Second, the above described fears rely on the assumption that conferences still constitute a vital element of the carrier strategy, and that carriers which cannot enter conference agreements are at a serious disadvantage in comparison to their business rivals, which may do so. It has been explained, however, throughout this study that carriers today rely less on conference agreements and more on consortia, especially in the form of modern alliances, as a means to ameliorate their market position. For this reason, the withdrawal from conference agreements does not burden the carriers serving Europe with any insurmountable difficulties. Development of shipping in the U. S. trades has shown that liner shipping markets may well operate without a system of common prices. The abolishment of the liner conference block exemp-

[8] Mercer, (1997), p. 138.
[9] OECD, (2002), p. 14.
[10] Temple Lang, ETL (1993), p. 408.

tion would merely constitute the logical continuation of the developments witnessed in the American trades after the enactment of OSRA. Finally, any fears concerning adverse government behaviour of third countries could be overcome if the U. S. and Europe agreed on how to deal with the issue of ending the special treatment of price fixing agreements in liner shipping. Such a step is not merely hypothetical, since the U. S. Congress has repeatedly considered legislative proposals with the purpose of withdrawing the current antitrust exemption from liner shipping since the enactment of OSRA[11].

The final reason, why the Commission should consider a cancellation of the liner conference block exemption is the incompatibility of Art. 3 Regulation 4056/86 with the EC Treaty. It has been explained in chapter six that joint price fixing of liner conferences is not acceptable under Art. 81 (ex 85) EC. Art. 211 (ex 155) EC confers upon the Commission the duty to "*ensure that the provisions of this Treaty (.....) are applied*". In pursuance of this duty, the Commission should initiate a legislative proposal with the intention of eradicating the liner conference block exemption. A possible course of action would be to abolish Art. 3 Regulation 4056/86 and all other provisions governing the liner conference block exemption without any form of replacement. The remainder of Regulation 4056/86, especially Art. 2 (technical agreements) and the procedural provisions contained in Section 2 of that Regulation, should be incorporated into Regulation 823/2000. Since the block exemption for consortia is approved by all parties involved and also conforms to the Treaty, it is not necessary to modify any of the provisions contained therein. The inclusion of the remainder of Regulation 4056/86 into what is now Regulation 823/2000 would have one additional advantage: the application of European competition law to maritime transport would then be governed comprehensively by just one Regulation.

[11] Hearing before the Committee on the Judiciary of the House of Representatives on the Free Market antitrust Immunity Reform (FAIR) Act of 1999 on March 22, 2000 and hearing before the Committee on the Judiciary of the House of Representatives on the Free Market Antitrust Immunity Reform (FAIR) Act of 2001 on June 5, 2002.

Bibliography

Judgements of the European Court of Justice and the Court of First Instance:

Case 6/64, *Costa (Flaminio) v ENEL*, (1964), ECR, p. 585 ff.

Joint Cases 56 and 58/64, *Consten SARL & Grundig-Verkaufs GmbH v Commission*, (1966), ECR, p. 299 ff.

Case 56/65, *Société Technique Minière v Maschinenbau Ulm GmbH*, (1966), ECR, p. 282 ff.

Case 14/68, *Walt Wilhelm and Others v Bundeskartellamt*, (1969), ECR, p. 1 ff.

Case 48/69, *Imperial Chemical Industries Ltd. v Commission*, (1972), ECR, p. 619 ff.

Case 22/71, *Béguelin Import Co. v S.A.G. L. Import Export*, (1971), ECR, p. 949 ff.

Case 167/73, *Commission v France (Re French Seamen)*, (1974) ECR, p. 359 ff.

Case 26/76, *Metro-SB-Grossmärkte GmbH & Co. KG v Commission (No. 1)*, (1977), ECR, p. 1875 ff.

Case 27/76, *United Brands Company and United Brands Continentaal BV v Commission*, (1978), ECR, p. 207 ff.

Joint Cases 209 – 215 and 218/78, *Heintz van Landewyck Sàrl and Others v Commission*, (1980), ECR, p. 3125 ff.

Case 322/81, *N. V. Nederlandsche Banden - Industrie Michelin v Commission*, (1983), ECR, p. 3461 ff.

Case 13/83, *European Parliament v Council*, (1985), ECR, p. 1513 ff.

Case 42/84, *Remia BV and Others v Commission*, (1985), ECR, p. 2545 ff.

Case 161/84, *Pronuptia de Paris GMBH v Pronuptia de Paris Irmgard Schillgalis*, (1986), ECR, p. 353 ff.

Case 75/84, *Metro-SB-Grossmärkte GmbH & Co. KG v Commission (No. 2)*, (1986), ECR, p. 3021 ff.

Joint Cases 209 - 213/84, *Ministère Public v Lucas Asjes and Others (Nouvelles Frontières)*, (1986), ECR, p. 1425 ff.

Joint Cases 89/85 104 /85 114/85 116/85 125 - 125/85, *A. Ahlström Osakeytiö and Others v Commission*, (1988), ECR, p. 5193 ff.

Case 66/86, *Ahmed Saeed Flugreisen and Silver Line Reisbüro v Zentrale zur Bekämpfung unlauteren Wetttbewerbs*, (1989), ECR, p. 803 ff.

Case C-41/90, *Höfner & Elser v Macrotron GmbH*, (1991), ECR I, p. 1979 ff.

Joint Cases C-395/96 and C-396/96, *Compagnie maritime belge transports and Others v Commission (CEWAL)*, (2000), ECR I, p. 1365 ff.

Case T-11/89, *Shell International Chemical Co. Ltd. v Commission*, (1995), ECR II, p. 757 ff.

Joint Cases T-68/89 T-77/89 T-78/89, *Societa Italiano Vetro v Commission*, (1992), ECR II, p. 1403 ff.

Case T-141/89, *Montepide SpA v Commission*, (1992), ECR II, p. 1155 ff.

Case T-148/89, *Tréfilunion v Commission*, (1995), ECR II, p. 1063 ff.

Case T-395/94, *Atlantic Container Line AB and Others v Commission*, (2002), ECR II, p. 875 ff.

Case T-86/95, *Compagnie générale maritime and Others v. Commission*, (2002), ECR II, p. 1011.

Case T-18/97, *Atlantic Container Line AB and Others v Commission*, (2002), ECR II, p. 1125 ff.

Judgements of other courts:

United States v. Hamburg- Amerikanische Packet - Fahrt - Actien - Gesellschaft et al, (1911), Circuit Court, S. D. New York, 200 F 806.

United States v. Pacific & Arctic Railway & Navigation Company et al, (1913), United States Supreme Court, 228 U. S. 87.

United States v. Prince Line Limited et al, (1915), District Court, S. D. New York, 220 F 230.

United States Navigation Co. v. Cunard S. S. Co. et al, (1932), United States Supreme Court, 284 U. S. 474.

Far East Conference et al v. United States et al, (1952), United States Supreme Court, 342 U. S. 570.

Federal Maritime Board v. Isbrandtsen Co. et al, (1952), United States Supreme Court, 356 U. S. 481.

Carnation Co. v. Pacific Westbound Conference et al, (1966), United States Supreme Court, 383 U. S. 213.

Federal Maritime Commission et al v. Aktiebolaget Svenska Amerika Linien, (1968), United States Supreme Court, 390 U. S. 238.

Federal Maritime Commission v. Seatrain Lines Inc. et al, (1973), United States Supreme Court, 411 U. S. 726.

The case of the SS "*Lotus*", (1927), Permanent Court of International Justice, PCIJ Reports, Series A, No. 10.

Decisions of the Commission and other Commission documents:

Grosfillex-Fillistorf, 64/233/EEC, 11th of March 1964, OJ 1964, 58/915.

Bendix, 64/344/EEC, 1st of June 1964, OJ 1964, 92/1426.

Dyestuffs, 96/243/EEC, 24th of July 1969, OJ 1969, L-195/11.

Papiers Peints de Belgique, 74/431/EEC, 23rd of July 1974, OJ 1974, L-237/3.

Preserved Mushrooms, 75/77/EEC, 8th of January 1975, OJ 1975, L-29/26.

GB-Inno-BM/Fedetab, 78/670/EEC, 20th of July 1978, OJ 1978, L-224/29.

Cast Iron and Steel Rolls, 83/546/EEC, 17th of October 1983, OJ 1983, L-317/1.

Zinc Producer Group, 84/405/EEC, 6th of August 1984, OJ 1984, L-220/27.

Wood Pulp, 85/202/EEC, 19th of December 1984, OJ 1985, L-85/1.

Welded Steel Mesh, 89/515/EEC, 2nd of August 1989, OJ 1989, L-260/1.

Far Eastern Freight Conference (FETC), 94/985/EC, 21st of December 1994, OJ 1994, L-376/17.

Trans-Atlantic Agreement (TAA), 94/980/EC, 19th of October 1994, OJ 1994, L-376/1.

Trans-Atlantic Conference Agreement (TACA), 1999/234/EC, 16th of September 1998, OJ 1999, L-095/1.

Europe Asia Trades Agreement (EATA), 1999/485/EC, 30th of April 1999, OJ 1999, L-193/23.

Far East Trade Tariff Charges and Surcharges Agreement (FETTCSA), 2000/627/EC, 16th of May 2000, OJ 2000 L-268/1.

Commission (1985), Progress towards a Common Transport Policy Report on Maritime Transport, COM (85) 90 final, March 6,1985.

Commission (1990), Communication by the Commission - Report on the Possibility of a Group Exemption for Consortia Agreements in Liner Shipping, COM (90) 260 final, June 18,1990.

Commission (1995), Commission Working Document on Regulation 870/95, at: http://www.europa.eu.int/comm/competition/antitrust/report_comm_reg_870_95_de.pdf

Commission (1997), Commission Notice on the Definition of Relevant Markets for the Purposes of Community Competition Law, OJ 1997, C-372/5

Documents of public interest:

Structure and Organisation of MaritimeTransport, Mercer Management Con sulting, Office for Official Publications of the European Communities, Luxembourg, (1996)

Analysis of Supply and Demand of Liner Shipping Services, Mercer Management and Consulting, (1997), at: http://europa.eu.int/comm/transport/extra/final_reports/waterborn/asdss.pdf

Economics of Liner Shipping Conferences, Meyrick & Associates Pty Ltd, (1999), at: http://pc.gov.au/inquiry/shipping/subs005.pdf

International Liner Cargo Shipping: A Review of Part X of the Trade Practices Act 1974, Productivity Commission of Australia, (1999) at: http://www.pc.gov.au/inquiry/shipping/finalreport

Submission of Brian Mankins to the Productivity Commission of Australia, (1999), at: http://www.pc.gov.au/inquiry/shipping/subs/sub004.pdf

Statement of Mr. H. Creel before the U. S. House of Representatives, Hearing before the Committee on the Judiciary of the House of Representatives, 106th Congress, 1st Session, May 5,1999, Serial No. 30, p. 6 ff

Statement of Mr. A. Danas before the U. S. House of Representatives, Hearing before the Committee on the Judiciary of the House of Representatives, 106th Congress, 1st Session, May 5,1999, Serial No. 30, p. 48 ff

Statement of Mr. J. Nannes before the U. S. House of Representatives, Hearing before the Committee on the Judiciary of the House of Representatives, 106th Congress, 1st Session, May 5,1999, Serial No. 30, p. 20 ff

Statement of Mr. D. Won before the U. S. House of Representatives, Hearing before the Committee on the Judiciary of the House of Representatives, 106th Congress, 1st Session, May 5,1999, Serial No. 30, p. 18 ff

Submission of the CSC to the OECD on Maritime Regulatory Reform, (2001), at: http://www.oecd.org/dsti/sti/transpor/sea/prod/CSC_Competition_Policy.pdf

Submission of the ESC to the OECD on Maritime Regulatory Reform, (2001), at: http://www.oecd.org/dsti/sti/transpor/sea/prod/ESC_Competition_Policy.pdf

Submission of the NITL to the OECD on Maritime Regulatory Reform, (2001), at: http://www.oecd.org/dsti/sti/transpor/sea/prod/NITL_CompetitionPolicy.pdf

Submission of the TACA to the OECD on Maritime Regulatory Reform, (2001) at: http://www.oecd.org/dsti/sti/transpor/sea/prod/TACA_submissions.pdf

Submission of the TSA to the OECD on Maritime Regulatory Reform, (2001), at: http://www.oecd.org/dsti/sti/transpor/sea/prod/TSA_Competition_Policy.pdf

Submission of the WSC to the OECD on Maritime Regulatory Reform, (2001), at:http://www.oecd.org/dsti/sti/transpor/sea/prod/WSC_Competition_Policy.pdf

The Impact of the Ocean Shipping Reform Act of 1998, Federal Maritime Commission, (2001), at: http://www.fmc.gov/OSRA_REPORT/OSRA_STUDY.pdf

Competition Policy in Liner Shipping; final report, OECD, (2002), at: http://www.oecd.org/pdf/M00020000/M00020755.pdf

Statement of Mr. H. Creel before the U. S. House of Representatives, Hearing before the Committee on the Judiciary of the House of Representatives, 107th Congress, 1st Session, June 5, 2002, Serial No. 88, at: http://www.fmc.gov/Speeches/Creel/HR1253%20statemetn.html

Books:

Baumol, William/Blinder, Alan, Economics, Principles and Policy, The Dryden Press, Fort Worth/U. S., 1999, 8th Edition

Bellamy, Christopher/Child, Graham D., Common Market Law of Competition, edited by Vivien Rose, Sweet & Maxwell, London/U. K., 1993, 4th Edition

Calliess, Christian/Ruffert, Matthias, Kommentar zu EU-Vertrag und EG-Vertrag, Luchterhand, Neuwied, 2002, 2nd Edition

Clough, Mark/Randolph, Fergus, Shipping and EC Competition Law, Butterworths, London/U. K., 1991

Craig, Paul/De Burca, Grainne, EU Law, Texts, Cases and Materials, Oxford University Press, Oxford/U. K., 1998, 2nd Edition

Deakin, B.M., Shipping Conferences, Cambridge University Press, Cambridge/U. K., 1973

Dolfen, Michael, Der Verkehr im europäischen Wettbewerb, R. v. Decker's Verlag, Heidelberg, 1991

Erdmenger, Jürgen, The European Community Transport Policy: Towards a Common Transport Policy, Gower Publishing, Aldershot/U. K., 1983

Eaton, Curties/Eaton, Diane/Allen, Douglas, Microeconomics, Prentice Hall Canada Inc., Scarborough/Canada, 1999, 4th Edition

Faull, Jonathan/Nikpay, Ali, Competition Law, Oxford University Press, Oxford/U. K., 1999

Gilman, Sidney, The competitive Dynamics of Container Shipping, Gower Publishing, London/U. K., 1983

Gleiss, Alfred/Hirsch, Martin, Kommentar zum EWG-Kartellrecht, Verlagsgesellschaft Recht und Wirtschaft mbh, Heidelberg, 1978, 3rd Edition

Goyder, D. G., EC Competition Law, Oxford University Press, Oxford/U. K., 1998, 3rd Edition, cit.: Goyder, (1998)

Grabitz, Eberhard/Hilf, Meinhard, EUV/EGV, Volume 1, (Maastricht Version), Verlag C. H. Beck, München, 1999 (13. Update)

Grabitz, Eberhard/Hilf, Meinhard, Das Recht der Europäischen Union, Vol. 1, Verlag C. H. Beck, München, 2002, (19th update)

von der Groeben, Hans/Thiesing, Jochen/Ehlermann, Claus-Dieter, Kommentar zum EU/EG Vertrag, Volume 1, Arts. 1 – 84, Nomos Verlagsgesellschaft, Baden-Baden, 1997, 5th Edition

von der Groeben, Hans/Thiesing, Jochen/Ehlermann, Claus-Dieter, Kommentar zum EU/EG Vertrag, Volume 2/1, Arts. 85 – 87, Nomos Verlagsgesellschaft, Baden-Baden, 1999, 5th Edition

von der Groeben, Hans/Thiesing, Jochen/Ehlermann, Claus-Dieter, Kommentar um EU/EG Vertrag, Volume 5, Nomos Verlagsgesellschaft, Baden Baden, 1997, 5th Edition

Herman, Amos, Shipping Conferences, Kluwer Law and Taxation Publishers, Deventer/Netherlands, 1983

Immenga, Ulrich/Mestmäker, Ernst-Joachim, EG-Wettbewerbsrecht, Volume 1, Verlag C.H. Beck, München, 1997

Immenga, Ulrich/Mestmäker, Ernst-Joachim, EG-Wettbewerbsrecht, Volume 2, Verlag C.H. Beck, München, 1997

Ipsen, Knut, Völkerrecht, Verlag C. H. Beck, München , 1999, 4th Edition

Jacobs, Andreas, Zur Vereinbarkeit von Kartellabsprachen der internationalen Linienschiffahrt mit Artikel 85 EWG-Vertrag, Nomos Verlagsgesellschaft, Baden-Baden, 1991

Jansson, Jan Owen/Shneerson, Dan, Liner Shipping Economics, Chapman and Hall, London/U.K., New York/U.S., 1987

Jones, Alison/Sufrin, Brenda, EC Competition Law, Texts Cases and Materials, Oxford University Press, Oxford/U. K., 2001

Koutsoyiannis, A., Modern Microeconomics, The Macmillan Press Ltd, London/U. K., 1979, 2nd Edition

Kühne, Eberhardt, Kooperationen in der internationalen Seeschiffahrt und europäisches Kartellrecht, Peter Lang Europäischer Verlag der Wissenschaften, Frankfurt am Main, 1996

Lenz, Carl Otto, EG-Vertrag Kommentar, Bundesanzeiger, Köln, 1999, 2nd Edition

Mankiw, Gregory, Principles of Economics, Harcourt College Publishers, Fort Worth/U. S., 2001, 2nd Edition

Marx Jr., Daniel, International Shipping Cartels, Princeton University Press, Princeton/U. S., 1953

Nicholson, Walter, Microeconomic Theory, Basic Principles and Extensions, The Dryden Press, Fort Worth/U. S., 1998, 7th Edition

Nicholson, Walter, Intermediate Microeconomics and its Application, The Dryden Press, Fort Worth/U. S., 2000, 8th Edition

Oppermann, Thomas, Europarecht, Verlag C.H.Beck, München, 1999, 2nd Edition

O'Sullivan, Arthur/Sheffrin, Steven M., Microeconomics, Principles and Tools, Prentice Hall, Upper Saddle River/U. S., (2001), 2nd Edition

Power, Vincent, EC Shipping Law, Lloyd's Shipping Law Library, London/U.K., 1992

Reisener, Wolfgang, Staatliche Regulierung der Linienschiffahrt in den USA, Veröffentlichungen des Hamburgischen Weltwirtschaftsarchivs, Hamburg, 1968

Ruffin, Roy J./Gregory, Paul R., Principles of Microeconomics, Addison Wesley, Boston/U. S., 2001

Streinz, Rudolf, Europarecht, C.F. Müller Verlag, Heidelberg, 1999

Schwarze, Jürgen, EU-Kommentar, Nomos Verlagsgesellschaft, Baden Baden, 2000

Sletmo, Gunnar K./Williams, Ernest W., Liner Conferences in the Container Age, Macmillan, New York/U. S., London/U. K., 1981

Articles:

Basedow, Jürgen, Europäische Seeverkehrspolitik, Dienstleistungsfreiheit und Seekabotage, in: Transportrecht, 1994, p. 85 ff

Braakman, August J., Some Observations on the Block Exemption for Consortia Agreements in Light of Regulation No 4056/86, in: European Transport Law, 1996, p. 265 ff

Brooks, Mary, Competition in Liner Shipping: Are National Policies Appropriate?, in: Ocean Yearbook, 1998, Volume 13, p. 142 ff

Brooks, Mary, Restructuring in the Liner Shipping Industry: A Case Study in Evolution, 2000, at: http://mgmt.dal.ca/cibs/%5B-papers/DP_176.pdf

Britain, Sir Leon, The EC's Competition Policy for Liner Shipping set in its Commercial and Political Context, in: European Transport Law, 1993, p. 337 ff.

Bunte, Hermann-Josef, Das Verhältnis von deutschem zu europäischem Kartellrecht, in: Wirtschaft und Wettbewerb, 1989, p. 7 ff

Butz, David, Ocean Shipping Economics: Free Trade and Antitrust Implications, in: Contemporary Policy Issues, 1993, Issue 3, p. 69 ff

Campbell, Thomas C./Shin, Thai S., Regulatory Reform, Ocean Shipping: The Shipping Act of 1984, in: Transportation Quarterly, 1987, Vol. 41, p. 151 ff

Casavant, Kenneth L./Wilson, Wesley W., Shipper Perspectives of the Shipping Act of 1984, in: Transportation Quarterly, 1991, Vol. 45, p. 109 ff

Clyde, Paul/Reitzes, James, The Effectiveness of Collusion Under Antitrust Immunity - The Case of Liner Shipping Conferences, 1995, at: http://www.ftc.gov/reports/shipping.pdf

Confavreux, Régis, Les transports maritimes dans le droit de la concurrence communitaire, in: Revue du Marché commun et de l'Union europénne, 1996, p. 369 ff

Davies, Peter N., British Shipping and World Trade: Rise and Decline, 1820-1939, in: Business History of Shipping, University of Tokyo Press, Tokyo, 1985

Erdmenger, Jürgen, Development and Prospects of the Maritime Transport Law of the European Communities, in: European Transport Law, 1988, p. 543 ff

Erdmenger, Jürgen, Zur Anwendung des EG-Kartellrechts auf die Seeschiffahrt, in: Festschrift for Peter Raisch, Carl Heymanns Verlag, Köln, 1995

Faull, Jonathan, Recent Developments in European Community Competition Policy in the Maritime Field, in: European Transport Law, 1995, p. 3 ff

Fink,Carsten/Mattoo, Aaditya/Neagu, Chrisina Ileana, Trade in International Maritime Services:How Much Does Policy Matter?, 2001, Policy Research Working Paper No 1522, (The Worldbank), at.: http://www.econ.worldbank.org/files/1338_wps2522.pdf

Fox, Ruth, An Oligopoly Model of Ocean Liner Shipping, in: Review of Industrial Organisation, 1994, p. 343 ff

Franck, Bernard/Bunel, Jean-Claude, Contestability, Competition and Regulation The Case of Liner Shipping, in: International Journal of Industrial Organisation, 1991, Vol. 9, p. 141 ff

Francois, Joseph/Wooton, Ian, Trade In International Transport Services: The Role of Competition, 2000, at: http://www.gla.ac.uk/Acad/PolEcon/pdf00/ShippingFeb2000.pdf

Van Ginderachter, Eric/Durande, S., EC Regulation 870/95: The Consortia Block Exemption, in: European Transport Law, 1996, p. 241 ff

Green, Nicholas, Competition and Maritime Trade: A Critical View, in: European Transport Law, 1988, p. 612 ff

Green, Nicholas, The Consortia Block Exemption, in: European Transport Law, 1993, p. 477 ff

Grewlich, Klaus W., Die UN-Konvention über einen Verhaltenskodex für Linienkonferenzen, in: Zeitschrift für ausländisches und öffentliches Recht, 1975, Vol. 35, p. 742 ff

Hautau, Ullrich, Die wettbewerbspolitische Regulierung internationaler Container-Seeverkehrsmärkte – US-amerikanische Reformen und EU-Regelungen im Vergleich, in: Zeitschrift für Verkehrswissenschaft, 2002, p. 25 ff

Heldring, Balt, Free Access to Ocean Trades, in: European Transport Law, 1988, p. 600 ff

Hoffmann, Jan, Concentration in Liner Shipping: Causes and Impacts, in: World Sea Trade Service Review, 1998, Volume 1, Third Quarter, p. 68 ff

Hummels, David, Have International Transportation Costs Declined?, 1999, at: http://www.gsb.uchicago.edu/fac/david.hummels/research/transport/declined.pdf

Kang, Jong-Soon/Findlay, Christopher, Regulatory Reform in the Maritime Industry, in: Impediments to Trade in Services, edited by Christopher Findlay and Tony Warren, Routledge, London/U. K., New York/U. S., 2000

Knebel, Hans-Werner, Die Extraterritorialität des Europäischen Kartellrechts, in: Europäische Zeitung für Wirtschaftsrecht, 1991, p. 265 ff

Kreis, Helmut W. R., Consortia in Liner Shipping, in: European Transport Law, 1995, p. 849 ff

Kreis, Helmut W. R., European Community Competition Policy and International Shipping, in: European Transport Law, 1992, p. 155 ff

Kreis, Helmut W. R., Maritime Transport and EEC Competition Rules, in: European Transport Law, 1988, p. 562 ff

Kröger, Bernd, Current Issues in EC Maritime Competition Law, in: European Transport Law, 1993, p. 423 ff

Kröger, Bernd, Europäisches Kartellrecht und Seeschiffahrt, in: Transportrecht, 1994, p. 7 ff

Lange, Dieter G. F./Sandage, John Byron, The Wood Pulp Decision and its Implications for EC Competition Law, in: Common Market Law Review, 1989, p. 137 ff

Lieberknecht, Otfried, Das Verhältnis der EWG-Gruppenfreistellungsverordnungen zum deutschen Kartellrecht, in: Festschrift für Gerd Pfeiffer Carl Heymanns Verlag, Köln, Berlin, Bonn, München, 1988

Lewis, Ira/Vellenga, David B., The Ocean Shipping Reform Act of 1998, in: Transportation Journal, 2000, Vol. 39, Issue 4 (electronic resource)

Meessen, Karl Matthias, Der Räumliche Anwendungsbereich des EWG Kartellrechts und das Allgemeine Völkerrecht, in: Europarecht, 1973, p. 18 ff

Munari, Francesco, Das Europäische Wettbewerbsrecht des Seeverkehrs, in: Rabels Zeitschrift für ausländisches und internationales Privatrecht, 1990, p. 627 ff

Munster, Marc, Confidentiality in "Service Contracting" under the Ocean Shipping Reform Act of 1998, (2001), at: http://www.wmcd.com/articles/maritime/reform.html

Necker, Karl-Hartmann, Die Seeschiffahrt im Europäischen Recht, in: Festschrift für Martin Luther, p. 113 ff, C. H. Beck Verlag, München, 1976

Pernice, Ingolf, Offene Märkte und Wettbewerbsordnung der EG im Bereich der Seeschiffahrt, in: Festschrift für Arved Deringer, Nomos Verlagsgesellschaft, Baden-Baden, 1993

Pirrong, Stephen Craig, An Application of Core Theory to the analysis of Ocean Shipping Markets, in: Journal of Law and Economics, (1992), Vol. 35, April, p. 89 ff.

Power, Vincent, EC Maritime Policy - A lawyer's reaction, in: European Transport Law, 1996, p. 179 ff

Prieß, Hans-Joachim, Zur Entwicklung des EG-Rechts betreffend die Seeschiffahrt, in: Europarecht, 1989, p. 369 ff

Rabe, Hans-Jürgen, Wettbewerbs-und Seeschiffahrtspolitik der EG: Ein ungelöster Widerspruch?, in: Transportrecht, 1994, p. 1 ff

Rabe, Dieter/Schütte, Michael, Die erste Verordnung des Rates zur Anwendung des EWG-Kartellrechts (Art. 85 und 86 EWG) auf den Seeverkehr, in: Recht der Internationalen Wirtschaft, 1988, p. 701 ff

Reitzes, James, Ocean Shipping Economics: Comment, in: Contemporary Policy Issues 1993, Issue 3, p. 81 ff

Reitzes, James D./Sheran, Kelli L., Rolling Seas in Liner Shipping, in: Review of Industrial Organisation, 2002, p. 51 ff

Rodriguez, Carlos/Craig, Ashley, Implementation of Ocean Shipping Regulatory Reform, 1998, at:http://www.hhgfaa.org/portal/dec_98dec24.asp

Ruttley, Philip, The Consortia Block Exemption, in: European Transport Law, 1993, p. 487 ff

Rycken, Willem, European Antitrust Aspects of Maritime and Air Transport, in: European Transport Law, 1987, p. 483 ff

Shashikumar, N., Intermodal Transport: Need, Strategies and Competitive Ramifications, 1999, at: http://www.bell.mma.edu/~nshashik/intermodal1.htm

Shashikumar, N./Schatz, G. L., The impact of U. S. regulatory changes on international intermodal movements, in: Transportation Journal, 2000, Vol. 40, Issue 1 (electronic resource)

Sjoström, William, Collusion in Ocean Shipping: A Test of Monopoly and Empty Core Models, in: Journal of Political Economy, 1989, Vol. 97, No. 5, p. 1160 ff

Temple Lang, John, Current Issues in EC Maritime Competition Law, in: European Transport Law, 1993, p. 405 ff

Vermote, Lieven, Le code de conduite des conférences maritimes et le compromis de Bruxelles, in: European Transport Law, 1986, p. 3 ff

Vermote, Lieven, The Application of the United Nations Liner Code within the European Communities, in: European Transport Law, 1988, p. 571 ff

Werner, Walter, Die Wettbewerbsverordnung der EWG für den Seeverkehr, in: Neue Juristische Wochenschrift, 1988, p. 2159 ff

Werner, Walter, Eine Wettbewerbsverordnung für den Seeverkehr, in: Wirtschaft und Wettbewerb, 1987, p. 796 ff

Williams, Charles, Adoption of Regulation 823/2000 Renewing the Block Exemption for Liner Shipping Consortia, in: Competition Policy Newsletter, 2000, No. 3, October, p. 44 ff

Wilson, Wesley W./Casavant, Kenneth L., Some Market Power Implications of the Shipping Act of 1984: A Case Study of the U. S. to Pacific Rim Transportation Markets, in: Western Journal of Agricultural Economics, (1991), Vol. 16, p. 427 ff.

Würdinger, Hans, Konferenzen der Linienschiffahrt und GWB, in: Wirtschaft und Wettbewerb, 1969, p. 655 ff

Zerby, John/Colon, R. M., Joint Costs and Intra-Tariff Cross-Subsidies: The Case of Liner Shipping, in: Journal of Industrial Economics, (1983), Vol. 31, Issue 4, p. 383 ff

Zerby, John, Regulating Ocean Shipping in the U.S.A: historical Perspective and Current Trends, (1984), at: http://www.library.unsw.edu.au/~jazerby/circle1.htm

Zuleeg, Manfred, Der Rang des europäischen im Verhältnis zum nationalen Wettbewerbsrecht, in: Europarecht, 1990, p. 123 ff

Speeches:

Danas, Andrew M., The Impact of the Ocean Shipping Reform Act on smaller Shippers and what they will demand from NVOCCs in the new Marketplace, speech held before the Journal of Commerce Symposium on NVOCCs (New York), October 7, 1998, at: http://www.gjcobert.com/danasjoc.html

Fitzgerald, Eric, Stability v Competitiveness, Speech held at the Transasia 99 Conference (Hong Kong), August 25 - 27, 1999, at: http://www.europa.eu.int/comm/competition/speeches/text/sp1999457_en.pdf

Van Miert, Karel, Competition Policy in the Maritime Sector, speech held at the International Maritime Conference (Antwerp), November 27, 1998, in: European Transport Law, 1999, p. 3 ff

Pons, Jean Francois, After TACA? Towards a more competitive and innovative Liner Shipping Market, speech held at the European Shippers' Council (Barcelona), October 29, 1998, at: http://www.europa.eu.int/comm/competition/speeches/text/sp1998_049_en.html

Pons, Jean Francois, Liner Shipping: Market Development and Government Action – The EU Competition Policy Perspective, speech held at the 1st International Shipping Convention (London), October 18 - 20, 2000, at: http://www.europa.eu.int /comm/competition/speeches/text/sp2000_019_en.pdf

Stragier, Joos, Recent Developments in EU Competition Policy in the Maritime Sector, speech held at the Shipping Forecast Conference, London, April 25 – 26, 2002, at: http://www.europa.eu.int/comm/competition/speeches/text/sp2002-015-eu.pdf

Wood, David, High Tides, Low Tides: The Scope of the Conference Group Exemption, speech held at the EMLO (London), January 29, 1999, at: http://www.europa,eu.int/comm/competition/speeches/text/sp/2000_002_en.pdf